Citizens and Soldiers

CORNELL STUDIES IN
SECURITY AFFAIRS

edited by Robert J. Art
and Robert Jervis

Citizens and Soldiers

THE DILEMMAS OF MILITARY SERVICE

ELIOT A. COHEN

Cornell University Press

ITHACA AND LONDON

Copyright © 1985 by Cornell University Press

All rights reserved. Except for brief quotations in a review, this book,
or parts thereof, must not be reproduced in any form without permission
in writing from the publisher. For information, address Cornell University Press,
124 Roberts Place, Ithaca, New York 14850.

First published 1985 by Cornell University Press.
Published in the United Kingdom by
Cornell University Press Ltd., London.

International Standard Book Number 0–8014–1581–0
Library of Congress Catalog Card Number 84–14266
Printed in the United States of America
Librarians: Library of Congress cataloging information appears
on the last page of the book.

The paper in this book is acid-free and meets the guidelines for permanence
and durability of the Committee on Production Guidelines for
Book Longevity of the Council on Library Resources.

Les lois sur le recrutement sont des institutions.

Marshal Gouvion St.-Cyr

Military service is at once a necessity, a good, and a danger. But it is primarily a necessity. By this I mean it is justified only as a means to an imperative end. It is not to be undertaken for itself, nor is it lightly to be adopted as a means.

Ralph Barton Perry

There has always been controversy as to how far a nation should maintain a standing army and how far it should depend upon levies raised for each special emergency; whether or not special levies of the latter sort should be raised by conscription or on a volunteer basis; and to what extent troops drawn from a particular locality should remain subject to the control of the local authorities. I mention these three questions because they have been especially troublesome in our own history. Each of our wars has raised them, and it can hardly be said that a definite public opinion has yet crystallized with regard to them. Substantially the same questions present themselves in broad forms. What sort of military organization goes best with democratic government and most conforms to democratic ideals of individual conduct and national policy? What is the connection between the obligation to military service and civic obligation in general? What is the relation between the military organization of a nation and its industrial, commercial, and political organization?

John Dickinson

Contents

[7]

Acknowledgments

The Center for International Affairs of Harvard University provided me with material support for which I am most grateful. Of the staff there, Janet Haochine and Linda Cohn were particularly helpful in typing early drafts, and I appreciate their diligence and cheerfulness. The National Science Foundation sustained me with a graduate fellowship, and the Harvard Department of Government with teaching fellowships, so that I could work in reasonable comfort. Quincy House, where I was a resident tutor and am now Allston Burr Senior Tutor, has always provided a comfortable and congenial place for work. I salute its dedicated Masters, Charles Dunn and David Aloian, its conscientious tutorial and administrative staffs, and, above all, its unquenchable students.

It was largely because my students insistently posed questions I could not answer that I joined the United States Army Reserve. A very part-time second lieutenant, I have learned much from military men and women, officers and enlisted, who knew me not as a researcher but rather as a very inexperienced officer. At the Army's heart are values for which I have the highest respect and admiration, and my thoughts are with those soldiers I have met who cherish those values.

The following friends and colleagues contributed valuable comments on portions of this manuscript: Ernest Evans, John Mearsheimer, Shep Melnick, and John Mojdehi. My long-time intellectual sparring partner, Stephen Rosen, was particularly helpful, not only because of his uncanny ability to find holes in my argument, but because of the remorseless good humor with which he did so.

The collegiality and intellectual stimulation provided over the past few years by the National Security Study Group of the Center for International Affairs has been invaluable. I am grateful to all of its members, and in particular to Steven David, Aaron Friedberg, and Joel Sokolsky.

Colonel Frank Partlow and Antonia Chayes engaged me frequently on the issue of women in the military, as well as on the broader issues involved in the study of military manpower. They took my admittedly extreme views on the subject with good grace and taught me much. Martin Binkin and Charles Moskos shared with me their encyclopedic knowledge of the modern American military. Having spoken with them as well as having studied their work, I have become conscious of the fact that I remain a novice in this field. I greatly appreciate their kind interest in my work.

I have been lucky in the matter of editors. Neal Kozodoy of *Commentary* sharpened my prose style considerably, and not only in the preparation of the article abstracted from an earlier version of the book. Robert Art's comments caused me to redraft some parts of the book substantially, resulting, I think, in great improvements. Brian Keeling's keen editorial eye caught many flaws of grammar and style. The patience and encouragement of Walter Lippincott of Cornell University Press have meant much to me: my thanks go as well to Michael Mandelbaum for introducing us.

Stanley Hoffmann provided acute criticism of this book in its first incarnation. Over the years I have learned much from his catholic approach to the study of politics. Samuel Huntington, who guided me throughout my graduate career, has not merely been exceedingly generous with time and help: he has provided me a model of intellectual rigor and academic conduct which I have taken very much to heart. My debt to him is great indeed.

My parents, my in-laws, and other members of my family have provided me throughout graduate school and my early professional career with many kinds of psychological and material support. Their sympathy and backing made this enterprise much easier than it might well have been.

My children Rafi and Michal do not know it, but their arrivals in 1981 and 1984, respectively, spurred their father to finish first a dissertation and then a book. My apologies to these treasures for my chronic grumpiness.

To my wife, Judy, I owe more than I can say. She gave me more solace and encouragement than I had any right to ask, and accepted more annoyance and irritation than I care to remember. She typed portions and proofread all of the manuscript and prepared the index for this book, but more important, she has supported me

Acknowledgments

for seven years with her affection, her wisdom, and her labors. I have been fortunate in many things, but in none more than our marriage. With love and gratitude I dedicate this book to her.

E.A.C.

Cambridge, Massachusetts

Citizens and Soldiers

Introduction

The broad purpose of this book is to provide a context for America's current military manpower debate, to analyze the nature of our difficulties and the extent to which we can master them. In particular, I seek to answer the question, Why has the United States, unlike every other twentieth-century Great Power and World Power, failed to settle on a durable system of peacetime military service?[1] To answer that question I must ask two others: How and with what results has the United States raised its military forces, under what constraints of domestic politics and exigencies of war? What alternative methods have other countries adopted, how well did they work, and could they be tried here?

For well over a generation this country has oscillated in its attitudes toward conscription and its practice of it. At various times universal military service, universal military training, selective service, a lottery draft, and an all-volunteer armed force have been either implemented or seriously contemplated. This instability has occurred because since 1945 the United States has confronted dilemmas that have prevented it (unlike the European Great Powers) from settling on a durable system of military service. The United States must prepare for two completely different kinds of war, large and small, which require, for political and military reasons, two completely different kinds of armies.[2] In addition, American ideology has always been peculiarly ambivalent toward conscription. Two strains of thought, Anglo-Saxon liberalism and democratic egalitarianism, accord with different varieties of peacetime military service. Moreover, both ideological strains run counter to the forms of military service best suited for large-scale war. These dilemmas of political-military necessity and ideology are, by their nature, intractable: in other words, it would be extremely difficult,

[15]

if not impossible, to create a system of military service that the American regime could live with for decades. In many other countries this is not the case—for example, Canada, Switzerland, Britain, and France all have retained their types of peacetime military service for nearly a century.

This book focuses on the United States, but it is essential to use historical and philosophical material from other states. In the case of some countries (France, Germany, and Switzerland primarily) it is important to do so because each of these countries either created or developed to its fullest a given type of military service. In other cases (Great Britain, Canada, and Australia) historical evidence can help because of the similarity between these regimes and the American one. The history of Great Britain provides particularly interesting material, not only because of the similarities between American and British notions of justice, but because America's role in the post–World War II period resembles that of Great Britain from 1902 to 1914.

The political philosophical part of the book (Chapters 5 and 6 in particular) also uses a variety of materials. Although I discuss the views of such crucial philosophers as Hobbes and Locke, I do not simply extrapolate from their arguments. Rather, I also examine the writings of eminent and theoretically inclined politicians (Abraham Lincoln and Woodrow Wilson in the United States, for example, and Adolphe Thiers in France) and academics (Ralph Barton Perry, for instance). In addition, I draw inferences from the often unstated political assumptions and premises that color national debates. For example, it is currently assumed in the United States that neither commutation (substitution of monetary payment for military service) nor a selective draft for a five-year term of military service would be acceptable to politicians of either the Democratic or Republican party, let alone to the public at large.

Military service is at once a subject for scholarly inquiry and a political issue of the first order. It is regrettable but unavoidable that today, as in the past, Americans turn their attention to military service only under the shadow of its forcible imposition by government. During peacetime, or at least when war is neither recent nor imminent, the citizen regards the study of military service as too mundane for anyone but experts, or as an interesting but purely hypothetical exercise in political philosophy. What holds true for the average citizen or politician holds true for the scholar as well; it was no coincidence that the two special issues of the *Annals of the*

[16]

American Academy of Political and Social Science dealing with conscription appeared in 1916 and 1945. The present book represents no exception to this observation, for today Americans face the possible reintroduction of a military draft, and young men must register for it. Yet we are lucky in that today we can consider issues related to a draft and other types of military service before a war has broken out; although the return of conscription looms close enough to be treated seriously, we are not confronted with the painful matter of deciding whose lives will be risked on the battlefield.

To treat these issues profitably, it is essential to take the broadest possible view of them. In so doing, I hope to inform and expand the current conscription debate, not to present a neat or definitive solution to America's military manpower problems. Newspaper editors, politicians, and pollsters pose the question all too simply: Do you favor a draft or do you oppose it? Rarely do they ask: What kinds of draft are possible? How should we go about selecting some men (and possibly women) for service, and not others? How will our methods of recruitment affect our foreign policy, our domestic politics, and our forces' performance in battle?

The public conscription debate, waged as it is in the editorial and letters columns of newspapers and journals of opinion, relies on instinctive belief, not elaborate discussion. To take but one current example, such philosophical arguments as we read in even the most sophisticated newspapers proceed from absolute understandings of military obligation—a young man must either serve two years wherever the government chooses, even as a combat soldier in an undeclared war overseas, or not at all. Intermediate notions of obligation (the militia concept, for example) have fallen by the wayside. Commentators offer proposals for national service without regard to their constitutionality or to the fundamental political and military differences between such schemes and various forms of compulsory military service.[3] A similar superficiality bedevils the discussion of the foreign policy implications of systems of military service: we read either that a draft makes an unjust war impossible (by reason of its reliance on citizen-soldiers) or that it makes such wars inevitable (by militarizing society and providing the armed forces with unstinted supplies of cannon fodder).[4]

The more durable literature on systems of military service falls into five broad categories. First, one has governmental studies of enormous bulk which concentrate, for the most part, on short-term problems of securing sufficient manpower for forces whose numerical strengths seem arbitrarily set. Examples of such works include the *Report of the President's Commission on an All-Volunteer Armed Force* (1970) and the *Defense Manpower Commission* report (1976), each a multivolume study replete with statistical tables and data of various kinds. In each case political factors, preeminent among them a desire to prove that an all-volunteer armed force could work, predetermined the reports' conclusion (see Chapter 8).

The issue of conscription has always evoked an enormous amount of polemical literature, and thus the second category of literature is that produced by pamphleteers. Such work varies greatly in quality, of course, but should not on that account be neglected. The pamphlets arising from the British conscription debate in the early twentieth century (Ian Hamilton's *Compulsory Service* and its target, Lord Roberts's *Message to the Nation*, for example) were the work of highly intelligent professional soldiers, as was Leonard Wood's 1915 pamphlet, *The Military Obligation of Citizenship*.

A third type of writing on military service comes from the pens of political philosophers. Such books as Ralph Barton Perry's *The Free Man and the Soldier* (1916) and Michael Walzer's *Obligations* (1970) are theoretical treatments of conscription, although it should be noted that both appeared during a time of political controversy and were written by politically engaged scholars. A fourth group are purely historical studies of conscription such as Richard Challener's *The French Theory of the Nation in Arms, 1866–1939* (1965) and Bernard Schnapper's *Le Remplacement Militaire en France* (1968). These studies rarely compare different countries, however, and usually shy away from attempts to answer the larger questions set forth above.

Finally, one has the smallest category, into which the present work falls: general studies of military manpower. Of these, the most important are John McAuley Palmer's *Statesmanship or War* (1927), Frederick Martin Stern's *The Citizen Army* (1957), and M. R. D. Foot's *Men in Uniform* (1961).

Governmental studies do not, for the most part, raise fundamental questions, such as the connection between foreign policy and conscription; polemical works are, by definition, tendentious and directed at an immediate set of proposals and problems; philosophical works ignore the practical necessities of war-fighting; historical studies do not look for larger truths; general studies are either outdated or insufficiently focused. The weaknesses of pre-

[18]

vious works lie not so much in their date of publication as in their choice of approach.

What sets this book apart from other general studies of military manpower systems? The most important difference is one of perspective. This book is informed throughout by a view of military organizations as, first, fundamentally *political*; and, second, fundamentally *institutional*. While there is nothing revolutionary-sounding in calling military service systems "political-military institutions," I know of no work that adheres to the view implied by that description. As such, it is not beside the point to linger a little over the application, in this context, of the two defining terms.

First, then, why does this subject fall within the purview of the political scientist rather than that of the soldier or historian? For one thing, the forms of recruitment and military service have an obvious and direct bearing on the military power of states, as well as on their willingness to use such power. The study of war belongs, in large measure, to the study of international politics, and to understand war we must understand systems of military service. In addition, the study of conscription raises in its most acute form the question, What are the obligations of the citizen to the state? For that reason, the study of systems of military service has long attracted the interest of students of political philosophy, particularly in states where the notion of complete obligation—the obligation to die for the state, if necessary—remains open to dispute. The role of peacetime military service as an inculcator of civic virtue and as a means of civic education offers subsidiary philosophical interest.

The comparative study of systems of military service can teach us about the similarities of and differences among regimes, in other words, comparative politics. In this book, for example, I will observe that the United States, Great Britain, Australia, Canada, and New Zealand, because of their similar political traditions, have grappled with the problem of conscription in comparable ways. On the other hand, some states whose internal construction is very dissimilar (France and Germany, for example) have adopted remarkably similar forms of military service. Thus, the study of systems of military service raises interesting issues in the study of comparative government.

Finally, the study of America's military manpower system is part of the study of American politics. America's conscription debates have been particularly sharp: during the War of 1812, the Civil War, and the periods 1914–1920, 1940–1950, and 1968–1973, conscription has been a highly divisive political issue. In short, few topics are more political, in the largest sense, than that of systems of military service.

Small wonder, then, that the view expressed in the epigraph to this book—"the laws governing recruitment are [political] institutions"—was once a commonplace. General Louis Trochu explicated Marshal Saint-Cyr's remark in 1867, saying that systems of military service must be treated as political institutions because of the "direct, powerful, and permanent effect they have on the dearest interests, aspirations, mores, and practices of the entire population."[5] Saint-Cyr's dictum has ancient roots. Polybius's description of the Roman republic contains a detailed analysis of the Roman legionary system, and Aristotle discusses at length the relationship between types of military service and the form of the regime.[6]

Yet the notion that one must study systems of military service to understand a state's foreign and domestic politics has fallen into desuetude. The classical approach proceeded from the assumption that a system of recruitment formed part of a constitutional edifice, and hence deserved the careful attention of statesmen and citizens. Consider, by way of contrast, the official and dominant opinion in the United States during the 1970s and 1980s. The Gates Commission, which recommended in 1970 the abolition of the draft, asserted that conscription is simply "a form of taxation," and its consultants conjured up elaborate formulas for assessing the dollar value of this taxation.[7] The Commissioners, their expert advisers, and many official and academic analysts since have treated the manpower problem as an economic, not a political matter. These men and women, most of them economists or systems analysts, have defined the problem thus: What is the least costly way of obtaining x number of persons having such and such characteristics for a fixed period of time (given, of course, that any departure from the principle of voluntarism is suspect)?[8] They have slighted those philosophical, political, and even military aspects of the question not susceptible to quantitative analysis. Richard Cooper's influential 1977 RAND study, for example, contains only one chapter on "Historical and International Perspectives of [sic] Conscription"—prepared largely by a research assistant.

Second, what is meant by speaking of military service systems as "institutional" in character? In the words of Samuel Huntington, one of the foremost students of political institutions, "Institutions are stable, valued, recurring patterns of behavior. Organizations

[20]

and procedures vary in their degree of institutionalization. Harvard University and the newly opened suburban high school are both organizations, but Harvard is much more of an institution than the high school."[9] A system of military service carries with it a freight of social and political values.[10] Like any institution, it possesses inertia and a life independent of its instrumental role. A system of military service has, whether we wish it or not, functions beyond providing sufficient armed forces adequately trained and equipped.[11] It flourishes or withers only in part because of its military utility; moreover, its influence may extend considerably beyond its primary function of providing modern states with trained soldiers.

Tocqueville's treatment of trial by jury will serve to illustrate my meaning.[12] Tocqueville held that the importance of jury trial in the United States was twofold: it served as a device to render judicial opinions of guilt or innocence, to be sure, but just as important—perhaps even more important—it trained Americans in the ways of responsible democratic citizenship. Now, to appreciate Tocqueville's insight one must consider the many ways of discussing the American jury system. A policy analyst might treat it as only one method (and a far from cost-effective one at that) of procuring judicial decisions; an historian could study jury behavior in particular trials, to understand the outcome of particular dispositions; a sociologist might inquire about the patterns of behavior and social origins of all jurors; a jurist might explore the question of whether jurors can understand complex cases. Each of these points of view has something to tell the student of jury trial, and indeed, I shall use analogous methods of inquiry in later chapters. Even so, none offers the comprehensiveness of an institutional point of view, and all run the risk of parochialism. The policy analyst and the jurist might find jury trial costly and inept, but they probably could not account for its larger utility or its durability. The historian and sociologist have much to teach about the system but could easily miss the bigger questions: whether the jury system does what it is supposed to do, whether alternatives exist, and what their usefulness might be. In short, an institutional approach offers us a method as catholic as the subject is multifaceted.

The analogy should make it clear why, although this book incorporates historical and theoretical materials, it is neither a history nor a disquisition on political philosophy. It is, rather, a work in the field of military politics, which is a branch of political science. Clausewitz's dictum that war is a continuation of politics by other means means much more than that war is a tool of statecraft. It means that politics pervades war and preparation for it; that, as I have argued, military institutions are political institutions.

This latter is a view well-developed by German students of Clausewitz such as Otto Hintze and Hans Delbrueck; however, it has only intermittently gained currency in the United States.[13] The most extreme form of the view that an army's nature is shaped by the society from which it springs was advanced by M. R. D. Foot in one of the first modern studies of military service: "Police states have police-ridden armies. Lackadaisical countries have lackadaisical armies. . . . Sturdy peasant armies [are] tough, wary, but under-equipped; and highly industrialized countries have highly industrialized forces, equipped with elaborate machinery staffed by skilled technicians."[14] In Chapter 3 we shall see that this argument can go too far, and thereby vitiate the peculiar strength of the institutional approach to systems of military service. On the other hand, a small but tenacious group of students of war have argued forcefully that much of war is independent of politics, that the human instruments of war can operate unaffected by political and social turmoil.[15] Indeed, one of the most interesting questions discussed in this book is: Under what conditions can a military organization maintain an ethos and character quite independent of that of the society from which it springs?

The book begins with a discussion of the broad classes of factors that influence the development of military service systems (Chapter 1). Chapters 2–4 and 5–6 (respectively) treat the external and internal dimensions of military service. As Michael Howard has pointed out, students of military politics and military sociology must never forget that armies exist, after all, to fight; hence, Chapters 2–4 explore how different systems of military service prepare nations for war. Chapter 2 examines the origins of modern systems of military service, Chapter 3 discusses low-intensity warfare, and Chapter 4 deals with large-scale war. I then discuss the internal dimension—the influence of ideology and principle—for it is as great a mistake to ignore the constraints posed by domestic conceptions of justice as it is to disregard the imperatives of war. Chapter 5 discusses the uniqueness of military service as a political obligation; Chapter 6, the tensions between liberal and democratic attitudes toward compulsory military service.

The last chapters (7–9) examine the military manpower dilemmas that have beset America since World War II (it is only since

[22]

Introduction

Table 1. Major Types of Military Service

System	Military Purpose	Length of Service	Method of Recruitment
expansible	training	long tour	voluntary
UMT	training	six months	universal
militia	home defense	part-time plus initial training	any
cadre/conscript	home defense or general purpose	short tour	universal, random, selective
AVF	general purpose	short tour	voluntary
ancien regime conscript	general purpose	long tour	class-based
professional	general purpose	long tour	voluntary, random
selective service	general purpose	long tour (duration of conflict)	selective

Expansible: A cadre of professional soldiers prepares in peacetime to train large masses of conscripts or volunteers in war. Example: the German Army (*Reichswehr*) 1920–1935.

UMT (Universal Military Training): All physically fit young men receive a short period of military instruction during high school or shortly after its completion. Examples: pre–World War I Australia; system proposed in the United States in 1948.

Militia: Men, selected by a number of possible methods, train sporadically during the year (e.g., a weekend a month) while pursuing civilian careers. These men perform active duty only in time of invasion or general war. Examples: United States National Guard, British Territorial Army.

Cadre/Conscript: A cadre of professional sergeants (noncommissioned officers, or NCOs) and officers trains and leads conscripts who then become part of a nation's standing forces. Examples: (home defense) Federal Republic of Germany today; (general purpose) United States Army 1948–1973.

AVF (All-Volunteer Force): The same as cadre/conscript, but with the exclusive use of volunteers, most of whom serve only one tour and then leave the military. Example: United States Army 1973–present.

Ancien Regime Conscript: Long tour compulsory military service for certain classes, e.g., day laborers and nobles. Statutory exemption of men from military service on the basis of class. Example: Frederician Prussia.

Professional: Officers and NCOs are long service soldiers, but unlike other systems, rank and file also regard military service as a career. Example: British Army from the 1700s to the present, with the exception of the World Wars.

Selective Service: A wartime measure. Men are selected for military service on the basis of overall usefulness to a total (i.e., economic and military) war effort. In other words, preference, luck, or attributes such as origin or wealth count for nothing. Example: the United States 1914–1918, 1940–1946. Note: The Selective Service System is also the name of the American draft agency; the importance of distinguishing between the type of service and the bureaucratic body which, in two World Wars, administered it, will be outlined in Chapter 4, and again in Chapters 8 and 9.

1945 that the problem has been chronic). These chapters focus on two turning points: Congressional rejection of Universal Military Training in 1948, which led to the extension of selective service into peacetime (Chapter 7); and the decision to establish an all-volunteer force in 1970 (Chapter 8). I conclude that neither measure—one the product of inertia, the other of expediency—met America's foreign and domestic needs. The final chapter (9) presents a possible solution to America's manpower dilemmas. Discussion of this proposal, however, serves mainly to further illuminate the practical and theoretical difficulties that will beset any reform of America's military manpower system, not to provide a final remedy to these difficulties.

Discussion of systems of military service often suffers from careless use of such terms as "professional army" and "conscript army." As remarked above, journalists and politicians often reduce the entire issue to one of being for or against "the draft." For clarity, therefore, we must begin by defining certain types of military service.

Three aspects of military service are particularly important in defining it: military purpose (training, home defense, general); length of service (six months, a short tour of one to three years, a long tour of more than three years, part-time reserve duty); and method of conscription (universal, random, class-based, selective). There is no need to generate a matrix of all the various permutations, for many of the theoretical possibilities (selective long-tour training, for example) have never existed and are wildly improbable. Moreover, countries often adopt hybrid manpower systems. Table 1, however, details the major types of military service.

Why these types of service are the essential ones, and why these criteria are the significant ones, will become clear later in this book. I will attempt to show how the various systems have very different political and military consequences, and to what extent these have changed over time.

[1]

Constraints: Necessity
and Choice

Nations adopt systems of military service to meet two kinds of demands, those of external necessity—the constraints placed on states by their participation in world politics, their status as sovereign members of the state system, and their location on the globe—and those of ideology.

IMPERATIVES OF GEOPOLITICS

Minor and Intermediate Powers

Perhaps the best (if crudest) predictors of a country's system of military service are the length of its land borders with potentially hostile neighbors and the size of its population relative to that of its neighbors. Countries such as Switzerland, France, and Germany, surrounded as they have been by powerful and occasionally malevolent Great Powers, have almost always required and depended on conscription to raise large standing armies to defend themselves. On the other hand, insular states such as Great Britain and Australia have only rarely faced a threat of invasion, and hence have almost never had occasion to raise large armies in peacetime in order to protect their frontiers.

One exception to this rule occurs in the case of a medium power with so many inhabitants that it can raise a large standing or instantly mobilizable force without resort to forcible induction into military service. China and India, always overpopulated, have never needed to raise their huge armies by conscription. The sheer bulk and poverty of their peasant populations have ensured that enough men would be attracted to military service by the lure of

[25]

glory, plunder, or, above all, sheer security, to meet any national emergency. Thus, as late as World War II India raised an army of over two and a half million by voluntary enlistment. The People's Republic of China maintains a regular force of four million today, also by voluntary enlistment.

For the small state, a rigorously enforced system of compulsory military service not only can ensure some degree of security against sudden onslaught: it can diminish or even eliminate entirely the advantages that would normally accrue to richer or more populous countries. Take, for example, the case of Israel: its population of four million men and women is dwarfed by that of Egypt (forty-two million), yet the two countries can, within a few days of mobilization, deploy approximately the same number of soldiers—450,000. In an earlier period, shortly before World War I, France managed to overcome its population inferiority of approximately two to three vis-à-vis Germany by introducing a three-year period of military service and progressively tightening its exemptions from the draft. In 1914 the active forces on both sides numbered some 600,000.[1]

We can find interesting exceptions to the rules that insular and heavily populated states do not require conscription and countries with small populations and long land borders do. Singapore, for example, is an island state that enforces a strict conscription. In that country, however, as in many others, conscription has other uses besides providing adequate land forces for national defense. More to the point, Singapore finds itself surrounded by ethnically different and by no means sympathetic states, most within easy striking range across narrow straits. Cuba is another example of a highly militarized island state relying on comprehensive conscription; other examples are modern Taiwan and nineteenth-century and early twentieth-century Japan. Nonetheless, in all of these cases (with the possible exception of Japan) a strong case can be made that an amphibious invasion is an acute threat, and hence that these nations find themselves in a state of insecurity similar to that faced by their landlocked brethren.

Another class of exceptions is comprised of small countries with relatively long borders for whom a large military establishment seems pointless, either because successful resistance to attack seems impossible (as in the case of Luxembourg, Costa Rica, and various African states) or because the threat seems so minor as to obviate the need for any sizable military force (contemporary New Zealand). Finally, some countries, though heavily populated

(Nigeria and Brazil, for example), still rely on conscription. In each of these cases there is a real land-based security threat, but one which by itself might not justify conscription. The reason for conscription in such cases is again a political one.

There is little correlation between a country's economic wealth and its reliance on conscription. Although the United States and Britain are as well off as their European allies, they maintain well-paid volunteer forces while the latter do not. Conversely, China and India are among the poorer nations in the world, yet they, like the Anglo-Saxon states, draw their regular military forces from voluntary enlistment.

Nonetheless, despite the political concerns alluded to above, most countries adopt some form of conscription primarily if they face the prospect of an invasion by a hostile neighbor across land borders or narrow straits. Minor powers that believe that they face a particularly acute threat of invasion by much larger states frequently adopt a *militia* system of military service, such as that introduced by Israel in 1948, and the system that has been in place in Switzerland for centuries. The advantages of such a system are two-fold: First, it enables a small state in the midst of real crisis to deploy forces comparable in sheer numbers (if still inferior) to those of the hostile state. Thus, on mobilization the Swiss Army today numbers 625,000 men, the Israeli Army 500,000. The United States, although its population is thirty-six times Switzerland's 6,370,000 and fifty-seven times Israel's 4,000,000, has an active military force only three to four times the size of the forces in these small states.[2]

A second advantage of a militia system for a vulnerable minor power is that it allows such a country to resist an invasion from the very beginning and throughout a national territory. A Finland or a Yugoslavia can hope to deter attackers by the prospect of a prolonged guerrilla struggle throughout its territory. Thus, reliance on a force of citizen-soldiers, no matter what its political attractiveness, also seems particularly apt for geographically large or physically rugged countries, whose terrain favors long-term battles of attrition.

A militia system also offers many advantages to the small state plagued by chronic, low-level security threats. Israel's militia system ensures that any limited incursion—even by a band of a few bomb-throwing terrorists—can be contained by the presence of armed citizen-soldiers. The old colonial militia system in the United States served a similar purpose, ensuring that every isolated settlement would have at least some capability for self-defense against small bands of marauders.[3]

For large, well-organized or less-threatened states, however, the militia system has many drawbacks, a number of which will be discussed in following chapters. Militias require a commitment to serious part-time training of a kind that few states have: the long-standing suspicion of American regular officers that reservists only gather for drills to drink and swap stories dates back to the colonial muster days, and has, it must be admitted, some basis in fact. A militia system works well only in two circumstances. It can wage conventional war only during very short, sharp conflicts (as in the Middle East wars) because any economy, urban or agrarian, will grind to a halt when suddenly deprived of the services of most of the young male population. Militias can sustain long wars only if the country has been substantially or even completely occupied by an enemy, in which case soldiers can, as it were, commute to war from home, and fight only part-time. Such militias (for instance, that of Yugoslavia in World War II) derive physical and psychological support from their localities, and without it lost their military effectiveness.

Thus, most states of intermediate size and population, confronted by potentially hostile neighbors of comparable size and power, resort to some form of conscription, primarily (since the late nineteenth century) the *cadre/conscript* system. As pointed out in Table 1 (see the Introduction), a cadre/conscript system inducts draftees for twelve to thirty-six months of training and military service, in units staffed primarily by professional noncommissioned officers (NCOs) and officers. To be sure, some of the junior leadership must come from the ranks of conscripts; nonetheless, in most cadre/conscript systems leadership rests in the hands of a professional elite.

A cadre/conscript system provides a state with substantial, immediately usable forces, and that fairly cheaply. Unlike militia forces, a cadre/conscript army can be expected to maintain high professional standards, because control rests in the hands of career soldiers. Unlike purely voluntary systems, it allows for the creation of a substantial reserve of former soldiers who can be recalled to the colors. In addition, a cadre/conscript system does not interfere with a country's economic life, because participants in it have usually not yet entered the work force: indeed, their value as workers may be enhanced by the vocational training they receive and such habits of discipline as they acquire while in military service.

[28]

The primary vulnerability of such a system lies in its dependence on professional (that is, career) soldiers. Unlike a militia system, a cadre/conscript system does not normally produce a body of reserve officers and NCOs: hence, when ex-soldiers are mobilized the small professional cadre is swamped and the quality of the army as a whole deteriorates. In addition, even in peacetime, when the army consists solely of conscripts on active duty, a country may be unable to attract sufficient numbers of high-quality NCOs and officers to train and lead the draftees. The modern Soviet Army, for example, suffers from a nearly complete lack of professional NCOs in the Western sense, and must rely instead on draftees in their second year of service and an extremely large officer corps to provide leaders.[4] Conversely, the strength of the German Army throughout the nineteenth and twentieth centuries rested heavily on a substantial corps of career NCOs.[5] Finally, the cadre/conscript system's reliance on a professional officer and NCO corps creates a host of potential problems for civil-military relations (discussed below).

As a general matter, then, we can expect to find two basic varieties of military service in small and medium states that believe themselves both threatened and capable of resistance. Small or more geographically vulnerable states will usually choose a militia-type system, in order to extract the maximum possible military power from limited population. Larger or more secure states will adopt a cadre/conscript system, trading military efficiency and flexibility for mere mass. In both cases, as we shall see below, political considerations may modify these general rules.

World Powers

Since the late nineteenth century most Great Powers (Germany, for example) and the smaller European states have found a satisfactory solution to their manpower needs in the cadre-conscript system. Since 1875, and despite various (sometimes interesting) hiatuses, these countries have raised large armies more or less on the principle of universal military service along the lines of the German model. As already remarked, such a system provides a state with large numbers of adequately trained men and usually at a reasonable cost, since conscripts have rarely been well paid. Such a system suits the principal military need of Great Powers—namely, the need to fight an intense war on short notice against an equally sophisticated neighboring state.

The World Powers have faced quite different problems. Great Britain was, and the United States is the preeminent state of this kind. Not only does the Anglo-Saxon liberal tradition of these two states present peculiar difficulties in the matter of conscription (as I shall argue below), but, because of their peculiar geopolitical position, they have considerable difficulty matching their military manpower systems to the kinds of war they must fight.

Unlike the medium and Great Powers, a World Power must prepare for two entirely different kinds of war: full-scale conventional conflicts on the continent of Europe, and smaller, politically and geographically limited contests in other regions. Because the manpower problems of large or total war differ completely from those of small war, the need to prepare for both presents serious difficulties for the manpower policies of the World Powers. The need to prepare for total war stems from what Michael Howard has termed a Continental Commitment to allies on the European mainland. This has raised a number of questions in itself: whether troops should be stationed on the European front lines in peacetime or move to their positions only when war becomes imminent; what sorts of mobilization commitments the insular powers should make; what should be done if the forces appear to be in danger of being cut off; whether these forces should serve only the interests of the allies or be available for other deployments as well.

But above all, Continental war is total war, that is, intense warfare requiring the entire panoply of modern weapons. It is war conducted in developed lands, near the home country (for the Soviet Union) or on the territory of a large and friendly ally (for the United States). It is war conducted with full national economic, psychological, and military mobilization. More often than not, the objective is the unconditional surrender of one's enemies. Total war is waged side by side with allies who must be accommodated and succored, but who offer psychological and material support. Such wars have as their epicenter western and central Europe, control of which has, since the sixteenth century, been the key to the global balance of power.[6]

World Powers must also, however, prepare to fight numerous small wars outside Europe on its periphery, in order to protect and further the global interests and resources on which their power rests. The physiognomy of such wars, and hence their manpower requirements, differ completely from those of large wars. World

Powers wage small wars against the inferior forces of a much weaker state, a guerrilla movement, or the proxy forces of another World Power.[7] These low-intensity conflicts do not engage the full energies of a World Power's armed forces or population, although the same need not be true of its opponent.

Indeed, rather than summon up all of its physical and emotional resources to win such wars, a World Power will often accept compromise or even a limited defeat. This was the case for the United States in Vietnam, as it was a century earlier for Great Britain in Afghanistan. Such wars are fought at the margin, for defeat need not lead to a loss of either independence or a large fraction of the national wealth, as is necessarily the case in total war. This does not mean, however, that such wars are easily won, either on the battlefield or on the home front.

World Powers often wage small wars to win the allegiance of a people, either to a client government or the World Power itself. Republics have waged such imperial wars as often as any other kind of regime has. The notion with which democrats flattered themselves, that republics cannot be imperial powers and hence can wage only wars of self-preservation, is incorrect. Athens and Rome were both what Raymond Aron has termed imperial republics, as is the United States today.[8]

An imperial power, whether or not it is interested in establishing colonies (Athens, for example, was not), must bear the burden of minor wars to save clients, fill vacuums of power, or protect some larger economic interests. It must do so in order to maintain a world order that it believes itself responsible to protect. Thus, small wars are both inescapable and vital to a World Power. When a country no longer has the self-confidence or resources to fight such limited wars its imperial days are numbered, as the British Cabinet belatedly discovered in 1956. When the world is bipolar—as in Thucydides' day and (to a lesser extent) ours—the World Power will have little choice but to use force at some point or other, for any loss is perceived as the opponent's gain. Pericles' admonition to the Athenians, "It may have been wrong to take it [your empire]; it is certainly dangerous to let it go,"[9] has been repeated in various forms in the councils of such states. Thus, even today, many erstwhile opponents of the Vietnam war are willing to contemplate the dispatch of the Rapid Deployment Force to the Persian Gulf to secure oil supplies less vital to the United States than to her dependent European and Japanese allies.

A World Power fights its small wars in distant lands, usually under difficult climatic and geographical conditions. Such wars may cost few casualties, but they are usually long wars. In Malaysia during the Emergency, for example, it took the British six years to "break the Communists' aggressive power, and six more to 'dig out the roots.' "[10] In the nineteenth and early twentieth centuries the French occupation and pacification of Morocco took decades.[11] As we shall see in Chapter 4, small wars are primarily light infantry wars, and hence require troops who are both physically and psychologically rugged. World Powers usually fight small wars without the cooperation of major allies; indeed, the more severe small wars (the Boer and Vietnam wars are examples) tend to isolate a World Power. Allies fear a diversion of the World Power's resources and attention, neutrals usually regard such morally ambiguous conflicts with suspicion, and rivals exploit the discomfort of both.

The great differences between the political-military requirements of large and small wars are revealed most clearly in the system of military service suited to each. For the one, a large, mechanized, conscript force offers the main, perhaps the only hope, of success. For the other, a smaller, lightly equipped, professional force seems best. The best and most recent example of this large war/small war military manpower dilemma comes from the Soviet Union, which has emerged only in the past two decades as a World Power capable of projecting its land, air, and naval forces across the globe. When it invaded Afghanistan in 1979 it deployed a Great Power army, a completely mechanized cadre/conscript force trained and equipped for war in central Europe. It quickly discovered, as had its Anglo-Saxon counterparts repeatedly in previous centuries, that such a force, suited though it might be for European war, could not hope to accomplish the delicate and extremely difficult chore ahead of it.[12]

IMPERATIVES OF IDEOLOGY

I have thus far discussed systems of military service as if they were determined solely by a state's geopolitical position, in other words, without reference to internal politics. The dimension of external necessity is always present, and plays a particularly important role in wartime, when many objections based on principle and ideology must give way to the demands of survival. Even in wartime, however, and more so in peacetime, considerations of domestic politics and justice strongly influence what system of military service a state will choose. This is particularly true in the American case, and compounds America's strategic dilemma.

Particularly in cases of the introduction of novel systems of military service (for example, the first modern large-scale conscription, during the French Revolution) or the retention of extremely old ones (that of Switzerland), it is difficult to determine which force has played the greater role, necessity or choice.[13] As we shall see in Chapter 3, both interpretations were placed on the use of conscription in the French Revolution, and both have some merit.

Military service touches the very essence of a polity in several respects, all of which may be divorced from considerations of foreign policy. Forced military service presents the most extreme demand the community can impose on its members, the requirement that they prepare to die on its behalf. In addition, military service, beginning as it must in young manhood, cannot help but be seen as a form of moral education. The German phrase *die Schule der Nation* suggests an appeal of military service which still holds true in the developing parts of the world, where military service seems to offer a shortcut to vocational training and a unified national spirit. Military organizations must inculcate such virtues as loyalty, self-sacrifice, and obedience to duly constituted authority. Small wonder, then, that statesmen and educators have seen in military service a means nor merely of protecting the community, but of fostering its moral strength.

For totalitarian states conscription has had peculiar attractions.[14] If one definition of a totalitarian system is a warfare or siege state, universal military service offers a peculiarly potent tool for cultivating a sense of impending struggle. If offers such states one more tool to organize and regiment the lives of their subjects, and it may help create the sense of constant and potent foreign threat against which one must always be on guard. Even rudimentary forms of military service offer a chance to make a population commit itself, willy-nilly, to the goals of a regime.[15]

Conversely, the limited autocratic regimes of the nineteenth and twentieth centuries have deliberately avoided any type of conscript system, preferring instead to create an isolated professional army that would have few compunctions about suppressing a popular uprising. The French Army that helped install Napoleon III, and maintained him in power until the disaster of 1871, was such a force, as was the Russian Army until the end of the nineteenth century. When, under pressure from internal reformers and a growing German and Austrian threat, the Russians created a conscript army along European lines, the government found itself in 1905 no longer possessed of an army easily available to suppress a restive population.

In the main, systems of military service based on some form of universal conscription seem uniquely suited to modern democratic states—that is, "democratic" in Tocqueville's sense. For Tocqueville, modern democracy was characterized by egalitarianism and individualism, but not necessarily by the growth of freedom. He saw universal military service as a natural outgrowth and concomitant of the great democratic revolution of modern times, an association that both fascinated and horrified him.[16]

It is misleading, however, to speak of democratic forms of military service as though they were a foregone conclusion, particularly in the Anglo-Saxon states.[17] Countries such as Great Britain and the United States face an internal political dilemma quite as serious as the external one referred to above. In the United States, as Tocqueville pointed out, the claims of liberty temper those of democracy. The result is an attitude toward military organizations that has always been stubbornly ambivalent.

Military service means participation in a total institution, an institution that can control every minute of a man's waking hours and every facet of his behavior. This total institution differs greatly from normal liberal-democratic society. Whereas such a society tolerates diversity of dress and behavior, the armed forces must insist on uniformity of both. Whereas society frowns upon or prohibits violence and killing, a military organization must prepare men for them. Whereas free societies tell their members that one citizen is the equal of any other, the military must insist on rank, order, and deference.

On the other hand, there is no denying the intermittent popularity of the military ideal in liberal-democratic societies. The popular literature of our own time and the popularity in bygone decades of amateur military organizations (the Volunteer regiments in Great Britain during the second half of the nineteenth century, for example) suggest this, and it is confirmed by studies of American veterans of World War II, most of which suggested that those who went through the military came away with surprising approbation for its good qualities and tolerance of its bad.[18] Indeed, many Americans believe that military service fosters habits of discipline,

[34]

self-sacrifice, and collective action which are vital to the health of a free society.

Thus, the virtues and habits of thought and behavior that the armed forces must inculcate at once contradict liberal and democratic values and appeal to many who live in societies shaped by those values.[19] At no point does this fact have greater import than when the question of conscription is raised. Professional soldiers and professional armies can adhere to peculiar codes of behavior and thought and flourish, even in the midst of an indifferent or hostile society.[20] But when society participates directly in national defense by sending its young men into the armed forces for a few months or a few years, the tension between, and the overlap of, military and civilian values cannot be ignored. The military ideal incorporates some of a liberal-democratic society's most precious values and some values utterly repugnant to it. If, as Tocqueville asserted, it is the mores of a country such as the United States more than its geographical position or its laws that keep it both free and democratic, military service, because of the mores it promotes or offends, cannot escape political controversy.[21]

IMPERATIVES OF WAR

Raison d'état and conceptions of justice place the major constraints on a state's system of military service. Both, however, are themselves subject to a third influence, that of war. A system of military service that might serve the needs of foreign policy (by creating an imposing armed mass or giving an impression of resolve) or a cherished view of the obligations of the citizen to the state (universal male military service, for example) might still fail the test of war, and do so in a number of different ways.

I have already noted one type of difficulty, that of maintaining a system of military service suited for short, large-scale conventional war which must also supply forces for a long counterguerrilla campaign. The French plight in 1914–1915 suggests another possible dilemma, that of a system that is designed to ward off or win a short, exceedingly violent conventional war but is not suited for a protracted war of attrition. As we shall see in Chapter 3, the French found themselves forced to demobilize tens of thousands of soldiers in order to maintain the military production necessary to sustain the forces at the front. Universal military service provided them with a substantial active army—one, as noted above, quite as large as that of their German enemies—and corresponded to French democratic-egalitarian ideals. It did not, however, meet the requirements of war, and hence had to be changed.

The greatest differences, however, are those bewteen the stresses of small war and those of large war. Each poses different challenges, and it is virtually inevitable that the army suited for one kind of war will find itself at a disadvantage in the other. During small wars, for example, professional armies can stay in the field because casualties are usually relatively few, and the problem of replacements is manageable. For large wars, however, few countries can afford to fight simply with the forces that they have waiting in barracks and camps; they must mobilize former soldiers, reservists, or civilians. Governments must decide how to raise and equip divisions and how to replace losses that appear in a flood, not a trickle.

In a period of all-out war some particularly thorny problems may disappear: the question of the duration of military service, for example, which occasioned furious debates in Europe during the late nineteenth and early twentieth centuries. During a total conflict soldiers serve, for the most part, until the war's end. During a small war, however, such difficulties may become far more acute than in peacetime: military necessity may suggest long tours overseas, while ideological constraints (a desire to spread the war burden equitably) may dictate a short period of service. This dilemma was particularly acute for the United States during the Vietnam conflict.

Distinctions that bulk large in peacetime—that between short-service conscripts and volunteer professionals, for example—may diminish sharply or even disappear in wartime. The influx of replacements and transfers of experienced personnel cause units to become hybrids composed of those who intend to make military service a career and those who have volunteered or been coerced into service for the duration. Above all, the experience of combat makes the difference between regular soldier and citizen-soldier, volunteer and conscript, unimportant. The crucial distinction becomes that between those who are combat veterans and those who are not. The shared horrors, hardships, and rare elation of the battlefield mean more to men than why they ended up there.[22]

To be sure, even in peacetime the difference between conscripts of any kind and volunteer professional soldiers can be erased by clever and arduous training conducted by resourceful leaders. An example of this is in Jean Larteguy's brilliant fictionalized account of the Algerian war, *The Centurions*. In it Colonel Raspeguy, a veteran paratrooper, takes a group of resentful, indeed mutinous, conscripts and reservists and by a variety of physical and psychological devices (isolation from civil society, special clothing, physical exhaustion, and constant propaganda) turns them into a tough and cohesive elite force.[23] The Raspeguys are few and far between, however, as are elite units such as the paratroops or, in the United States, the Marines, who can use institutional mystique to indoctrinate and motivate new members. In peacetime or during a period of low-intensity conflict—as, in fact, the Algerian war proved—the differences between conscript and professional are acute, although not always destructive.

Armies always undergo a drastic transformation when they embark on a full-scale war. No army since the beginning of the nineteenth century has fought a major war successfully without calling into service vast numbers of civilians, whether or not they have had previous military experience. Invariably, the officer corps finds itself shaken by purges, as incompetent officers lose their commands and junior officers—often including former civilians—find themselves promoted with unheard-of rapidity (Generals Dwight Eisenhower and Omar Bradley, for example, began World War II as fairly junior colonels and ended as five-star generals). For conscripts who might under peacetime circumstances have had little or no chance of achieving high rank, new opportunities appear, for wartime armies find themselves short of leaders. The dull routines of peacetime are replaced by compressed training and sudden commitment to the battlefield. Strict financial accountability gives way to staggering and occasionally uncontrolled expenditure; safe and predictable training gives way to dangerous but necessary realism, as blanks give way to live ammunition. As a result of all of these factors, military service in wartime bears little resemblance to that in peacetime. If it is more dangerous it is also less constricted, less stultifying, and above all, more readily accepted by those who undergo it.

The effects of wartime can vanish as swiftly as they appeared in the first place. A good example of this is the demobilization problem faced by the victorious Western powers in 1919 and 1946.[24] Whereas only a few months earlier soldiers had accepted orders that would doom tens of thousands of them to injury or death, suddenly the British and American armies found their soldiers close to mutiny because of delays of a few weeks in demobilization. Generals who had been able to make their dispositions without reference to any particular concerns of equity or abstract justice found themselves confronted with the necessity of dismantling armies posthaste. Although sound military practice and prudent foreign policy would have dictated demobilization by unit, so as to retain an effective force, generals found themselves compelled to yield to the demand for fairness, demobilizing those who had served longest first. The result, of course, was the systematic stripping from all units of their experienced cadres.

Wartime constraints on military service are, like war itself, violent and unpredictable. In 1944, for example, Canada found itself plunged into a conscription crisis because of the sudden need for infantry replacements in Europe. Hitherto an uneasy compromise—conscription for home service only—had prevented the differences bewteen anti-conscription French Canadians and the largely pro-conscription English Canadians from breaking out into the open. A solution was found (limited shipment of draftees overseas), but only at the expense of domestic turmoil and, in a few cases, near-mutiny in the Canadian Army.[25]

THE AMERICAN PREDICAMENT

For many countries, the choice of a system of military service presents few difficulties. For them, the claims of raison d'état and ideology can be easily reconciled, and the demands of actual warfare seem comfortably remote. Four examples can demonstrate this. The Federal Republic of Germany is exclusively a Continental power, one whose primary reason for having a military force is to deter or repel a small or medium attack by the Soviet and East European forces on its border; failing either of those objectives, it must seek to make the conflict sufficiently long and bloody to allow the conventional nuclear forces of its allies (preeminent among them the United States) to come into play. It requires, therefore, a large mechanized force, and has returned to the cadre/conscript system traditional to post-1815 Germany.

Switzerland is a small, democratic, neutral country. It has always needed large forces to deter invasion, but no more: for that purpose an elaborate, compulsory militia system is adequate. Such a system works in large measure because Switzerland is not liberal in the Anglo-Saxon sense, as proven by the virtual prohibition of conscientious objection. Under such conditions, and (unlike Germany) with an army which has never encountered any serious domestic criticism, Swiss citizens accept the approximately thirty years of military service that the Swiss Army requires.[26] In a troubled century the large, defensively oriented Swiss militia has served its purposes admirably, and remains perhaps the most popular institution in Swiss society.[27]

Canada is a liberal, predominantly Anglo-Saxon state that faces no threats from contiguous states, and whose military consists of an extremely high-quality but small professional force. If the need again arises for large Canadian forces to fight in western Europe, Canadians can reasonably hope that they will have time to mobilize their forces behind the protection of American and European land and naval power. In addition, the high professionalism of Canada's forces makes them particularly suited to the trying mission of peacekeeping to which the Canadian government frequently assigns them.

Finally, Israel, a democratic state small both in geography and population, surrounded by much larger and wealthier hostile states, has adopted a uniquely rigorous system of military service. This system combines the cadre/conscript system with a Swiss-type militia organization, providing Israel with a quickly mobilizable and powerful force suited both for short all-out conventional wars and the chronic security mission of border protection. The sheer magnitude of the Israeli security problem removes virtually all major ideological restrictions on her system of military service: the simplicity of the primary threat makes the structuring of forces to cope with it far easier than is the case in other countries.

Until 1945 the United States also possessed an armed force compatible both with American foreign policy requirements and her liberal-democratic ideology. A small, volunteer, professional army and Marine Corps sufficed to police the American empire (the Philippines, for example, and the Caribbean) and the Western frontier. The voluntary state militias served as an admittedly shaky second line of defense, but one that reassured the population that an ample, essentially civilian force existed both to reinforce the regulars and to ensure their subservience to the larger community. In addition, until 1945 the United States could expect to have time to mobilize if it became involved in a large European war. The oceans insulated America from all Great Powers that lacked first-class navies, and Canada served as a hostage for the good behavior of the greatest naval power of them all, Great Britain. The other countries in the vicinity of the United States (Mexico, for example) posed no military threat. Finally, the construction of a powerful American Navy during the Civil War and its permanent reestablishment thirty years later meant that the United States could guarantee its possessions and its shores against any maritime foe.

All of this changed in 1940. Not only was there again, as during 1914–1917, a prospect of American intervention to restore the European balance; the Western Hemisphere, or at least North America, seemed directly endangered. For the first time in history it seemed possible that the British Navy might succumb to the forces of a land power, that Britain herself might be occupied or subdued. The rise of new naval powers, particularly Japan, coupled with the development of air power, ended America's military isolation from the Continent.[28]

After 1945, the United States accepted a host of new and wholly unprecedented commitments to foreign states in all corners of the globe. For the first time it permanently stationed troops in the territory of friendly states, and created a peacetime military establishment that only one other country in the world could rival. With world power came the military burdens discussed above, the necessity of preparing for both small and large wars. To fill the ranks of the largest peacetime army it had ever fielded, the United States for the first time in its history faced the prospect of a prolonged peacetime draft of some kind. The rival claims of liberalism and egalitarianism, which hitherto had been heard only intermittently over such issues as commutation during the Civil War, were now expressed continuously, culminating in bitter opposition to the draft during the Vietnam War.

For a variety of reasons which I shall take up in Chapter 9, the United States found itself able to alleviate this dilemma temporarily by creating a large but all-volunteer force in the early 1970s. For almost a decade the question of military manpower receded to the background of national political life, as the ranks of the armed forces were easily filled owing to poor economic conditions and favorable demography (a surplus of young men aged seventeen to twenty-one). To be sure, there were occasional expressions of alarm and discontent by the professional leadership of those armed forces, but by and large the country seemed to have returned to pre–World War II conditions.

As I shall attempt to demonstrate in the final chapter, this condition cannot last without causing either a serious deterioration in the American military establishment (with concomitant effects on

American foreign policy) or a disruptive and difficult debate about a return to some form of conscription. The goal of the chapters that follow is to explain why (and predict in what ways) the constraints sketched above will continue to impede America's search for a durable system of military service.

[2]

Military Service and the
Mass Army: 1776 to 1914

The foundations of most modern types of military service were established during the years 1776–1914. Study of this period is essential because fundamental attitudes toward conscription are still shaped by divergent understandings of the origins of the modern mass army. To understand both the history of mass military service and our perceptions of it—why, for example, most Europeans find the notion of an effective army without conscription laughable—we must understand the impact of the French Revolution on systems of military service.

In addition, many authors make the argument that the historic change in the standard European system of military service—itself the product of a change in people's conception of politics—transformed both politics and the art of war. Needless to say, this view has met resistance. The arguments advanced by both parties in this debate remain pertinent to an understanding of how and why states have chosen and will choose systems of military service.

THE DEBATE OVER THE MILITARY SIGNIFICANCE
OF THE FRENCH REVOLUTION

The standard interpretation of the military history of the French Revolution can be summarized as follows. The introduction of conscription in France decisively altered the Continental balance of power. It led to the introduction of new and simpler but more effective tactics, but above all, it endowed the soldiers of the Revolutionary armies with an invincible élan. The soldiers raised by the *levée en masse* had far higher morale than their mercenary foes

[42]

because they fought for the rights of man, rather than for fear of their officers. The quality of generalship improved, because lead-ership was no longer foolishly confined to a caste of dissolute and amateurish aristocrats. Thus, the ancien regime armies, composed of the dregs of European society, were technically, tactically in-ferior to those of Revolutionary France; similarly, their leadership suffered from a fatal timidity and amateurishness.[1] As Alfred Vagts put it: "The small rigidly drilled but spiritless armies with which they [European monarchs] had been accustomed to playing fine games of strategy were no match in size, tempo, or tactics for this [French revolutionary] onward sweep of fire-spreading crusaders."[2]

This view gained greatest currency around the turn of the twen-tieth century, when it was made with particular force by such influential historians as Hans Delbrueck. The larger significance of this interpretation stems from its fundamental premise, which is that a state's military apparatus is always a faithful reflection of its polity and society. Thus, R. R. Palmer wrote nearly a half-century later, "the military revolution was at bottom a political revolu-tion."[3]

This view can be, and has been, taken to extremes. In the end, one can argue that military victory stems from possession of a superior, or at least a more modern, political and social structure than that of one's opponent. The victory of the Revolutionary ar-mies is a sign of the superiority of the Revolutionary regime to the limited monarchies that opposed it. From here it is but one step to an interpretation of war based on Social Darwinism, according to which victory goes to those who, in a sense, deserve it.

The existence of mass drafted armies, of course, facilitates this interpretation of military and political history: what more obvious transmission belt between society and army can there be than con-scription? The attraction of this line of argument remains strong. When the American officer corps began to acknowledge the deteri-oration (or, as some argued, the disintegration) of the U.S. Army in Vietnam, they resorted to arguments similar to those advanced by Delbrueck, Palmer, and Vagts about the French Revolution. How, they asked, could the army avoid the problems of race relations, drug abuse, and shaky individual integrity when American society as a whole had to wrestle with the same problems?[4] Surely, these officers maintained, an army of conscripts merely reflected the society that had reared them.

Many officers rejected this "transmission belt theory," however, and argued that the myriad failings of the U.S. Army had purely military sources, having to do with a corruption of the officer corps quite unrelated to events in the civilian world.[5] Similarly a small group of military historians rejected the more general arguments advanced by Delbrueck and his supporters. Jean Colin, a French General Staff historian at the turn of the century, and Cyril Falls, an official historian of the British Army in this century, claimed that historians and political scientists must look for narrower explanations of the military successes of Revolutionary France. Falls tartly ascribed views such as Palmer's to a perverse desire to prove that wars are won by everything but the most obvious factor— fighting.[6] He argued that "tactical considerations are all important in most wars," and asserted that most historians find themselves too entranced by discussions of strategy and politics, and too bored by the literature of tactics, to study war properly.[7] In short, in this view much of war is independent of politics; nationalism and revolutionary spirit do not necessarily create superior armed forces; military proficiency has little connection with the regime; political revolution does not necessarily lead to tactical change, let alone tactical superiority.

Both points of view have some merit, and both contain some exaggerated claims. Both have peculiar importance for the study of systems of military service. If Delbrueck, Palmer, and Vagts are correct, a country is doomed to adopt a system of service suited to its domestic political institutions, whether or not such a system answers its military needs. The weaknesses of its army will flow from those of society, and hence lie beyond the power of statesmen or professional soldiers to ameliorate. If, on the other hand, Falls and Colin are correct, a state should first assess its military needs and then seek a system of military service that will meet them efficiently. In this view an army's weaknesses result from the failings of its leaders, not from those of its society.

We begin therefore by studying the armies of the French Revolutionary period in search of answers to the following questions: Is the modern mass army the product of a change in people's conceptions of politics, or the product of military necessity created by changes in the implements and techniques of war? To what extent does a system of military service shape tactics and discipline? Do revolutionary armies adopt revolutionary tactics, and are they superior? Finally, can a system of service created under one set of technological and tactical conditions (in this case, the armies of the pre-1789 ancien regime) adapt to a wholly new set of circumstances?

THE ARMIES OF THE ANCIEN RÉGIME

The European standing armies of the eighteenth century consisted of volunteers or conscripts, depending on the country in question.[8] Men served for varying lengths of time, but their terms lasted at least five years, and often considerably longer—from eight years in France to twenty-one in Great Britain. In Russia each village had to furnish one recruit for every dozen households, and a young man's departure was often accompanied by a funeral ceremony, since he served for twenty-five years (as of 1793) and had little chance of ever returning to his native hamlet.[9] In some countries, particularly Prussian and Austria, recruits were allowed to ply civilian occupations for ten or eleven months a year, but remained liable for call-up at any time. Because of lifelong service and the haphazard methods of recruiting, the armies of the ancien regime contained boys barely beyond adolescence as well as greybeards; war was not simply a young man's activity.

In England and France military service in the line was voluntary—although, as many contemporary and later observers pointed out, recruiters often resorted to trickery such as getting potential recruits drunk or making false promises in order to fill their quotas; at times they simply kidnapped their victims. Many armies contained large numbers of foreign mercenaries, exiles, and adventurers. The Prussian army under Frederick the Great's father, Frederick William I, consisted of roughly one-third foreigners, and by 1768 the proportion had risen to over two-fifths.[10] In the pre-Revolutionary French Army one-quarter of the regiments were made up entirely of foreigners—Germans, Swiss, Scots, Irish, and Flemings.[11] Frederick the Great laid it down as a rule of thumb that foreigners could be mixed in with natives up to the proportion of one-half, although he opposed their use in separate units.

It is hardly surprising that the system of voluntary enlistment and hiring of mercenaries produced armies that were, in Frederick's words, "for the most part composed of the dregs of society—sluggards, rakes, debauchees, rioters, undutiful sons, and the like, who have as little attachment to their masters or concern about them as do foreigners."[12] Although recent research indicates that

[45]

eighteenth-century armies attracted more than vagabonds and semi-criminals, it is true that the middle classes of eighteenth-century society did not usually serve.

What was unique about the ancien regime system of military service was not so much that it was conscript (it was not in all countries) as that it brought men into service from the lowest classes and for long periods of duty. The officers, on the other hand, derived from the nobility and often served for shorter periods of time, or only sporadically. The best ancien regime army, and the prototypical one, was that of Frederician Prussia.

The Prussian monarchy specifically exempted merchants, artisans, manufacturers, men who lived on rent or off a capital of six thousand thalers, and their sons from military service. In addition, a number of cities such as Berlin were relieved of the burden of military service.[13] The Prussian conscripts served with the regiment assigned to their cantons for varying periods of time, sometimes as briefly as two or three months a year, but military obligation lasted at least ten or twelve years. A similar system was used by the Austrian Empire.[14] The Prussian Army thereby drew on a small slice of the peasant population, foreign adventurers, and those Prussians foolish enough to enlist voluntarily.[15]

The officer corps of Prussia, like the officer corps of other eighteenth-century armies, consisted mainly of nobles: in fact, Frederick the Great preferred foreign-born nobles to his Prussian-born bourgeoisie.[16] He went so far as to purge his army of base-born men, although (as in most European armies of the time) a commoner could make a career in the technical branches of the armed forces, particularly in the artillery and engineers.

The nobility dominated the officer corps in almost all countries, although only in Prussia was military service regarded as an inescapable duty. The result in England and France was a swollen officer corps composed of many men for whom bearing arms was not a profession but an indication of social position. In 1775 the French army contained 170,000 men, of whom 60,000—more than a third—were officers.[17] Toward the end of the eighteenth century the nobles' control of the upper echelons actually increased, as French ministers of war introduced new and stiff requirements for proof of aristocratic birth and abolished the venality of commissions.[18] It should be noted that these reactionary measures were accompanied by real and intelligent reform, including a purge of incompetent noble officers, a melioration of discipline, and a wide-ranging set of tactical and organizational improvements.

[46]

A harsh discipline riveted together the peasant or underclass soldier and his noble officer. Frederick the Great told his officers that the common soldier must fear them more than the enemy, and obedience was enforced by the whip, the gauntlet, and the hangman's noose.[19] For their part, eighteenth-century soldiers deserted at extraordinary rates: in the Prussian Army even such mundane decisions as where to camp were made with a view to minimizing loss by desertion.[20] In that army, and to a lesser extent in the British, discipline was harsh; in the French Army, by contrast, a culprit might receive a score of blows from the flat of a sword for an offense that would have incurred hundreds of lashes in other forces.

It is tempting, however, to exaggerate the relative brutality of eighteenth-century armies. Some commanders refrained from cruel punishments, and the populace at large was accustomed to treatment far more ruthless than that of later periods. Furthermore, the complement to draconian discipline was often adequate feeding and housing during a period when the lower classes could not be certain of either. Frederick's instructions to his officers contain frequent exhortations to care for their men properly, and there is good evidence that such commands were heeded.[21]

For the most part, governments relied on standing armies, although they sporadically raised militia units for home defense (in England, for example) or in order to provide a pool of conscripts for the regular army (France). In general, these units did not serve overseas and existed for brief periods only. As time went on even less reliance was put on militia units, save in England and her colonies and Switzerland.[22]

Armies were small: Maurice de Saxe, one of the greatest of eighteenth-century soldiers, concluded that the optimal size of an army in the field was 34,000 infantry and 12,000 cavalry—a force only a fraction of the size of the hosts that fought such battles as Austerlitz and Borodino.[23] On the other hand, armies as a whole in relation to population were not that much smaller than in modern times. In 1786 Prussian kept 1 soldier per 29 inhabitants, and Austria 1 per 96; in 1789 France fielded 1 per 144. By comparison, in 1981 the United States had 1 serviceman per 109.[24]

Soldiers were precious and scarce, to be sure, but the tools of war were fairly cheap: weapons (even warships) had an effective service life of well over a generation, ammunition expenditure was low, and in garrison soldiers could be required to grow their own vegetables or even conduct small businesses. In the field, armies often supported themselves by foraging and living off the country. The Great Powers did indeed build large magazines and depots to feed their troops, but these did not provide all, or even the major part, of their needs in the field.[25]

Eighteenth-century warfare was indeed limited in the sense described by Clausewitz—limited in its political aims—but eighteenth-century battle was as murderous an affair as anything known until World War I. Marshal Saxe remarked, "I have always noticed that a single campaign reduces an army by a third, at least, and sometimes by half."[26] Many died from sickness, to be sure, but battles killed as well: at Fontenoy in 1745, for example, the Allied forces under the Duke of Cumberland suffered 15,000 dead and wounded.[27]

The prevalent technology of war made such losses inevitable, for weapons were extremely lethal, but only at short ranges. The armies of the ancien regime fought mainly in linear formations, lines three or more deep blazing away at enemies who generally stood as close as fifty or sixty yards away. The advantage went to those armies (such as the Prussian) whose men could load and fire rapidly and maneuver in line while sustaining heavy losses.[28] Extraordinary discipline was needed so that the volley could be delivered at the last possible moment (that is, after receiving the enemy's volley) and then immediately exploited with a bayonet charge.

The leaders of eighteenth-century armies reacted to these conditions as best they could, and some of them (Saxe, Marlborough, Suvorov, Frederick, and Wolfe, for example) certainly equaled Napoleon's marshals in military skill. Again, if they did not shatter kingdoms it was because war did not have ideological aims, and because the astute balance of power politics of the time prevented any one nation from gaining mastery.

Lesser-known but equally important figures (many of them Frenchmen active in the period 1770–1789) gradually improved military tactics, technology, and organization.[29] Partly as a result of the experiences of the American Revolution, German and French theorists developed a doctrine that called for light troops to skirmish ahead of the main forces. Others developed a simple set of evolutions to enable a marching column to form a line quickly: since the column formation maximizes speed and maneuverability, and the line maximizes the application of firepower, the result was a supple, easily learned drill, which greatly enhanced tactical mobility. Military technology improved, particularly in monarchical

France, where such men as Jean Baptiste de Gribeauval (inspector-general of artillery in the 1760s and 1770s) standardized cannon calibers, improved aiming sights, and developed light and sturdy cannon caissons. This development created the mobile firepower that Napoleon would use to smash a hole in an enemy's line.

Organizational reformers experimented with breaking armies up into divisions—small sub-armies composed of infantry, cavalry, and artillery—that could advance on separate routes although under one command. As a result, a greater portion of the countryside could be drawn on, and greater numbers of soldiers supported. In addition, divisional organization simplified the task of the army commander, who could now concentrate on the direction of a few large units rather than attempt to coordinate many small ones. Divisional approaches along multiple routes, however, were workable only because of much larger changes in Europe. Economic underdevelopment had inhibited eighteenth-century warfare as much as the political aims of those who waged it. Late eighteenth-century changes, foremost among them the development of roads, the growth in agriculture and manufacture, and the refinement of such vital auxiliary sciences as cartography, provided the preconditions for the swift movements by large forces which characterized Napoleonic warfare.[30]

Given eighteenth-century warfare as I have described it, the ancien regime system of military service—long service by conscripted or volunteer peasants, foreigners, and adventurers, leadership by a cast of nobles—made sense. Eighteenth-century battle required discipline of a peculiarly rigid kind: men had to fight shoulder to shoulder, look their enemies in the face, and execute a complicated set of operations even as a quarter or a third of their comrades fell by their side, shattered by bullet and cannonball. To load and fire the musket (which needed nearly a dozen steps, from tearing open a cartridge to ramming it home) was a matter of exact practice, in some ways far more complicated than the loading and firing of twentieth-century weapons.[31] Only long practice and discipline could enable troops to fire as many as four rounds per minute and to maneuver in paradeground order on the battlefield. Frederick the Great succeeded in developing armies of such quality, and with them he won the battles of Leuthen and Rossbach. Small wonder, then, that the soldier who had had two years' training—who had become a reliable automaton, in effect—was far more valuable to the Prussian king than two or three who had had none. Such precious assets were to be conserved by good care and a severe but equable discipline. At the same time, it seemed sensible (as contemporary economists pointed out) that only the dregs of society be used for such purposes, and that the more productive members of society, particularly the middle class, should concentrate on the production of national wealth.[32]

Similarly, the exclusive use of aristocrats as officers had much to be said for it. Frederick believed that their intensely personal sense of honor would lead them to perform their duty on the battlefield; he doubted that bourgeois officers could acquire a corporate sense of honor, that is, a code of honor applicable to officers as officers.[33] Moreover, as Tocqueville later pointed out, aristocrats had further advantages: they were accustomed to command, and they posed no threat to society, for their interests were at one with it.[34] Eighteenth-century officers might not have been particularly intelligent or diligent, but they were rarely cowards and virtually never a threat to the regime. The same could not always be said of their successors in democratic armies.

THE FRENCH REVOLUTION AND ITS CONSEQUENCES

During the course of the Revolution the French Army, which contained large numbers of unemployed artisans from the cities, succumbed to the blandishments of Revolutionary agitators. The leaders among the disaffected, who subsequently rose to high commands under Napoleon, were primarily noncommissioned officers and non-noble junior officers, many of whom had risen from the ranks. By the end of 1789 radicals in the National Assembly were proposing drastic military reform, including universal military training along Spartan lines, in accordance with republican ideals.[35] At the same time, the major cities formed National Guard units, volunteer associations composed primarily of bourgeois citizens and their elected officers.

In addition, in the period 1790–1793 units of Volunteers were formed, who were separate from the army, better paid, and more ideologically reliable, but less numerous (in December 1792, for example, the regular army numbered 112,000 men and the Volunteers only 44,000). Gradually, the exigencies of foreign wars forced the National Assembly to draft National Guards into the regular army (July 1792). Finally, on 23 August 1793 the levee en masse was declared, which provided for the conscription of all unmarried men aged eighteen to twenty-five, without exception of substitution. The National Guards, the conscripts, and the regular army (amalgamated with the Volunteers in February 1793) swiftly grew in size, from 264,000 men in 1793 to 749,000 by September 1794.[36]

To keep these numbers in perspective one must remember that France was easily the most populous country in Europe with the exception of Russia, and that muster rolls were undoubtedly inflated by poor or self-interested accounting. Nonetheless, the introduction of conscription clearly enabled the French regime to field a force five times the size of the old royal army. It was, however, the nucleus of the royal army that won the critical early battles fought by the Revolutionary armies against their European opponents. Throughout this period the cadre of the old royal army—junior officers and sergeants—provided the backbone of the new conscript armies. Above all, the Revolutionary armies used the weapons and tactical doctrine of the old army: the regulations governing tactics in 1785 remained in effect through the Napoleonic period.[37]

The French revolutionary armies did introduce tactical innovations in their use of a thick line of skirmishers, who sought cover in hedges and ditches and fired more or less at will. Some authorities attribute this to deliberate policy, others to the zeal of soldiers to close with the foe and the inability of officers to keep them under control.[38] One typical encounter was the battle of Hondschoote on 8 September 1793, in which some 9,000 Hanoverians, enduring the musketry of 22,000 French troops for four hours, suffered a casualty rate of one-third. Neither the orderly bayonet charges of the Germans nor their volleys made an impression on the scattered French, who fired from behind hedges and buildings at the enemy troops.

Interestingly enough, the Hanoverians retreated in good order, despite their heavy losses and extreme numerical inferiority. The Revolutionary armies were, no doubt, more ardent than their enemies, but more volatile as well. One French general sourly remarked in 1794 that the troops charged crying "Vive la republique!" and "ça ira!" but at the first shot shouted "Nous sommes perdus!" and when the enemy attacked, "Sauve qui peut!" In short, the ancien regime armies displayed little tactical flexibility, but greater determination and steadiness; their French opponents more ingenuity but less solidity.[39]

The virtues of the French Army created by the levee en masse were primarily those of the late eighteenth-century royal army—simple and flexible tactics, superior artillery and doctrine for its employment—carried to their logical conclusion by an officer corps that steadily improved in quality. Superior mobilization enabled the French to swamp opposing forces and replace losses quickly; here is where the system of military service adopted by France made its greatest contribution. Above all, however, the French benefited from the geographic and political disunity of the coalitions that opposed them. Prussia feared Austria almost as much as it did France, Austria suspected Russia, the English had far less interest in the outcome of Continental battles than in control of the high seas. At no time until the climactic campaigns against Napoleon in 1813–1815 were the powers hostile to France willing to exert themselves to the full to crush the Jacobins and their successors. The tepidness of their enthusiasm for the war against France was reflected in the constricted instructions they gave their generals, their cautious dispositions, and their limited strategic designs. When they allowed an able commander independence of action, however, as they did Suvorov in Italy, they gained substantial victories.[40]

Napoleon did not initially rely heavily on conscripts (in the period 1801–1804 he took only 30,000 regulars and as many reservists), but by 1813 he had drafted nearly 2,500,000. Although the term of service theoretically lasted only five years, in practice men were forced to serve for the duration of the wars, which lasted until Napoleon's overthrow.[41] As time went on, conscription became increasingly unpopular: indeed, even in the earlier period of the Revolution the royalist uprising in the Vendee gained strength from popular resistance to conscription. Nonetheless, the virtues of Napoleon's armies remained those of the Revolutionary armies, with the qualification that hero-worship may have replaced ideological fervor.

The popular interpretation of the relative merits of the ancien regime and French armies must explain why the Allies eventually beat down the Napoleonic regime. Some writers observe that the French were eventually beaten by mirror-image armies, and note that all of Napoleon's opponents eventually adopted conscription. This argument seems most forceful in the case of Prussia, which, according to some historians, reacted to the defeats of 1806 by creating a vast short-service reserve army, thereby evading the restrictions imposed by the French and making use of their example. In the words of Gerhard Ritter, "Technical and strategic tricks were of no avail here. . . . The most important change that was needed was to replace that soulless, time-honored power instrument, the thoroughly venal professional army, with a whole nation in arms."[42] Indeed, shortly after the calamitous defeats of Jena and Auerstaedt, General Gneisenau advocated "boldly rifling the armory of revolution," and Minister of War Scharnhorst proposed the abandonment of the small mercenary army for a citizen militia.[43]

What is often forgotten, however, is that King Frederick William III rejected these proposals, doubting their military efficacy and fearing their political consequences. He turned instead to such political conservatives as General Yorck, who purged the officer corps, increased the number of light infantry, reformed infantry and combined arms tactics, and meliorated discipline.[44] The citizen militia (Landwehr) numbered barely 20,000 poorly trained and disciplined men when Prussia reentered the war in 1813; the regular army numbered 65,000 or only 10,000 more than in 1806. At that point a general mobilization of 120,000 men into both the Landwehr and the regular army took place. Here too, the Prussians relied on the old regular army to train those without military experience, and to provide the cadres for noncommissioned and regular officers.[45] Following the war, the Prussian government returned to a modified form of ancien regime–type conscription, and slowly eroded the independence of the largely middle-class Landwehr.

The Russian Army maintained its traditional form of conscription throughout the early nineteenth century, although local militia units were raised to harass the French invaders in 1812. The most interesting ancien regime army, however, was that of England, which posed the greatest threat to France proper and won the culminating victory at Waterloo. As in past wars, the home defense of the British Isles rested with a large conscript militia (some 200,000 men doing four weeks' training a year and a smaller standing force of regular militia in which men enrolled for several years at a time). Some of the men in these units, animated by patriotism, greed, or a desire for adventure, enlisted in the regular army, which fought the campaigns on the Continent.[46]

The British Army of 1815, therefore, contained much the same human material as it had in the 1750s, including large numbers of foreigners (in April 1813, for example, Wellington had 75,000 troops, of whom 26,000 were Portuguese, 5,000 German, and 1,000 French). It was the Iron Duke himself who coined the description of the rank and file which has come to be identified with all ancien regime armies, "the scum of the earth"—although we rarely hear the remainder of that famous remark: "It is really wonderful that we should have made them the fine fellows they are."[47] The harshness of discipline, though relaxed from earlier days, was still severe. Flogging was common, although more frequent in some units than in others. Nor was it entirely unpopular: one old soldier of the Black Watch argued that whipping served to protect the exemplary soldiers from the scoundrels in the ranks. In response to philanthropists, he wrote: "The good soldier thanks you not for such philanthropy; the incorrigible laughs at your humanity, despises your clemency, and meditates only how to gratify his naturally vicious propensities."[48] In addition (although this is rarely remarked), Wellington and many of his subordinates went to great lengths to ensure that the troops were decently fed and housed. They established unprecedented levels of hygiene, and attempted to provide some recreation and amusement for the troops.[49]

Wellington coped with French tactics by shrewd use of the ground, hiding his troops behind hillcrests until after the opening artillery duels. Above all, he used to advantage the extraordinary steadiness of British troops, a steadiness acquired through years of drill. Thus, he could afford to thin his lines out to two ranks (instead of three) and withhold his fire until the very last moment, with psychological effects that were almost always decisive.[50] To neutralize the swarm of French skirmishers (*tirailleurs*) he deployed superbly trained riflemen and light infantry, who had been trained by one of Britain's most remarkable nineteenth-century soldiers, Sir John Moore.

Moore, who had served in America during the War for Independence and thereafter in Egypt, Italy, the West Indies, and Ireland, introduced into the British Army remarkably advanced notions of training and discipline.[51] In 1802 at the camp at Shorncliffe he began to train the regiment that would eventually form the nucleus of the Light Division, the British Army's force of light infantry in the Peninsular War. The material he was given was no better than that of the rest of the British Army: of the thirteen regiments asked to supply forty or more men, at least six carefully selected the misfits and troublemakers. Moore took these men and introduced a new type of training, which required of the officers "real knowledge, good temper, and kind treatment of the men." He drastically reduced corporal punishment and verbal abuse, emphasizing instead tactical exercises and physical training, and stressing throughout the importance of individual initiative.[52] He described his approach this way: "The essential thing required was not a new drill but a new discipline, a new spirit that should make of the whole a living organism to replace a mechanical instrument."[53]

[54]

It is interesting to note that Moore strongly opposed the introduction of short service (which meant, at the time, anything less than the standard twenty-one years). Not only did he think the troops content with the long enlistments; he believed such terms essential for military proficiency and good discipline:

> The discipline of the mind is as requisite as that of the body is to make a good soldier. The English are less prepared for this in their civil state than other nations and are more likely to acquire it when they enter the service for life than for a limited period. The impression on the mind at his entrance into the service that his profession is demanded for life, tends as much to the happiness of the individual as it does to make him a good soldier. He considers the officers and soldiers of his regiment as the persons with whom he is to pass his life, and he endeavors to gain their friendship, and good will, and to distinguish himself by the qualities which are likely to gain their approbation.[54]

Moore died a hero's death at Corunna, but through the officers who served with him his influence over the British Army lasted for decades. His accomplishments at Shorncliffe showed the range of capabilities of an ancien regime system of military service based on the long service on enlisted men and a paternalistic officer class.

CONSCRIPTION UNTIL 1914

Following the close of the Napoleonic wars, Europe returned to the ancien regime system of military service. Even in Prussia, where the greatest institutional changes had been made, less than half the annual cohort served the three-year term of obligation. Moreover, the son of a wealthy man could enlist as an *Einjaehrig-Freiwillige*, or one-year volunteer, who paid for his own support and clothing and thus escaped the rigors of prolonged service. In France the Law of Recruitment of 1832 provided for conscription for up to seven years' service. Theoretically, the entire male population was eligible for military service, but in practice only the poor had to serve, since there was a large market for substitutes (often former servicemen).[55]

France's return to the ancien regime system of military service had a number of roots. The reactionary and conservative politicians of the Restoration and the July monarchy undoubtedly feared the effect of massive, short-service conscription in a country where suffrage was limited to the wealthy few. They desired a reliable professional force that wuld not balk at suppressing insurrection or rebellion. But there were military arguments as well for the return to ancien regime conscription, arguments worth examining in some detail, since they incorporated a study of the wars of the Revolution and Napoleonic period with an understanding of the trends of modern warfare. More important, they proceeded from views about military psychology which still have some merit.

General Thomas Robert Bugeaud, the conqueror of Algeria, had served in Spain against the British and there developed a profound respect for that army, particularly its regimental cohesion. He deprecated the value of patriotic ardor, saying of the Marseillaise, "I like the song very much, but I do not think that it alone gives victory. I find, gentlemen, that the troops sing it before battle but not during it."[56] He argued that a seven-year period of service was necessary because the short-term man (with three years' experience or less) could never feel himself a true soldier:

> It has been thought that it suffices to teach a recruit his exercises to make him a good soldier: this is an error. Exercise is the least thing in the education of a soldier. One is not a soldier until one is no longer homesick; until the regimental flag is as familiar as the village steeple; until one loves that flag; until one is prepared to draw one's saber whenever the regiment's honor is attacked; until one has complete confidence in one's superiors, in one's neighbors on right and left.[57]

Bugeaud's arguments were based on a long and varied experience as an officer; those of Colonel Ardant du Picq were based in part on practical knowledge acquired in the Crimea and elsewhere, but more on reflection and study. His *Combat Studies* was the first modern investigation of the psychology of combat; he came to his conclusions after scholarly research and careful use of questionnaires distributed among the French officer corps.

Du Picq described combat as a "dreadful pasquinade" in which men are torn between fear, discipline, and vanity. He documented the phenomenon (rediscovered by S. L. A. Marshall during World War II) that in modern combat a fairly small percentage of men fire their weapons or advance into enemy fire.[58] Du Picq foresaw greater difficulty in forcing men to fight as weapons improved: the percussion cap and the cylindro-conoidal bullet (adopted by European armies in the period 1830–1860) allowed fast and accurate rifle fire at ranges of up to eight hundred yards, or four to eight times the range of the Napoleonic musket. As a result, battle degenerated into action at the company, platoon, or even squad level, because greater masses (the eighteenth-century battalion column, for example) would suffer horrendous casualties and disintegrate long before reaching enemy lines. Soldiers needed psychological cohesion more than ever before, because they would have to move in extended order over great distances in apparent isolation from neighboring units.

Du Picq held that only long-service troops could develop the mutual trust and instinctive cooperation, the self-confidence and initiative, to succeed on the mid-nineteenth-century battlefield. He contemptuously described reliance on short-service conscripts as "the theory of the big battalions" and attributed to conscription the Austrian defeat in Italy in 1859 at the hands of French regulars.[59] There was little point in bringing masses of men to the battlefield if they dissolved into a passive or (worse) a panicked mob when firing began. A well-paid mercenary army would fight well, if properly motivated by a sense of honor and professionalism; in mass armies, on the other hand, democratic notions of equality and individualism could only erode sound discipline.[60]

The Prussian Army that decisively defeated the French Army in the war of 1870–1871 approximated that of the modern cadre/conscript type. True, only about half of the annual contingent of eligible young men served, and the upper classes could ease the burden of conscription by enrolling their sons as one-year volunteers. Nonetheless, the victory of Prussia was seen by both contemporaries and historians as the triumph of a modern over an outmoded system of military service. Eventually the statesmen of the Third Republic, preeminent among them Adolphe Thiers, reluctantly conceded the need for conscription along Prussian lines.[61]

The chief advantage the Germans gained from conscription was one of numbers, an advantage of almost two to one against the French, who had a small regular army and virtually no reserves. Equally important was the poor generalship of the French commanders, their deficiency in artillery (and mishandling of what they had), and their lack of practice in large-scale operations. At the tactical level, however, French soldiers did display the virtues that du Picq and Bugeaud had claimed for them, namely cohesion and steadiness under fire. On a number of occasions (the battle of Gravelotte, for example) they repulsed superior forces brilliantly.

Although many conservatives in France and Britain clung to Bugeaud's and du Picq's views of military psychology, the new military psychology took its lead from the German general, Colmar von der Goltz. He argued that youthful conscripts made the best soldiers by virtue of their physical resilience and above all their naïveté.

> Those soldiers are, as a rule, the bravest who know no danger. . . . It is only the young that depart from life without pangs. They are not as yet fettered to this earth by the thousand threads that civil life winds round us. . . . Their yearning after experience rouses their ardour for war. Rest and enjoyment and the aims and aspirations of riper years are as yet far removed.[62]

It is difficult to imagine modern generals making such an argument as candidly as did this nineteenth-century Prussian, but they may well feel its force (hence, perhaps, military organizations' propensity to accept illegal, but enthusiastic, underage volunteers).

Psychology, however, played a small role in the death of the ancien regime armies and their replacement by forces modeled on those of nineteenth-century Prussia. Rather, considerations of sheer mass—above all, the need for reserve forces of former servicemen to replace losses and raise new armies—forced the development of mass armies. The difficulties France encountered in attempting to raise citizen armies after losing virtually its whole regular force at Sedan and Metz in 1870 indicated that soldiers needed at least a modicum of prewar training to be useful in wartime. In addition, the Industrial Revolution, and the development of the railroad in particular, gave modern states the capacity to sustain vast armies without needing to draw on limited local sources of food.

Democratic fervor, in other words, played little or no role in the European states' adoption of the cadre/conscript system in the period 1870–1900. The principle of obligatory service in the defense of the state had been accepted early in the eighteenth century. In addition, social peace was purchased by permitting members of the middle class to escape military service, albeit at some cost in organizational strength, since it meant the loss of large numbers of potential junior officers and NCOs. A type of conscription similar in its effects to that of ancien regime conscription bought a few years of social peace for the United States during the Vietnam war period. There too, the removal of a large pool of potential junior leaders hurt military efficiency; and ultimately, such discrimination could not work in a society far more egalitarian than that of the early nineteenth century.

[58]

In addition, the military arguments for the ancien regime system deserved some respect, based as they were on psychology rather than technology. It is particularly important that the discipline of an ancien regime army did not require Frederician brutality and *Kadavergehorsam* (corpse-like obedience). As du Picq argued and Moore demonstrated, capable officers could, by humane treatment, bring out intelligence and initiative from troops recruited from the lower orders of society. This was possible, however, only under the conditions of stability and near familial relations created by long service, a deeply rooted regimental tradition, and above all a devoted and capable officer corps. Under such conditions, but under such conditions only, ancien regime armies could cope with new technology and tactical conditions.

Thus, Colin and Falls were right to insist on the study of more purely military factors to understand the outcome of early nineteenth-century wars. Delbrueck and his school are correct, however, if we take the longer view. The adoption of mass conscription in Europe did not have political/ideological roots, but it did have very substantial political effects. The modern cadre/conscript system spread throughout Europe because of its military utility: it provided the major states with much larger armies than were hitherto thought possible. The Russian Empire, for example, adopted Prussian-type conscription in 1874 but paid the political price in 1905, when its short-service force of draftees proved unreliable against the crowds opposing the government.

Since 1870 the cadre/conscript system has been the norm for all of Continental Europe, so much so that in many countries no other system of military service is conceivable. On the other hand, the cadre/conscript system, durable though it has proven, is but one type of military service suited to modern warfare. In the next chapter I will compare it with others, which have their own peculiar merits and defects.

[3]

Systems of Military Service
and Total War

In Chapter 2 I examined the origins of the modern mass army, and in Chapter 1 I argued that America's contemporary manpower dilemma stems in part from the need to maintain a large army for total warfare. In this chapter I will examine the various systems capable of meeting a modern state's need for conventional forces in all-out war: in particular, the only three modern systems—cadre/ conscript, militia, and expansible/selective service—capable of raising and training armies that may number in the millions.

First, however, it is necessary to establish that modern conventional warfare still requires the mass army as it evolved in the late nineteenth and early twentieth centuries. Some students of military affairs assert that the nation in arms came to an end in 1918, or at the latest 1945, and that large armies now serve few purposes save those of domestic politics. Nor is the debate a purely academic one: one of the arguments advanced in the United States in the 1970s for the All-Volunteer Force was that the technological sophistication of postwar weaponry made war the business of mature technicians, not postadolescent conscripts.

THE DURABILITY OF THE MASS ARMY

In a recent essay titled "The Decline of the Mass Army," Jacques van Doorn argues that modern armies need fewer and fewer fighting men, that an increasing proportion of the military apparatus exists to service and maintain complicated machines that require considerable expertise to use. Doorn ascribes these developments to larger transformations in industrial society. The technological nature of modern warfare places less of a premium on traditional martial virtues than it does on mechanical competence: "The pilot, the artillery man, and the tank crew do not have to 'fight bravely,' in the strict sense of the expression; in the same way, the crane operator and the rolling machine operator do not have it as their prime obligation to 'work hard.'"[1] In this view the mass army was the product of certain nineteenth-century technological developments, in particular the railroad, which allowed the mobilization and supply of large masses of men, and the mechanization of such industries as textiles and agriculture which allowed them to be clothed, fed, and equipped. The military basis of the mass army was the simplicity and standardization of weapons, primarily the bolt action rifle of the late nineteenth century.

It is interesting to note that this line of reasoning is an old one—in fact, nearly a half-century old. In the two decades following World War I a small group of English, French, and German soldiers advanced theories of war supporting small professional armies in lieu of the masses who had died, seemingly for little or no purpose, in the trenches of the Western Front. All of these authors resorted in some measure to technological arguments to support their views. Thus, an examination of their arguments may shed light on the validity of the notion that technology constrains a state's choice of a system of military service, an argument as popular today as it was in the late 1920s and early 1930s.

The first and most influential of these figures was Major General J. F. C. Fuller, the architect of Britain's Plan 1919, the plan for the climactic invasion of Germany never used because of the collapse of Germany's resistance in November 1918. It envisioned the use of massed formations of tanks and aircraft to puncture the enemy's front line and run amok in his rear areas, in a fashion similar to that of the early blitzkrieg campaigns of World War II. Following the war, Fuller pioneered the theory of armored warfare and, through his writings, unintentionally exercised considerable influence over the German Army.

Drawing on his learning in military history, especially of the campaigns of Alexander the Great, Fuller argued that "the scientifically organized, well-armored, superbly disciplined, highly offensive and wonderfully mobile *little* army invariably destroyed the *horde*" (emphasis Fuller's).[2] Armored warfare would involve the use of small, totally mechanized forces, although this would largely be the result of expense: "In the next war it is highly improbable that any nation will be able to put in the field more than a

[61]

few thousand tanks."[3] The immobile masses of World War I–type armies—slow and vulnerable because of their sheer size—would be sliced to ribbons by standing armies of professional armored troops.

> Spengler's idea is: "The place of permanent armies as we know them will gradually be taken by professional forces of war-keen soldiers; and from millions we will revert to hundreds of thousands." Though my argument differs, my idea is the same: mechanization will force the small army to the fore by rendering the mass army useless. The age of the *condottiere* will return.[4]

These views were echoed by Fuller's fellow Englishman and sometime friend, B. H. Liddel Hart, a better-known but perhaps less influential theorist of armored warfare, who also argued that "in modern war, weapon and motor power count for more than manpower." Additionally, however, both men believed that small professional armies could win because of their superior esprit and discipline. Both were admirers of Sir John Moore (Fuller wrote two scholarly studies of him) and were convinced that a happy medium could be found between the rigidity of traditional discipline and the indiscipline of quickly raised citizen armies. Moore's paternalistic but inspirational type of discipline seemed particularly suited to modern military technology. It found its practical expression in the oft-noted informality of bomber and submarine crews in World War II. There mutual reliance was vital and technical competence necessary, and physical proximity to other crew members combined with isolation from the environment to create a small and cooperative community.[5]

Similar arguments were also advanced by Charles de Gaulle when he was a rising colonel in the French Army in the early 1930s. De Gaulle agreed that conscript armies, because of their size and frequent turnover in personnel, required training by the book, but "a professional army needs a different leaven."[6] He too believed that technological complexity dictated military professionalism. He noted that by the end of World War I the infantry fought with fully fifteen different types of weapons, and opened his most famous prewar book with the sentence, "Helpful friend at all times, at present the machine controls our destiny."[7] Like Fuller and Liddell Hart he was smitten by the tank; small wonder, then, that he believed that "the time has arrived of elite troops and special equipment."[8]

[62]

The most thoroughly argued case for a professional army came from the pen of Colonel-General Hans von Seeckt, commander of the German Army (the *Reichswehr*) during the 1920s. An extremely successful staff officer and commander on the Eastern Front during World War I, Seeckt created from the remnants of the defeated German Army the nucleus of Hitler's *Wehrmacht*, and this despite the restriction of his forces to 100,000 men without modern equipment. He was also a sincere advocate of a relatively small professional army backed by a larger conscript militia.[9]

Seeckt maintained that modern technology would make weapons too expensive for mass production. Moreover, the rapid progress of weapons technology resulted in swift obsolescence, which placed mass armies in the position of either expending vast sums of money to periodically re-equip their forces or accepting technological inferiority. Although he did not himself foresee the development of armored warfare, he enthusiastically supported the surreptitious experimentation of the Reichswehr with aircraft, motorized vehicles, and modern wireless equipment.

Seeckt also agreed with Fuller and the rest about the need for a new kind of discipline, one that could grow only from long professional association. He had been particularly impressed by the superior fighting qualities of the British Army at the opening of World War I, when he had served in Kluck's First Army on the Western Front during the battles of August 1914. He noted that professional British troops animated by esprit de corps did not surrender until wounded, but that French troops motivated by patriotism laid down their weapons when still capable of resistance.[10]

For all four of these men—who brought both trained intellects and military experience to bear on the problem—technological arguments reinforced less tangible reasons for turning to professional volunteer armies; the moral and psychological benefits of long service and the spirit, versatility, and cohesion of professional soldiers weighed as heavily with them as technical reasons. In short, their analysis of the problem was more subtle than that of those who simply declared "the Wars of the Nations" to be at an end. As World War II subsequently demonstrated, the difficulties lay not in the lack of technical proficiency of conscript troops, but in their lack of cohesion and morale.

Contrary to the expectations of virtually all experts, the technology of mid-twentieth-century warfare posed no insuperable obstacles to the raising of mass armies. During the first part of the war, for example, Great Britain administered the Commonwealth Air Training Program, which, in short order, produced 11,000 pilots, 6,300 observers, and 10,700 radio-operators and gunners a year. Careful selection of personnel (to include making use of their civilian skills) made it possible to reduce training time for pilots to nine months and that for subsidiary crew members to three.[11] The United States accomplished similar miracles as it raised an armed force of some twelve million men, provisioned with types of equipment for which only prototypes existed a few years before the war. In August 1941, for example, the Army Air Force had seven times as many pilots as it had had less than two years earlier, before full mobilization. Several months before America's entry into the war, General John McAuley Palmer wrote:

> There has always been a great deal of buncombe about the time required for training. There can be no arbitrary rule because so much depends upon the characteristics of the recruit. I began to drive an automobile at the age of sixty-two and it took me nearly two years to become a competent and confident chauffeur. My grandson began at the age of sixteen and within a month was a better chauffeur than I can ever hope to be. A lumberjack who can haul big logs over a rocky forest trail with a tractor is well on his way to be an effective tank driver.[12]

Technological complexity is, as General Palmer observed, something relative to the skills and knowledge of the average soldier.

Similarly, when the newly raised mass armies failed it was not because of the technological complexity of their tasks. The experience of the least combat-ready division in the American Army in 1945, the 65th, reveals the relative unimportance of mechanical or technical factors as opposed to morale and practice in the art of military cooperation. Although activated in the summer of 1943, it was the victim of drafts for other units and individual replacement pools: many of its rank and file were disgruntled draftees shunted into the division from disbanded units. The division was virtually worthless not because its men could not operate the machinery, but because they were not yet a team. The official historians record that the 65th should have benefited from all of the planning and training expertise so painfully acquired by the American Army in three years of mobilization; instead, personnel turbulence reduced the unit to a mere "hodge-podge."[13]

It might be suggested that modern military technology has ad-

vanced so far beyond that of World War II that the lessons derived
therefrom need not apply. On the other hand, sophisticated technology often *decreases* the amount of technical training needed by
fresh troops. For example, the Tube-launched, Optically tracked,
Wire-guided (TOW) antitank missile, the main antitank weapon of
the United States inventory, requires only a week or so of training.
The actual use of the weapon is simplicity itself: the soldier need
only hold the enemy in his sights until impact.[14] Similarly, modern
jet aircraft may be easier to repair on forward air fields than were
their predecessors because of the use of modular construction, the
building of complicated technical parts into removable boxes. Yet
another example is the use of rugged micro-computers (as in the
army's TACFIRE artillery fire direction system) to eliminate tedious
and exacting chores.

Doorn and others argue that many military specialties are no
longer combat-related; in that sense, at least, the bulk of the fighting is done by relatively few "specialists" in combat arms, backed
by a mass of service and support personnel who might as well be
civilians.[15] They point to the progressive reduction of the percentage of enlisted in the line-combat occupations in the American
Army from 90 percent in the Civil War to 40 percent in World War I
to 29 percent in World War II and something like 25 percent today.
This analysis does not, however, account for the fact that the
United States in World War II had to create and maintain a vast
logistical structure overseas. Whereas in World War I American
troops served on one relatively accessible front, using the logistical
infrastructure of their allies, in World War II American armies
fought around the globe and had to support a host of dependent
armies, including the French, the Chinese, and even (in some measure) the British and Russians. As for pre–World War I experience,
it should be noted that in that period much of the service support
was provided by civilian contractors—often with disastrous
results.

Furthermore (and here the case for elite professional armies also
breaks down), one must confront the problem of casualty replacements. For example, by 31 January 1945 almost all the infantry
regiments in nineteen American divisions had lost between 100
and 200 percent of their initial strength in battle casualties. As a
rule of thumb a division could expect to take 100 percent losses in
its infantry regiments every three months. Men inducted after 1943
were trained primarily as combat replacements, and in fact over
twice as many soldiers were trained for combat specialties as were

assigned to units at any one time. Even so, the U.S. Army, like the Canadian and British Armies, ended the war desperately short of trained infantrymen, and was forced to raid service units and special college training programs for footsoldiers.[16]

Finally, the argument that fighting is now done by "specialists" ignores the fact that under conditions of modern warfare rear area or support troops (engineers, for example) are often subject to the same combat stresses from artillery fire or air attack as are front-line troops. Moreover, rear area troops must often suddenly convert themselves to infantry to fight off airborne or deep penetration forces, as the Burma campaigns (and, in Korea, the retreat of the First Marine Division) demonstrated. Rear area troops must, therefore, be physically and mentally prepared to serve as infantrymen, even if they are only infrequently called upon to do so.

The mass army flourished in World War II and flourishes today, as a survey of the systems of military service of such powerful states as Vietnam and Israel suggest. In World War II, technology presented no insuperable barrier to the raising of vast, quickly trained armies. The undeniable qualitative advantages of professional armies simply could not compensate for their inability to cope with substantial losses. The question was, and remains, how a state can raise the mass army it needs—and will continue to need—for large-scale warfare.

THE CADRE/CONSCRIPT SYSTEM

Clearly, then, the mass army—defined as armed forces composed of a large proportion (say, a quarter of more) of the young male population, and composed primarily of soldiers ready for war—remains necessary for the prosecution of large wars. As already observed, most European states after 1871 turned to the cadre/conscript system to create mass armies, modeling their forces along the lines of the victorious Prussian Army.[17] It proved serviceable in World War I and, for Russia and Japan, during World War II as well. It remains the dominant system of military service among the Great Powers of the world, and of one of the World Powers—the Soviet Union.

Under this system young men are drafted at a fixed age (anywhere from eighteen to twenty-one), although some may have their service deferred. In most countries some sort of effort is made to ensure that a bulk of the healthy male population undergoes military service. Military service thus becomes a rite of passage, something to be expected, and in some cases even welcomed, by young men. Service usually lasts between a year (as in some European countries) and thirty-six months (in particularly hard-pressed states), after which soldiers serve as reservists. This latter status may require them to attend periodic training assemblies or none at all; in an event, the military maintains a central listing of former soldiers eligible for recall in the event of emergency.

This is a key point, because the essence of all-out war is that it mandates the use not only of active duty forces, but of reservists and civilians without prior military training. Insofar as the military planners of a cadre/conscript system plan for the use of reservists (the Germans in both World Wars did so extremely skillfully), they make full use of its potential. When states fail to do so (the French, for example, consistently undervalued reserve formations before World War I) they only deceive themselves about their ability to win a war with forces on hand. Depending on the variant of the cadre/conscript system adopted, even minor operations may require reserve mobilizations: the Soviet invasion of Afghanistan in December 1979 being a case in point.

As its name suggests, a cadre/conscript system relies on a relatively small corps of professional noncommissioned officers (NCOs) or sergeants and officers to train and lead the drafted rank and file. To be sure, some draftees must be used, usually as junior reserve officers to provide low-level leadership in the event of a full mobilization. Nonetheless, a cadre/conscript system usually has the effect of creating a separate military caste whose way of life, interests, and views often differ quite considerably from those of the enlisted mass.[18] However successful a cadre/conscript system might be in ensuring civilian control of the military (French conscripts in Algeria in 1960 foiled a coup attempt that had the sympathy of a goodly portion of the officer corps), it does not ensure mutual understanding, much less an integration of the officer corps into society.

The advantages of the cadre/conscript system are straightforward. It provides a large standing force of young and therefore vigorous men. As conscripts finish their period of active duty they can enter a reserve, and hence provide a state with the means for quick mobilization in wartime. Unlike professional soldiers, conscripts need not receive good pay or other compensations. Unlike

[67]

militiamen, they can enter battle fresh from the barracks, without need for preliminary refresher training.

On the other hand, conscription for this type of service has a number of drawbacks. For one thing, a draftee is forced to set aside his career and normal pursuits for a period of between one and three years, which may make him a disgruntled and inefficient soldier. If service is not universal or nearly so, those selected for military duty may feel that they are victims of fate rather than citizens performing a civic obligation. The result may be either attempts to evade service or a general distaste for it that can poison civil-military relations. In any event, a sense of ill luck may increase the resentment caused by low pay, disagreeable housing, and the strictures of military discipline.

Most European states have sensed this and, in periods when more men have been available than the armed forces required (the 1960s, for example), have shortened the length of service in order to keep up the sense of universal service.[19] Because in peacetime military service is often as much a political institution as a method of procuring men for the armed services, nations will accept penalties in military efficiency in order to preserve military obligation as an integral part of citizenship. When, in peacetime, parliaments desire to reduce military spending without upsetting political institutions, the great temptation is to reduce the duration of military service rather than transform the system itself. This was the case in interwar France.

Short service, however, confronts armies with serious challenges to military effectiveness. They face two unpleasant alternatives. Either they train conscripts in complete units, which means that only a small proportion of a nation's total forces will be in peak military condition at any given time, or they spread new recruits throughout all units, a practice that undermines unit cohesion through personnel turbulence. The Soviet Army, for example, drafts and releases recruits twice a year; service lasts two years, and recruits are parceled out to various units in the field. As a result, one-quarter of the troops in any full-strength Soviet division have probably served less than six months with that unit. This level of personnel turbulence is remarkably similar to that which crippled the U.S. Army's 65th Division (cited above).[20]

Although man-for-man a cadre/conscript army is likely to cost less than a professional army, it usually costs far more than a militia or expansible army. Even if conscripts are poorly paid, they must still be sheltered, fed, and trained, all at considerable expense. The sheer bulk of a cadre/conscript army, with its appetite for equipment and training materials, further increases its cost.

A serious difficulty for many cadre/conscript armies lies in the need for a substantial and well-trained NCO corps. One great strength of the German Army from the late nineteenth century through World War II, for example, was the unusually long average length of service of its NCOs. Conversely, one great weakness of the Soviet Army is its lack of such an NCO corps, and hence its reliance on second-year conscripts to fulfill many of their functions, a practice fraught with disciplinary hazards.[21]

A cadre/conscript system is probably best for fighting a relatively brief but intense offensive war on short notice. During a protracted war, countries using the cadre/conscript system must improvise some form of selective service, as we shall see later in this chapter ("The Militia System"). This is difficult for a system founded on universal service or even some sort of lottery-based selective service. During both World Wars, for example, France had to demobilize some recalled reservists in order to restore production in key economic sectors. The great merit of the cadre–conscript system is that it produces an effective army, one much larger than a professional force and, if well-led, nearly as proficient, in a far shorter time than either the militia or expansible systems can.

From the point of view of the insular Anglo-Saxon world powers, however, this system of military service has two major drawbacks. First, it is radically unsuited to the demands of small war (see Chapter 4). To create two armies, one tailored for each kind of war, is a possible solution to this difficulty, but it raises considerable problems of cost and officer and NCO recruitment. The British considered and rejected this possibility in the early twentieth century. The French did create a dual army system in the late nineteenth century, but the result was an overworked and overstretched officer corps. Moreover, France, unlike Great Britain in the past or the United States today, made no effort after the middle of the nineteenth century to maintain a first-class navy, a prerequisite for World Power status.

Second, it is difficult to reconcile a cadre/conscript system with American notions of military obligation (see Chapter 6). Historically, the Anglo-Saxon states have had difficulty maintaining peacetime conscription of this kind. Resistance to a draft of the European kind is not merely traditional; it has roots in the nature of the American regime. For these reasons, most Americans who have treated the problem in depth have argued for either the militia system or the expansible one.

THE MILITIA SYSTEM

Three salient characteristics define a militia system: it requires only brief periods of active service from those who participate in it; it draws its strength from a large, organized force of citizen-soldiers who train periodically (weekly or monthly) in peacetime; and at all levels except the very highest it relies on an officer corps of part-time, as opposed to professional, officers. Some militia systems have been conscript, others volunteer, but that is less important than the fundamental notion of an armed force that exists as such only in time of war. In some states militias have served as a supplement to other systems—in the United States, for example, where the National Guard is the lineal descendant of colonial militias. In other states, however, it has served as the major, if not sole, source of military manpower.

The best-known of all militia systems is that of Switzerland, which has provided a model for military reformers since the time of the American Revolution.[22] Although foreign observers have agreed that of all countries relying on this system of military service Switzerland provides the best example in terms of training, doctrine, and equipment, it is a system that has not been tested in battle since the beginning of the nineteenth century. One must study it in some depth in order to weigh the merits of a defense completely based on a citizen army.

The fact that the Swiss Army has not had to fight gives some indication of its effectiveness. Contrary to popular belief, Swiss defense does not rely primarily on the geographical advantages of a mountainous country: the northern half of Switzerland (the *Mittelland*, which contains the bulk of the country's population and industry) is wooded and hilly but hardly impassable, and contains numerous excellent roads. This is, moreover, the area most likely to be invaded in the past by Germany or France attempting to outflank each other, or today by Soviet forces seeking to envelop the Federal Republic of Germany. During each of the three major Franco-German wars since 1870 Switzerland mobilized its forces to protect its territory.

Nor were the threats to Swiss neutrality chimerical. Before

[70]

World War I the German General Staff examined the possibility of an attack on France via Switzerland rather than by the route used in 1914, that passing through Belgium. Count von Schlieffen, architect of German war plans, rejected this option, saying, "I prefer that we should leave alone this people whose military organization is so solidly based."[23] For the purposes of this study, however, it is more important to study Swiss military capacities in World War II and thereafter, when technological progress might seem to call into question the workability of the Swiss system.

On 1 September 1939 Switzerland mobilized its 435,000-man army, representing over one-tenth of the entire population; thereafter it kept 100,000 men under arms at all times until the end of the war. This force initially was deployed opposite the German frontier, although the events of May 1940 subsequently forced the construction of defensive lines throughout the Mittelland. During the invasion of France, Swiss citizen-pilots took to the air (in fifty recently purchased German Me-109s, ironically) and shot down seven German aircraft, losing only one of their own.[24]

During the summer of 1940 Hitler ordered his generals to prepare for operation *Tannenbaum,* the invasion of Switzerland. The moment seemed propitious, since the Swiss has neither fortified the French frontier nor yet redeployed their forces (they were busy preparing plans for a withdrawal to the so-called Alpine Redoubt). Switzerland could expect no support, even from the air, from the British or anyone else, and indeed the Italians could be expected to invade the southern regions of the country as the Germans entered the north, east, and west. Moreover, German forces were fresh from the dazzling victories of 1940, and had not yet been committed to major campaigns in the east.

Why attack at all? Hitler's table talk reveals a visceral dislike for the Swiss: neither the discovery of their prewar joint planning with the French nor their aggressive defense of their airspace had endeared them to him. Second, Switzerland was the only German-speaking area of Europe not yet absorbed into the Reich, and indeed a number of pro-Nazi movements had existed there during the 1930s. Third, control of Switzerland would have give Hitler access to valuable industries and their workers; only later in the war did the advantage of having productive neutrals nearby become apparent. Finally, control of Switzerland would have ensured secure communications with Italy.[25]

Given Switzerland's small size, the certainty of its air inferiority, and its thoroughly unfavorable strategic position, the forces that the German Army claimed it would require to subdue her were huge. By October 1940 the use of some twenty-one divisions, including three or four panzer divisions plus airborne units, was envisioned.[26] By contrast, the Germans used only six divisions to conquer Norway and Denmark in the face of local and British and French naval, air, and ground forces. The terrain in Norway was, if anything, more difficult than that of Switzerland, and the lines of communication fewer and more exposed. The Germans held back from invading Switzerland for a number of reasons, some of which had nothing to do with the quality of the Swiss militia. But their plan for employing such large forces surely reflected a healthy respect for the ability of the Swiss to fend off a conventional assault.

In the years after World War II, Swiss strategists evolved a theory of total defense (*Gesamtverteidigung*) involving not merely military defense but provision for civil defense and civilian resistance in the event of war. The keystone of Swiss defenses, however, remains the militia system, which continues in its essentials to be that which obtained during the World Wars.

The Swiss system rests on the thirty-year service of all able-bodied men—which explains why it can today field an army of 625,000 on two days' notice, out of a total population of 6,300,000.[27] The country's standing forces consist of 3,500 professional officers and NCOs who serve as instructors and 15,000 civilians who maintain aircraft and installations. There is also one squadron of pilots (the *Ueberwachungsgeschwader*) to perform surveillance of Swiss airspace. Basic training (*Rekrutenschule*) lasts seventeen weeks—a month and a half longer than in the U.S. Army—and is supplemented by refresher courses throughout the Swiss citizen's military career, particularly the first twelve years. NCOs attend four weeks of special training and then return to a full term of Rekrutenschule as squad leaders; officer candidates do all of the above, then attend a seventeen-week officers' course and again go do Rekrutenschule, this time as platoon leaders.[28] This education (spread over several years) provides all officers and NCOs with leadership experience of an unusually appropriate kind: that is, learning how to teach fellow citizens how to be soldiers, a task that officers in other armies must often perform without such preparation. There are, in addition, specialized types of training, such as flight school, which lasts seven months. In general, the Swiss exert themselves to assign soldiers specialties that most resemble their civil professions or trades.[29]

[72]

The Swiss system must meet two geopolitical requirements: rapid mobilization (within two days) and defense of all Swiss territory. What are required, therefore, are large fighting forces that have the advantage of very short lines of communication and familiarity with the terrain. As a result of its policies, Switzerland can field a force of six infantry, three mechanized, and three mountain divisions, plus twenty-three independent brigades—a force roughly as large as the active U.S. Army.

Although the Swiss Army is designed for territorial defense, it is neither a guerrilla army nor a fortress garrison. The Swiss have over eight hundred tanks, in addition to armored personnel carriers and self-propelled artillery. Their forces are conventionally organized—that is, by the divisional formation of fifteen thousand men or more. The air force contains over two hundred moderately sophisticated ground attack aircraft, in addition to a smaller interception force. This is, then, very much a conventional army.[30]

This is not to suggest that the Swiss Army is as capable of mobile warfare as, say, the U.S. or German armies. Swiss strategists recognize the limits the milita system places on development of maneuver forces; they are particularly sensitive to the difficulty of large-scale armored maneuver with inexperienced troops, and hence intend to deploy their mechanized divisions as a sort of general reserve, using battalions or regiments of armored troops in support of larger formations.[31] Other constraints as well, however, have led to Swiss reluctance to adopt a strategy of mobile warfare. They regard the expense of first-class armored forces as excessive, particularly because massed use of such forces would probably require that Swiss airspace be dominated by the Swiss Air Force, which would then require large acquisitions of expensive fighter aircraft. Swiss terrain—even in the Mittelland—is not suited to the same kind of wheeling movements that, for example, the Sinai peninsula is. Switzerland possesses no large uninhabited training areas; military exercises must be conducted in the countryside, which is thickly settled.[32] Finally, the purpose of Swiss military policy is to deter any violation of its territory; therefore, its strategy is one of presenting any possible intruder with the prospect of a long series of battles of attrition (*Abnuetzungsgefechten*). A quickly mobilizable heavy infantry force thus suits Swiss policy far better than a force that might be able to annihilate an enemy army but is also more vulnerable to disruption itself.[33]

The Swiss adhere rigidly to the militia system for a number of reasons, not the least of which is its vitality as a Swiss political and social institution. It is a system that few other countries need—or would wish—to imitate in all respects; not all countries need to be able to mobilize vast and effective forces in two days, or have to rely on a reserve force containing no cadre composed of veterans of two- or three-year terms of active duty. The militia system undoubtedly causes the Swiss to pay some penalties in terms of military efficiency, as the Swiss have been the first to admit.[34]

Other countries have military systems roughly similar to that of Switzerland. Sweden, for example, has also repudiated guerrilla and static linear warfare in favor of a mobile, territorial defense.[35] The problem in Sweden, as in Switzerland, is that these forces have not engaged in battle, or at least modern warfare in which the full panoply of convential forces has been used. The examples of militia forces (forces composed of citizen-soldiers) that have done so are relatively few. The Norwegian Army in April 1940 consisted of some 120,000 militiamen with only scanty training (barely eight weeks' worth) and exiguous and obsolete equipment. Moreover, by seizing key cities and ports at the very outbreak of the campaign, the Germans completely disrupted Norwegian plans. Only 50,000 Norwegians participated in the battle for their homeland, and that in a disorganized and disjointed way. The campaign highlighted one crucial defect of militia systems, their vulnerability to paralysis by an *attaque brusque* that prevents their mobilization.[36]

Other Nordic states, however, had militia systems organized and trained along sounder lines. The Finnish Army in both the Winter War of 1939–1940 and World War II gave a good account of itself. It too was a militia force, organized on a territorial basis, although its initial period of training was considerably longer even than that of Switzerland (a year as opposed to seventeen weeks).[37]

The British militia, the Territorial Army, conducted major operations in France during the campaign of 1940. The five Territorial divisions, particularly the 51st (Highland), acquitted themselves well: the opposing German forces recorded that "certainly the Territorial divisions are inferior to the Regular troops in training, but where morale is concerned they are their equal."[38] The fighting retreat of the 51st Highland Division (assigned to a different sector than the rest of the British Expeditionary Force) was an epic of skill and endurance.

What are the characteristic strengths and weaknesses of militia armies? One advantage stems from the inevitable territorial organization of militia type armies: the men who belong to any given unit are probably neighbors and often know one another socially; in any event they possess the homogeneity of regional origin. Such territorial basing was a source of solidity and cohesion in the old British Army, which recruited each of its regiments from a particular locale. In addition, reserve or militia units have the great advantage of sustained existence as a unit, and far less personnel turbulence than cadre/conscript units. Thus, at all levels officers and men know one another well, having worked together for many years. In their classic analysis of the sources of combat cohesion, Edward Shils and Morris Janowitz pointed out the importance of regional homogeneity and long-standing familiarity in developing small-unit solidity.[39] A drawback is that during a war some regions of a country will likely suffer exceptionally high casualties. The counterargument (which may not be convincing to small towns whose male population has suffered instant decimation) is that territorial recruiting, by creating more cohesive units, lowers the overall casualty rate.

A second strength of the militia army stems from its full use of a country's military talent, as opposed to cadre/conscript systems, in which "only the brawn of the people is prepared for war, there being no adequate provision for developing the latent military leadership and genius of the people as a whole."[40] A good example of the citizen-officer is Sir John Monash, an Australian militia colonel in 1914 who, by 1918, was the extraordinarily popular and successful commander of Australia's five divisions in Europe. He was, by the agreement of contemporaries and historians, "a first class general in command of first class troops."[41]

A third advantage of the militia system stems from its need to confront in peacetime the problem most armies must face in war, the problem of disciplining an army of part-time soldiers. After all, a professional soldier soon adopts and absorbs the ethos of the professional army. A conscript doing a two-year term of duty is usually young enough to be malleable; the army can play on certain vulnerabilities that are less characteristic of older men—desire for approbation, fear of failure, an urge to prove one's masculinity. Unburdened by cares and family responsibilities, the young man is more open to the appeal of military glory and self-sacrifice. The older soldier, particularly the mobilized reservist or militiaman, has more obligations to others and other sources of psychological support than those proffered by military society.

The problem is by no means insoluble, of course. The Swiss, Australian, and Israeli armies have all evolved informal types of discipline without dealing crippling damage to battle discipline.

They have, at the same time, developed junior leaders capable of displaying initiative, and men responsive to such exercises of initiative.[42] Moreover, under certain conditions the morale of milita units can exceed that of cadre/conscript forces. Whereas the conscript waits out a two-year term (more or less) of service during which he is burdened by the petty chores and drudgery of garrison duty, the militiaman spends most of his time doing only one kind of duty, training. This is the part of soldiering that men, including short-service conscripts, enjoy most. In the U.S. Army, for example, it has been found that soldiers look back on basic training as a rewarding experience, despite (indeed because of) its stressful nature.[43] A further morale booster can be the recognition, prestige, and approbation generally accorded the part-time soldier by his community (and not only in local parades and ceremonies). The short-service soldier, by contrast, spends most of his time in garrisons and casernes that are usually not near his home, where he has little contact with the civilian world and where his relationship with civilians is likely to be an exploitative or suspicious one.

On the other hand, militia systems are peculiarly vulnerable to subversion of discipline, through political interference and other means. The former was a particular problem for the National Guard in the United States, where appointments and promotions often depended on cronyism.[44] At a more subtle level, the seemingly inevitable informality of militia units occasionally subverts the need for obedience that war requires; an officer whose men call him by his first name rather than "Sir" can, in most cases, expect less instant compliance with his instructions than can his professional counterpart.

Mobilization presents other difficulties for the militia system. As in the case of Norway in 1940 (or Israel in the first day or two of the 1973 Yom Kippur War), militias are vulnerable to the surprise attack that interrupts or disorganizes a call-up. In addition, militia troops simply cannot be as practiced as standing units. Here the most important defect of militia or reserve formations is their lack of practice in combined operations, which require less technical skill than teamwork and experience in joint action. Thus, in 1975 some 90 percent of the United States' Air Force Reserve and Air National Guard units were ready for action instantly; most Army National Guard units were rated marginally ready or not ready at all. The Air National Guardsmen have to maintain and operate complicated modern aircraft; their skills are primarily individual and technical in nature. The Army Guardsmen, infantry and armor

[76]

troops primarily, require less individual skill, but a great deal of practice in coordinated action.[45]

The complete mobilization of a militia army threatens a country with economic collapse (this was a factor in the Israeli decision to attack in June 1967 after a crisis lasting only a few weeks). The political difficulties of mobilization are almost as severe: particularly in democratic states, a government cannot pluck civilians away from their normal careers without good reason. Thus, the resentment produced in the United States by the call-up of several hundred thousand reservists in 1961 convinced many in the Johnson administration that a reserve call-up to fight the Vietnam war was politically impossible. Because of the sacrifices a mobilization of reservists entails, a country cannot easily use call-ups for diplomatic bargaining and signaling.

Finally, a militia system is unsuited for small war for the same political reasons that apply to the cadre/conscript system. It is hard enough to secure a draft of eighteen-year-olds to fight an obscure limited war; the call-up of prominent citizens, of civilians with full-time jobs and family obligations, cannot be done with equity satisfactory to all. Militias are best suited to the fighting of wars on or near the home country, and to large wars only when they are fought on the defensive, or after a lengthy period of refresher training. These are also virtually the only wars for which militias are usable from a political point of view as well.

THE EXPANSIBLE/SELECTIVE SERVICE SYSTEM

Expansible Armies

The final system to consider is that of the United States from the turn of the century until 1940 and of the German Army in the interwar period, namely the expansible system. Its distinguishing features are: in peacetime, a small professional army prepares itself to expand geometrically; the leadership of the wartime army rests in the hands of the professional officer corps, but (unlike in the cadre/conscript system) the shortage of regular officers mandates the swift promotion of citizen-soldiers. Because of the time required to field an expansible army, few states have adopted this system purely voluntarily. It is, nonetheless, one with peculiar merits and advantages.

The British Army in World War II conducted a substantial expansion, and with reasonable efficiency, even granting that it started from a more considerable base than that of other states. A relatively compact army was raised from the Territorial divisions, whose numbers were doubled. Here the British learned from their experiences in World War I, when the decision was made to expand the army by creating entirely new units (the so-called "Kitchener Armies") from scratch, rather than building on the framework of existing forces. Still, the British expansion is less striking than that of other states, because so many of its forces were diverted to home defense (including air defense) rather than offensive operations.

The experience of the German Army from 1919 to 1933 offers more telling lessons. The Reichswehr had always secretly planned to expand its size if the restrictions of the Versailles Treaty could be subverted. Even under Seeckt's original scheme the professional army would have doubled in size and a vast militia would have been raised. Thus, the Reichswehr prepared to serve as the cadre for both regular and militia forces; it became a *Fuehrerarmee*, an army of leaders. To this end all officers and NCOs were trained for at least one rank above that which they held, and enlisted men were prepared for NCO status.[46]

When Hitler came to power he had four options for the expansion of the German Army: the creation of a revolutionary Nazi Army (a course of action pressed by the storm troop leader Ernst Roehm); the expansion of the Reichswehr as a professional volunteer force; the creation of a cadre/conscript army; or the creation of a militia along the lines originally envisioned by Seeckt.[47] In the end Hitler chose a mixed type of expansion: between 1933 and 1935 the professional army grew by voluntary enlistment, in 1935 he reintroduced mass conscription, and by the end of the war a large proportion of the army (and some of its best units) were Nazi divisions (*Waffen SS*). In the most important period, 1935–1941, the Seeckt plan held sway: the army's elite (its airborne and armored divisions) consisted mainly of volunteer regulars. Behind them were the infantry divisions, mobilized, trained, and passed into the reserves by "waves." Seeckt's insistence that all officers be well-trained generalists paid off, and even though the army had to mobilize former officers and train many new ones, the old Reichswehr provided the vital core that made the Wehrmacht an extraordinarily efficient military organization. It took, nonetheless, over four years of effort to prepare an army capable of defeating Poland and then France; in 1938, for example, the General Staff had barely created twenty-seven divisions out of the ten in the Reichswehr.

Throughout this period, then, the German Army was incapable of handling a first-class opponent, which accounts for the General Staff's nervousness about Hitler's foreign policy.

Yet if expansion meant a prolonged period of weakness, the prior existence of a small but fundamentally complete professional army had had major advantages. Unlike their American and even their British counterparts, the German Reichswehr generals were practiced in handling complete divisions. Unlike their French counterparts, they had the advantage of working with superlative human material, well trained and motivated. Because the men were regulars, their officers did not have to waste time continuously reteaching the basics. Because they knew they were drastically outnumbered and outgunned, they had to cultivate mobility and tactical excellence to have any hope of survival in war. Seeckt had inculcated a new type of discipline in the Reichswehr, one that carried over into the Wehrmacht and that was key to its successes, based on a paternal kind of concern for the soldiers' welfare.[48] The small, cohesive officer corps (which dominated the Wehrmacht as well) shared the advantages of mutual familiarity and a common approach to warfare. The benefit was, as Liddell Hart discovered when he interviewed German generals after the war, "a background common to all, [a single] mold in which their doctrine was cast."[49]

The American expansion in World War I had been remarkable enough, from an army of 120,000 and a National Guard of 80,000 in April 1917 to a force of almost a million less than a year later. This achievement was dwarfed, however, by that of World War II. The army numbered scarcely 190,000 men before the introduction of conscription in 1940, and its plans only called for the creation of a 1,200,000-man force. By the summer of 1941 it became clear that this force would be too small, and plans were drawn up for the final expansion to a force of over eight million.

The expansion took time; despite the mobilization of the National Guard and thousands of reserve officers as well as the introduction of the draft in 1940, it was a full year and a half (October 1941) before *one* infantry division was ready for service. It was only in 1943 that the United States disposed of several dozen combat-ready divisions.[50] The time required was comparable to that in Germany, but the quality of the final product was not, as the initial battles in North Africa demonstrated.

One critical difficulty was that of officer procurement: many of the National Guard officers were second-rate, and had to be purged despite political counterpressures. A May 1942 survey of one National Guard and two regular divisions found that over half of the privates who were former National Guardsmen were convinced that promotions were won by "bootlicking or politics" as compared with a quarter who thought they were won by ability; whereas in the two regular divisions the proportions of responses were just the reverse.[51] The Officer Reserve Corps (graduates, for the most part, of officers' training programs in college), though well motivated and technically competent, lacked the leadership skills necessary to quickly train a citizen-army.[52] A second difficulty stemmed from the prewar American practice of maintaining half-strength divisions and scattered garrisons. No wonder, then, that it took time to develop competent battalion, regiment, and divisional officers—unlike their counterparts in the Reichswehr, the regulars were learning their jobs at the same time the citizen-soldiers were. Time was wasted because half- and quarter-strength divisions were brought to full strength and then passed through a complete training cycle, to include seventeen weeks of basic training, thirteen weeks of unit training, and fourteen weeks of combined arms training. This system created effective combat divisions, but the prior training of the regulars and Guardsmen went to waste, since they, like everyone else, had to repeat the whole training cycle.[53]

A final complication was the army's need to have on hand an intervention force of two divisions or more to cope with an expected Nazi assault on Brazil. The official history records the pernicious consequences of

the continuing uncertainty of when or whether the training of the mass Army might be interrupted to supply a complete, trained, volunteer corps as an initial expeditionary force. The uncertainty of the prewar training objective, which could be altered almost without notice by a shift in state policy, continued for many months one of the most serious handicaps to that training program.[54]

Unlike the German Army, which could concentrate on orderly expansion, the U.S. Army had to prepare for both immediate and long-term contingencies.

Nonetheless, the creation by the United States of a vast and fairly capable ground army within the space of only four years was an extraordinary achievement. Two factors help account for it. First, the army educational system was reasonably well prepared to train masses of civilians and help the army absorb new technology. The training manuals and devices proved adequate for the task in large part due to the efforts of men like Chief of Staff George C. Marshall, who had long foreseen the need to prepare for the absorption of masses of citizen-soldiers.

A second asset—and one of a kind that obtained even more strongly in the Reichswehr—was Marshall's intimate knowledge of the officer corps. His swift elevation of Bradley, Eichelberger, Hodges, Collins, and above all, Eisenhower revealed a sure knowledge of the strengths and weaknesses of the more junior officers in the small prewar army. The value of knowing the personalities, quirks, and working habits of one's peers and subordinates in wartime cannot be exaggerated.[55]

Yet remarkable as the expansion of the German and American armies is, neither case is quite so astonishing as those of the British Dominions—Canada, Australia, and New Zealand—which produced large and effective armies from minute prewar regular forces (4,200, 3000, and 500 men respectively). The prewar:wartime size ratio of the U.S. Army was 1:45, that of Canada (which deployed some half a million troops), 1:125.[56] The key to success in each British Dominion was a substantial voluntary militia force (Canada—60,000 men; Australia—70,000; New Zealand—10,000). These forces, and above all their officers, provided the cadre of leaders for the mass armies of the war—in 1945, for example, three of Australia's six divisional commanders and all but one of her brigade commanders were former officers in the militia; and similar figures held true in Canada and New Zealand.[57]

Two factors help explain the extraordinary success of these armies. First, all three countries used the British regimental system to recruit and organize troops: "The units of the Active Service Force of 1939 were units of the Canadian Militia, wearing the badges and the titles of regiments long familiar to the public in their districts, and inheriting traditions and *esprit de corps* which were a part of Canadian history."[58] From the very beginning of training, therefore, soldiers had a sense of identity denied most American conscripts stumbling off the trains at army training bases far from their home towns.

Perhaps most crucial was the presence of a large and experienced cadre of officers and NCOs, men experienced not so much in the technology of modern warfare (the weaponry of the prewar Dominion militias was, like that of the American National Guard, hopelessly obsolete) as in the leadership and management of men.

[81]

Also, unlike in the state-controlled American National Guard, local politics did not interfere with officer selection.

Selective Service

Thus far I have discussed the standing forces that provide the framework for the mass citizen armies of large war; I now turn to how those armies are recruited. The type of conscription that the generals—and most of the political leaders—in all of the countries under discussion favored can be referred to as a form of selective service. It is a concept fundamentally different from the type of military service that exists in peacetime. In peacetime military service is often so much a political institution that nations sacrifice military efficiency in order to ensure universality of service; in wartime, efficient use of manpower has the highest priority. In peacetime active service is confined to young men, usually bachelors; in wartime men up to the age of fifty and beyond, fathers and heads of families, may go to war. In most countries peacetime military conscription appears at worst as an unpleasant interruption of one's life; in wartime many more drastic controls (rationing, control of movement, even conscription of labor) are tolerated. Finally, in peacetime service lasts for a short, fixed period; in wartime it lasts for the duration.

One characteristic of modern warfare is its dependence on industrial war production, production impeded or even disrupted when key workers join the armed forces. France found herself forced to demobilize tens of thousands of reservists in both World Wars in order to maintain shell production (which actually dropped in the early months of the war). Similarly, in England crucial industries suffered because large numbers of workers volunteered for service. Selective service is needed in wartime less to find sufficient numbers of soldiers for the armed forces than to allocate manpower rationally. Voluntary enlistment (which provided two and a half million men for the North during the Civil War, and as many for England in 1916) may provide adequate forces for the first year or two of an all-out war, but it may equally well cripple the industrial sinews of a state at war.

It was America in 1917–1918 that provided a model for the intelligent use of military manpower in wartime. The Selective Service system, composed of over 4,600 local and 155 district draft boards, registered and classified all American males aged eighteen to forty-five in two days. The directing intelligence behind this extraor-

[82]

dinarily successful effort was Provost Marshal Enoch Crowder, who, like most of his countrymen, wished to demonstrate that the American republic could organize a military machine far more efficiently than its allies. "The ultimate goal of America was to organize not only an army, but a nation for war. . . . Every man within the draft age had to become either an effective producer or a soldier."[59]

Selective service contradicted and rejected utterly a virtue that men generally, and military men above all, hold precious, namely voluntarism. In the United States from 1940 to 1942, for example, both the Navy and Marine Corps fought tenaciously for the right to take only volunteers, and lost with ill grace. Nonetheless, in all of the states influenced by American practice (particularly the Dominions and Great Britain), efforts were made beginning in 1939 to prohibit indiscriminate voluntary enlistment. General Crowder (who in 1917 secured a prohibition on any voluntary enlistment by draft registrants) put his case this way after World War I:

> The volunteer system destroyed all calculation. It took its toll from all classes and from all walks of life. It had no eye for the industrial life to be maintained behind the armies, without which those armies could not live. It envisioned war as a struggle of arms, not as a struggle of whole nations. It was not fitted for a modern war. It could not organize the nation; it could not even organize its armies.[60]

The logical concomitant of selective service was some form of labor conscription, variants of which were indeed implemented by Britain, Canada, and Australia during World War II. This was a development predicted by Seeckt and Fuller with approval, by Liddell Hart with horror. It received some support in the United States, where Secretary of War Henry Stimson argued in January 1944, "Certainly, the nation has no less right to require a man to make weapons than it has to require another man to fight with those weapons."[61] Nonetheless, in all of the Anglo-Saxon countries liberal scruples prevented the extension of such obligations to their logical limits. The complete regimentation of a society that national service would require seemed to many (George Orwell among them) apt to lead to creeping totalitarianism in the Allied countries. As we shall see in later chapters, it was the continuance of Selective Service—a system as utterly unfitted for peacetime as it was admirably suited to total war—that helped foster the American draft crisis of the late 1960s.

[83]

One critical aspect of the joint expansible/selective service system concerns the timing of conscription. To expand too late is, at worst, to invite the preemptive assault of a better-prepared enemy, and at best to create a clumsy, hastily trained mass army. To expand too early is to expend vast sums, drain the country of skilled manpower, and risk violent political opposition.

One might think that the commanders of expansible armies would press early on for the introduction of conscription. In fact, the pre–World War II armies of Germany and the Anglo-Saxon allies were given conscription before they needed it or their generals had pressed for it. The latter usually preferred a thorough classification of manpower while they expanded their small professional forces and established the training facilities needed to handle mass armies. In all of the countries under consideration a flood of volunteers—motivated by patriotism, a love of adventure, or ambition—more than met the armies' immediate needs.

Political leaders chose to introduce conscription for purely political reasons. Hitler, for example, announced conscription and the expansion of the Wehrmacht to thirty-six divisions to gratify domestic opinion and to gain bargaining leverage with the French and Germans. His generals preferred voluntary enlistment to expand to a strength of only twenty-one divisions.[62] The British Military Training Act of 1939, which provided for six months of active and forty-two months of reserve duty (a militia draft, in fact), stemmed from the government's need to bolster courage at home and reassure the French. The British Army was, however, simply unprepared to cope with the influx of trainees. Similarly in Canada conscription was adopted in June 1940 because, in Prime Minister Mackenzie King's words, "provision should be made for the feeling in the country that every able-bodied man should be used in some part of the war effort."[63] In New Zealand the Prime Minister proclaimed: "Apart from everything else, however, the country feels at the present time in this crisis that the voluntary system, even if completely successful, does not apply fairly and does not embody that spirit of service that the country demands."[64] In the United States the draft was reintroduced primarily as a result of a civilian preparedness campaign led, like that of 1916, by civilians such as Grenville Clark. General Marshall scrupulously avoided public support for the measure, erroneously fearing a public backlash, correctly fearing an influx of men before there were sufficient resources to house, equip, and train them.

Selective service, in short, is both uniquely suited to the demands of large-scale war and uniquely dependent on its peculiar domestic politics. The former demands a rational marshaling of all of society's resources; the latter the appearance of total effort, and equity in its administration. Ironically, in the early stages of war its immense political appeal detracts from the military rationality that informs it.

CONCLUSION: LIMITED SOLUTIONS

Only two states—the United States and Britain—have ever attempted to fight total wars by use of voluntary enlistment; both (the former in 1864, the latter in 1916) ultimately resorted to conscription to fill the ranks of their armies and organize their economies for war. The question faced by nations such as the United States, therefore, is what system of conscription is best suited to the demands of all-out war.

The answer depends largely on the amount of time available for mobilization. An expansible/selective service system is cheap and efficient. It allows the professional force to create and test new weapons and doctrine, so that when conscription *is* introduced recruits have no outmoded doctrine or obsolete prior training to unlearn. Under such a system, a nation can begin war making the most intelligent use of its manpower, and can reduce the economic dislocation of mobilization to negligible proportions. The expansible/selective service system was suited in theory (if not completely in practice) to the United States when she could rely on months or even years during which to assemble and train her forces.

The theory for such a system of military service was advanced most cogently by Major-General Emory Upton in his posthumous but highly influential *The Military Policy of the United States*, published in 1904. He urged the peacetime use of half-strength units to be brought to full strength in wartime by volunteers or conscripts, and bitterly opposed any reliance on militia forces. The opposing view—put forth most cogently by Brigadier John McAuley Palmer, aide to both Pershing and Marshall—favored a small standing army and a large, centrally controlled militia.[65] Upton's formula cannot answer for a state that must prepare to wage full-scale war months, let alone weeks, after mobilization; and Palmer's was never tried, in large part because of the entrenched position of the state-controlled National Guard, and the skepticism of professional officers toward militia and reservists.

Perhaps the best system for short but total conflicts is that of Israel, which combines the cadre/conscript system with a militia organization and spirit reflected in the style of discipline and the composition of the officer corps. The Israelis deliberately modeled their system on that of Switzerland (which Israel's Chief of Staff visited in 1949) and retain many of its features, including the use of senior reserve commanders.[66] Nonetheless, the Israeli system has yet to cope with a prolonged conflict requiring full mobilization, and it is indeed one of her leaders' major tasks to prevent that eventuality.

The truth is, however, that none of the three major systems of service offers an ideal solution to the problem of all-out war: some offer immediate strength at the price of delayed weakness, others domestic political harmony in peace without strength in war. Above all, each responds to only some of the peculiar military *and* political conditions of all-out war, conditions not often found in peacetime or even (as we shall see in the next chapter) during smaller conflicts.

[4]

Systems of Military Service
and Small Wars

The military manpower requirements of small wars pose a unique set of challenges to World Powers. Many European states, particularly France, have found themselves engaged in military operations overseas, yet for most of them such conflicts have been as peripheral as they have been infrequent. To be sure, in some cases (France in 1954–1961, Portugal in 1964–1974, the Netherlands in 1946–1949) these wars have briefly convulsed the body politic, and warped military systems dedicated primarily to Continental warfare. Nonetheless, World Powers alone *chronically* find themselves forced to prepare for or wage such wars. In addition, World Powers must retain their strength through naval predominance, supplemented since the late 1920s by large air forces. The need to create and maintain these forces—whose manpower requirements and institutional ethos are quite different from those of armies—creates further constraints on systems of military service.

This chapter, therefore, focuses on the experiences of the two major World Powers of the past century and a half, Great Britain and the United States. Not only did the United States and Great Britain face the same geopolitical constraints; they faced the same domestic political and ideological constraints as well. In both, peacetime conscription has been an historical anomaly, voluntary enlistment the norm. In both, an unfettered press and a powerful and independent legislature have publicized and critized the prosecution of far-flung military conflicts. Finally, public opinion in both has powerfully affected whether and how wars have been fought.

I will begin by discussing the classic doctrine of small war, both as it evolved in Great Britain at the end of the nineteenth century and as the Americans applied it in their war with Filipino insurgents. In a second section I will look at how each World Power was eventually affected by the need to raise armies suited for total as well as small war. In the case of Britain I will examine the period 1904–1914, when British power was at its height, albeit coming under ever graver challenge. In the case of the United States I will look mainly at the years 1950–1970, a time when the United States accepted worldwide military responsibilities (many devolved from the withering British Empire) and found itself engaged in several small wars.

The major contrast between British manpower policy and that of the United States is that the former chose to build a system around the small-war problem, the latter to build one focused on a large-war problem. Both systems were terribly strained by occurrences of the kinds of war they had not prepared for—Britain by World War I, the United States by Korea and Vietnam. The question for the future is, are better compromises conceivable, and if so, are they feasible?

Some readers may object to the use of the historical analogies contained in this chapter, arguing that the lessons of nineteenth-century warfare between imperial powers and underarmed colonial peoples have little relevance to modern limited warfare. Throughout this chapter I will attempt to show why this view is incorrect. To be sure, we must treat all historical analogies and, even more so, historical lessons with care. Nonetheless, the military and in many respects the political problems inherent in devising a durable system of military service for a World Power have remained constant.

PROFESSIONAL ARMIES AND SMALL WARS

British Small Wars in the Nineteenth Century

Following the Napoleonic wars, Great Britain turned its back on a military commitment to the Continent and concentrated exclusively on the defense and (in some areas) the expansion of its vast, global empire. In 1891 the secretary of state for war codified the responsibilities of the British Army. These were, in order of priority: the support of the civil power in the United Kingdom; the garrisoning of India; the garrisoning of fortresses and coaling stations at home and abroad; the maintenance of approximately two corps of regulars and militia to defend against invasion; the ability to raise an expeditionary force of two army corps with support troops.[1] These missions, even though the last two of them were not entirely met until after the Boer War, strained the British Army sorely. That it met them, and succeeded in providing enough reserve force to meet a host of minor imperial contingencies (for example, the occupation of Egypt in 1881), is a tribute mainly to Sir Edward Cardwell, secretary of state for war from 1869 to 1874 and the father of the modern British Army.

Cardwell abolished the traditional twenty-one-year enlistment, substituting instead an active duty time of seven years with a reserve obligation of five. Numbered regiments (for example, the 72nd of the Line) gave way to territorial designations (for example, the Middlesex regiment), usually incorporating the name of the county in which the regiment had a depot and from which it recruited its troops. Each regiment—an administrative, not a tactical organization—now consisted of two battalions. Under this so-called linked battalion system one battalion served abroad while the other remained at the depot, training recruits, providing replacements for the overseas battalion, and serving as part of the garrison of the United Kingdom.[2]

When Cardwell came to office, more than half of the British Army was serving abroad, a situation that made recruitment difficult and obstructed the creation of a home defense force. Part of his reforms, therefore, included redeployment of troops from the Dominions to Britain, India, and strategic bases or chokepoints such as Mauritius and Suez. Even under his system, however, the home battalions frequently degenerated to the status of mere recruiting offices, as their ranks were constantly depleted to send replacement drafts overseas. Home defense rested on these units and a heterogeneous group of auxiliary military units. These included the Volunteers (prosperous but haphazardly organized townsmen) and their country cavalry equivalents, the Yeomanry; and the Militia, units of which were affiliated with the local regimental depot. Although the militia had the most rigorous training (six weeks initially and four weeks each summer), they were far from a solid force: on average, of twenty enlistees seven would join the regulars, four would desert, five would be discharged, and only four would complete their six-year enlistment.[3]

The final component of the imperial armies was local native forces, of which the most formidable were the Indian Army and the volunteer militias of the white Dominions—Canada, Australia, New Zealand, and South Africa. The problem with these forces was that none of them were necessarily available for service outside their region of the Empire. Nonetheless, they too were turned into effective forces by adoption of variations of the regimental system devised by Cardwell. This achievement was most notable in India, where, despite the Mutiny, the British succeeded in raising a loyal force at least twice the size of their own.

The core of the British military system, therefore, was a small force (about a quarter of a million men at the end of the nineteenth century) of volunteer professional soldiers, organized along the lines of the regimental system. It was a force deficient in some of the arms required for European warfare, particularly medium and heavy artillery, and one that was not organized (like its European counterparts) into standing divisions, corps, and armies. Small wonder that Bismarck referred to it dismissively as a *veraechtliches Armee* (a negligible, or contemptible little army—hence the regulars' ironic reference to themselves as the Old Contemptibles).

It was, however, an army well suited to small war and well practiced in it, for Victoria's long reign knew only one year of imperial peace. Many historians have underestimated the complexity of Britain's military problems in the nineteenth century and her skill in dealing with them. The British Army had to fight a wide variety of opponents, many of them neither primitive nor cowardly, in some of the harshest terrain in the world, and for political ends quite different from those obtaining in European warfare.[4]

A very good source to examine for an appreciation of the kinds of military problems faced by the British, and for an understanding of the peculiarities of small war generally, is Colonel C. E. Callwell's *Small Wars*, a treatise prepared under the auspices of the General Staff in 1906. Callwell defined small wars as "all campaigns other than those where both the opposing sides consist of regular troops."[5] He asserted that imperial campaigns differed completely from European ones, and were characterized by a diversity of terrains, climates, and opponents without parallel in European warfare. He reminded his readers that many of the opponents of the British displayed conspicuous military virtue: the Zulus, for example, were both fanatically brave and highly disciplined; the Afghans were natural marksmen at least as skilled as the British. During the Tirah campaign of 1897 Sir William Lockhart told his troops:

> We must remember that we are opposed to perhaps the best skirmishers and the best natural shots in the world, and that the country

they inhabit is the most difficult on the face of the globe. The enemy's strength lies in his thorough knowledge of the ground, which enables him to watch all our movements unperceived and to take advantage of every height and ravine.[6]

Moreover, imperial troops had to be prepared to adapt swiftly to new situations, as they were dispatched to different corners of the Empire and as new opponents entered the field. Callwell pointed out that in three short years British troops in South Africa had to cope with the completely different strategic and tactical problems involved in fighting the Transkei Kaffirs, the Zulus, and the Boers.[7] Feckless or poorly led imperial troops risked, and suffered, defeat, as at Majuba and Insandlwhana.

Against all opponents regular troops had to attack, because the political objectives of small wars are "to wipe out an insult, to repress a rebellion, or to consolidate a conquest." In addition, the imperial forces had to convince their opponent that resistance was hopeless: "prestige is everything in such warfare." One great victory would not suffice, however, for that would allow irregulars to regroup or revert to guerrilla warfare. Rather, a continuous but dispersed offensive was needed to overawe and overwhelm the enemy, and an unflagging pursuit to end his power of resistance.[8]

This meant, of course, a great deal of hard marching and fighting in oppressive climates, the kind that only seasoned men could perform. For this reason the British Army did not send soldiers overseas until they were twenty years old and had had at least one year of service. The physical demands were enormous: the regulars had to compensate for the natural mobility of the irregulars, who knew the country better, had at least the passive support of a friendly population, traveled light, and were often extremely fit (as on the Northwest Frontier) or well-mounted (as were the Boers). Moreover, small wars are, according to Callwell, preeminently "campaigns against nature," climate and terrain exposing troops to more than usual fatigue and disease.

Imperial troops required military skills quite different from those of the European conscript. The British Army discovered in the late nineteenth century the need for marksmanship in order to counter the extremely accurate fire of Afghan and Boer snipers, who often had modern precision firearms—in some cases (for example, the Boers' Mauser rifles), better weapons than those carried by the British. Even before the Boer War British soldiers were taught to shoot at moving targets and shot seven times as much ball am-

munition per man in training as the average conscript in any Continental army.[9] Good shooting and fire discipline also prevented
British troops from spraying away large quantities of ammunition,
thereby avoiding unnecessary strain on the precarious logistics of
small, detached units, and allowing the withholding of fire until
the moment of maximum psychological impact.

The British system of military service created the rugged and
skilled forces needed for small wars; equally important, it provided
the psychological framework needed to sustain them. Kipling's
soldier begins his tribute to the ferocious and cunning Sudanese
with a phlegmatic, "We've fought with many men acrost the seas,
/ and some was brave, and some was not . . ." Such psychological
resilience—the ability to adjust to vastly different climates and
opponents—was needed, because almost all operations of small
war were, and are, more psychologically taxing than those of large
war. For example, in small war regular British troops frequently
had to withdraw under fire, particularly in hill country after the
completion of a short punitive operation. At this point discipline
and cohesion were of utmost importance. Regular forces traveled
more slowly than their nimble indigenous enemies and often had
to run a gauntlet of fire to safety. In addition, no matter what the
operation, the wounded could not, as in regular warfare, be left to
the care of the enemy (although here the Boer War was an exception), nor could they be swiftly evacuated to rear-area hospitals.
The strain of such retreats (which occasionally ended in disaster, as
in Afghanistan in 1842) can be imagined.[10]

The British soldier did not always have the comfort of being
surrounded by masses of friendly troops and the vast logistical and
technical apparatus of modern war. He and his fellows were often
dispersed in small units—companies or battalions—far from
friendly support. Here too, mutual confidence and familiarity were
vital.[11]

Finally, small wars were rarely won in one or two decisive campaigns or by virtue of a sustained national effort of the kind seen in
the Napoleonic wars or World Wars. They were often long and
seemingly inconclusive, waged far from home, in inhospitable regions, against seemingly invisible enemies, and without great public support. The grit that soldiers needed to fight such wars could
not be found in short-service conscripts:

> The aching nausea of home-sickness; the exasperation to the strained
> nerves of the ceaseless danger and intermittent crackling of muske-

try; the sheer physical revolt from dirt and rags and starvation; the enervating dreams of decent food and of the girls they left behind them; all these influence conscript campaigners in double or treble degree.[12]

The regimental system cushioned the regular soldiers against the sense of isolation and abandonment that plagued French conscripts in Vietnam in the 1880s and their American counterparts there eighty years later. The regiment of the Cardwell system resembled "the large, comfortable Victorian county family, from which some of the officers came and to which the rest would have liked to belong."[13] The soldiers' psychic satisfactions came not from their pay or the recognition they would win at home, but from the esteem of their comrades, the paternalistic care of their officers, and their attachment to their unit, a military tribe united by traditions, rituals, and mannerisms.

When the Boer War broke out in 1899 the British system of military service was put to a hard test. An initial force of 70,000 regulars was swiftly dispatched to "subdue 90,000 mounted riflemen in an area of 430,000 square miles over extensive stretches of which a horseman could ride in any direction for weeks on end." Such a force was insufficient: ultimately 250,000 regulars, 100,000 militia, and tens of thousands of British and colonial volunteers served in South Africa.[14] The European powers looked with contempt on a state that took three years to win in a war against a rabble of armed pastoralists. In so doing they failed to understand the difficulty of Britain's task. This was the first war fought with smokeless high-powered rifles that could kill a man at a distance of over half a mile, small arms that revolutionized tactics. The Boers had Mauser rifles and light artillery superior to that of the British, and the terrain was suited to the long-range sniping and hit-and-run tactics at which these hunters and farmers excelled. In addition, the Boers were a zealous religious community, animated by their faith as well as by nationalism. Finally, the task of the British was not simply to destroy Boer military power but to come to terms with them, to achieve a victory that would not require permanently stationing large forces in South Africa to keep the Boer states in check.

The war strained the British system of military service but did not break it. The slightly expanded regular army did the bulk of the fighting, but the militia and volunteer units (which served for a year at a time) occupied and held conquered territory. British naval supremacy protected the Empire (which had been stripped of most of its regular troops) and prevented European intervention or logistical support for the Boers. Nonetheless, the initial defeats suffered by the British Expeditionary Force, the weaknesses in imperial defense that the war exposed, led to a reevaluation of the British system of military service, which I will discuss presently.

American Small Wars until 1950

Until the mid-twentieth century, and with the exception of the Civil War and World Wars, the American Army was a small, professional force, whose main task was the protection of the Western frontier against the Indians. A brief examination of perhaps its most difficult small war, the campaign against Filipino insurgents at the turn of the century, will show interesting contrasts with the army that struggled in Korea and Vietnam, and not necessarily to the advantage of the latter.

The Army consisted in 1897 of some 25,000 men, a force noted for the hardiness of the officers and men and their high level of intelligence and tactical skill. As in the British Army, high-level (divisional) organization was deficient, as was preparation for large operations; only the oldest officers had Civil War experience, and mostly at a fairly low level. The Indian wars had developed a force used to operating in small detachments and in extreme conditions (the blazing heat of the desert Southwest as well as the winters on the Great Plains, when many of the decisive anti-Indian campaigns took place). State militias, numbering some 114,000 men in units of varying size, equipment, and efficiency, served as a second line of national defense.[15]

It is not necessary to elaborate here the reasons for or the history of the Spanish American War or the seizure of the Philippines. Because of a mixture of motives—a sense of manifest destiny, fear of other powers seizing the islands, and the natural consequences of the Spanish naval defeat in Manila Bay—the U.S. government decided to occupy first Manila and then the rest of the Philippine islands. A small expeditionary force grew to a total of 20,000 men in February 1899, when the Filipinos began fighting their liberator-conquerors. Of these, 5,000 were regulars and 15,000 volunteers who had enlisted for the duration of the Spanish-American War.

The Filipinos, numbering about 30,000, were poorly armed but under the command of a charismatic leader, Emilio Aguinaldo, who had made his reputation as a guerrilla commander against the

Spanish. This loosely organized force swarmed around Manila, which was occupied by General Elwell Otis's force (almost all of which was eligible for discharge). As tensions between Americans and Filipinos mounted, Otis's men voluntarily deferred their return home until replacements had arrived from the United States.

When hostilities broke out it was clear to the American president and his secretary of war, Elihu Root, that a substantial force would be needed to quell the insurgency. Therefore, on 2 March 1899 the president obtained Congressional authorization for an increased regular army of 65,000 men and a volunteer force of 35,000 enlisted to serve until the beginning of July 1901. These volunteers were not, as the volunteers for the war against Spain had been, inexperienced civilians possessed by a sudden and evanescent thirst for military glory. Root ordered the army to adhere to rigid physical and psychological standards in recruiting men. In July 1899 alone, 11,100 out of a total of 14,000 applications for enlistment were rejected. In the words of one historian, "The character of volunteers obtained under this act has never been surpassed in our service."[16] In total, some 112000 men served in the Philippines between July 1898 and July 1901. American strength in the Philippines peaked at 70,000 men in 1901. Given that the U.S. population was about 80,000,000, an equivalent effort in 1970 would have been maintaining an expeditionary force of roughly 180,000 men overseas for a period of two years. Total casualties numbered 4,200 dead and 2,800 wounded a 5.5 percent casualty rate or the equivalent, in 1970 terms, of about 11,000 dead and 6,000 wounded.[17] In short, this was a war smaller than Vietnam or Korea but not by an order of magnitude. Like both wars, it was long, lasting three years and five months, including some two and a half years (February 1899 to June 1901) of heavy fighting.

The political-military problem was a formidable one. The Americans set out to subjugate seven thousand islands containing seven million people seven thousand miles from home. The leaders of the insurrection came from the upper classes of the island, were experienced in guerrilla warfare, and knew of domestic opposition in American to the prosecution of the war. They adopted sophisticated revolutionary tactics: establishing a parallel government, often suborning officials the Americans had appointed, and enforcing their decrees by torture and execution. Their understanding of the theory and practice of guerrilla war was considerable.[18]

The American Navy isolated the insurgents by imposing an effective (although permeable) blockade of the islands. As a result,

American troops certainly outnumbered *armed* Filipino insurgents. However, as one American general put it:

> The insurgents provided with rifles were, of course, far short of this number [70,000 men], but their knowledge of the country, their mobility, their control over the population, either through sympathy or fear, and, above all, their habit of passing from the status of guerrilla soldiers to that of non-combatants really gave them an advantage that more than made up for the disparity of numbers.[19]

In three years American troops fought over 2,800 battles and skirmishes, in most of which they were ambushed. Particularly at first, the Americans suffered severely from the climate. Many of the marching columns reported 30–50 percent sick from amoebic dysentery and grueling physical exertion in the steamy heat. Patrols slogged through mud in regions that received up to seventy inches of rain a year.[20]

And yet the Americans won, and did so in a way that, despite the atrocities on both sides, won Filipino respect and loyalty—a respect and loyalty revealed in Filipino resistance to the Japanese during World War II. The Americans engaged in a dual policy of repression and benevolent civic action, including road and sewer construction, legal and tax reform, and, above all, education. General Arthur MacArthur (father of General Douglas MacArthur) recommended from the very beginning that "the archipelago be submerged immediately under a tidal wave of education."[21] At the same time he subjected the rebels to constant military pressure— American troops established some five hundred outposts and patrolled ceaselessly. Small detachments, most of them platoon-sized (well under fifty men), insulated the population from the guerrillas, denying the latter food and moral support. In addition, the Americans developed indigenous paramilitary forces so that by July 1901 American strength could be reduced to 50,000 men, and in December to 37,000.[22] Thus, even in areas where Americans outnumbered their antagonists by only two-to-one (as opposed to the ten-to-one margin dictated by orthodox counterguerrilla theory), they were able to suppress a well-led and tenacious insurgency.

How did the system of military service—the use of a professional force accustomed to counterguerrilla warfare, augmented by volunteer American and native auxiliaries—help the Americans achieve this outcome? For one thing, it precluded some of the violent domestic protest that accompanied the Vietnam war by avoiding any kind of conscription. As it was, the was as an unpopular one: Samuel Gompers and his organization, the American Federation of Labor, opposed it; William Jennings Bryan, the Democratic presidential candidate in 1900, opposed it; Mark Twain, Charles W. Eliot, and perhaps the majority of the literary and intellectual elite opposed it. The primary historian of the opposition to the war traces the failure of the antiwar groups to their inability to rally the urban middle class against the war, despite the reservations many Americans had about the colonial rule of distant lands, and the horror many felt at stories (all too many of them true) of torture committed by American troops.[23]

The resistance on the part of the government to sending too many troops is noteworthy. The army operated under clearly understood limits on manpower, knowing in advance the approximate number it would have available and how long it would have them (some 35 percent of the troops were two-year volunteers). Thus, commanders had a sense of both urgency and predictability. Because they could not hope, like their counterparts in Vietnam sixty years later, to smother their opponents with sheer numbers, they wasted no time recruiting and training a suitable indigenous force to augment their own.

In addition, the expeditionary force was a high-quality one, for only the hardiest and most stable were sent. The Philippines war was preeminently one of patrol and ambuscade; it required physical and psychological hardiness, the former to survive the climate and terrain, the latter to endure the isolation and boredom. The two-year period of service assured the American commander of having a stable, experienced, and acclimatized force, all advantages lacking in Korea and Vietnam.

Finally, the relatively small size of the Philippine expeditionary force and its careful recruitment ensured a uniformly high quality of leadership. This was particularly crucial in a war fought primarily by lieutenants and captains operating independently. The officers of the American Army adapted quickly to an astonishing variety of missions, from patroling to schoolteaching, from raiding to establishing public hygiene. Only an intelligent and elite corps of officers could do this.

The campaign in the Philippines was the last waged by the old Indian-fighting army. In the years following, Elihu Root implemented a series of reforms that produced the pre–World War I army, a force preparing for conventional warfare waged by a swiftly raised citizen-soldier force. The quasi-colonial function was taken over by the Marine Corps, which conducted several difficult, and on the whole reasonably successful, campaigns in Central America and the Caribbean.[24] This division of labor, which lasted uneasily until the 1960s, reinforces the general argument that total war and small war require completely different kinds of military establishments. It was no accident, therefore, that the small-war mission devolved on the small, tough, and professional light infantry of the Marine Corps until the 1960s.

THE MILITARY DILEMMA OF THE WORLD POWERS

Great Britain, 1902–1914

Great Britain prosecuted the Boer War successfully, but the duration of the war and its human and financial costs persuaded many in Britain that military reform was called for. On paper in 1899 the British Army had well over 650,000 men available for military service, including regulars, reservists, militia, Volunteers, and yeomanry. And yet the British found themselves hard pressed to scrape together the initial expeditionary corps of 40,000 men. Moreover, during the course of the war the regular garrisons even of Britain itself were reduced to the slenderest proportions. In addition, the war revealed Continental hostility to Great Britain— particularly on the part of Germany—that made further military efforts essential.[25]

In 1904 the Norfolk Commission, appointed to inquire into the status of the militia and the Volunteers, recommended the adoption of conscription for home service. It was an idea bandied about in a number of circles, most notably that of the secretary of state for war, Arnold-Foster. Arnold-Foster and the conscriptionists (most notable among them Lord Roberts of Kandahar, perhaps the most famous British soldier of the day) were influenced by a number of factors, including the growth of the German Navy and the slowly evolving Continental commitment (in April 1904 Britain arrived at her entente with France, and in August 1905 the Committee on Imperial Defence asked the general staff to investigate the feasibility of dispatching an expeditionary force to Belgium). This official movement toward a European military commitment matched, and in some cases simply followed, public fears of Germany expressed in the popular literature of the time.[26]

It was in these circumstances that one of the most interesting war ministers in Great Britain's history, Richard Burdon Haldane, took office in December 1905. A lawyer and student of German philosophy, Haldane immersed himself in military studies (including Ardant du Picq's *Battle Studies*, Bronsart von Schellendorff's authoritative description of the German General Staff, and Elihu Root's reports as secretary of war) before acting on any question of defense policy. When Britain's senior generals first asked him what kinds of reform he would seek, "My reply was that I was as a young and blushing virgin just united to a bronzed warrior, and that it was not expected that any result of the union should appear until at least nine months had passed." When they pressed the question a few months later, asking what kind of army he desired, he replied "A Hegelian Army," after which (as he told it) "the conversation . . . fell off."[27]

The essence of Haldane's reform was the following: while maintaining imperial forces at their 1905 levels he assembled a British Expeditionary Force of six infantry divisions and one cavalry division, plus attendant support. This force consisted of regulars and reservists, together numbering 170,000 strong, and could be sent to Belgium within two weeks of mobilization. The Militia, Volunteers, and Yeomanry were reorganized into fourteen Territorial Army divisions, each with a cavalry brigade and light artillery. Territorials enlisted for four years at a time and did eight to fifteen days' yearly camp plus weekly drills and voluntary extra work (particularly the NCOs and officers). In the event of war this force would mobilize for home defense, provide the basis for expansion of the wartime army, and, in extremis, serve overseas. In addition, Haldane created a Special Reserve of men with six months' training who, together with regular reservists, would flesh out the British Expeditionary Force (BEF). Finally, he created Officers' Training Corps at British public schools and universities, to help increase the size of the cadre for expansion in the event of war.[28]

To appreciate Haldane's successes we must understand the constraints under which he operated. One constraint was financial: Haldane's Liberal colleagues were not disposed to increase the army budget over its current level of twenty-eight million pounds. Parsimony alone did not dictate this state of affairs, as Parliament demonstrated by steadily increasing the Naval Estimates, from eleven million pounds in 1883 to thirty-four and a half in 1903 to over forty million in 1910. Haldane accepted this peacetime order of priorities, saying, "You cannot ride two horses at once, and no more can you possess in their integrity two great conflicting military traditions."[29] He by no means resigned himself to an army held static in time of war, as we shall see, but he accepted peace-time austerity as inevitable, indeed wise, given the finite resources of the British economy and the strict priorities required to deal with her geopolitical problems.

Secondly, Haldane understood the domestic political constraints peculiar to Great Britain at the time:

> To raise armies under the stress of war, when the people submit cheerfully to compulsion, and when highly intelligent civilian men of business readily quit their occupations to be trained as rapidly as possible for the work of every kind of officer, is one thing. To do it in peace time is quite another.[30]

To create the Territorial Army out of the hodgepodge of auxiliary units (all of whom had powerful protectors in Parliament) required great political skill. Haldane created the County Associations to help recruit and support the new Territorial units, co-opting the part-time officers who cherished the independence and dis-tinctiveness of their local units. He then used their support to overcome the opposition of regular soldiers, who had little use for the "Terriers," as Sir Henry Wilson (commandant of the Staff College) contemptuously referred to them.[31]

Haldane's opponents in the National Service League (founded in 1902) argued that his measures did not go far enough. They held that the Territorials should have to undergo some preliminary basic training, and that the ranks of the Territorial Army should be filled by conscripts. Branches of the National Service League agitated for similar measures in the Dominions, and in Australia they had some success.[32]

The dispute between Haldane and the National Service League produced heated debates and some brilliant pamphleteering, including Lord Roberts's *Facts and Fallacies* and *Address to the Nation* on the one hand, and a fascinating work by Ian Hamilton (a military aide to Haldane) on the other. The latter work, *Compulsory Service: A Study of the Question in the Light of Experience*, is of particular interest, since Hamilton disingenuously attacks proposals for creating a cadre/conscript army, rather than the mixed professional/militia system at the heart of the National Service League's program. Haldane rejected that program because he feared that it would be unpopular, too costly, and damaging to recruitment for the regular army. He also maintained, on rather dubious grounds, that volunteers would devote more energy to the mastery of military skills than would draftees.[33]

In retrospect, however, it appears that Haldane and his critics agreed about the fundamentals of British security needs and even of the system of military service required to cope with them. All agreed with the influential military correspondent of the *Times*, Charles à Court Repington, who wrote:

> No nation on earth is sufficiently rich or powerful to pretend to dominate both the sea and the land . . . a Power which commits itself to the futile pursuit of this chimera will find itself inferior in each element in turn after beggaring itself in the quest.[34]

Second, all agreed that only a long-service volunteer force could successfully police the Empire and fight small wars. Third, all recognized the need for an auxiliary military force to defend Great Britain proper and provide the structure for a mass army in the event of war. Fourth, all supported the creation of an expeditionary army capable of fighting in Europe, India (along the border menaced by Russia), and other unforeseeable locales—Australia, for example, which was menaced by Japanese invasion. "Wars of the second or third magnitude," as Lord Roberts called them, might be fought at great distances under difficult climatic and geographical conditions.[35]

Such middling wars—the Boer War being but the most recent example—would require a substantial professional force. Thus, the French system of having a small colonial army (some 56,000 men according to Hamilton, and almost half of those kept at home) and a mass cadre/conscript one could not apply to Great Britain, which had to keep over 115,000 abroad and prepare to send just as many overseas, and quickly. The BEF (the British equivalent of America's Rapid Deployment Force in the 1980s) would have to be of the highest quality, for it might have to fight under the severest of physical circumstances, and outnumbered to boot.

Finally, all of the interlocutors in the conscription debate accepted the notion that conscripts could not be sent overseas except in the direst emergency: "It is inadmissable that one recruit would spend his days in the decorative security of St. James's and another in the fever-swamps, the sun-blistered plains or barren rocks, of some outpost of Empire."[36] This sensitivity on the part of sober and calculating imperial strategists is remarkable. How many in the 1960s and 1970s were willing both to endorse America's war in

Vietnam and to argue that it was immoral to send conscripts to fight it? To be sure, those in Britain who expressed such views could rely on the undoubted proclivities of Britons to volunteer for overseas service, as in the Boer War. Nonetheless, the awareness—and, more important, the acceptance—of political-moral restraints on military service reflected by such sentiments remain rare indeed.

The Haldane system worked well enough, but it could not fully cope with the demands put upon it by World War I. In part, the difficulty lay in the method of expansion devised by the then secretary of state for war, Lord Kitchener, who created entirely new armies rather than divide each Territorial division into three or four cadre units. Such Territorial units as did go to France performed well; many, however, mistrusted as they were by the professional leadership of the British Army, simply went overseas to replace garrisons of regular troops. A year after the outbreak of war the British had only half a million troops in France, a force only a fraction the size of that of its European allies. Only by 1917 had the new divisions reached a level of training and skill to enable them to launch successful assaults on enemy lines.[37]

Haldane's measures had been intended to straddle the British manpower dilemma; they met with only partial success, but that was all that could be expected. Ultimately, his priorities, and those of Great Britain as a whole, were correct. Overwhelming naval superiority was required to maintain imperial communications and even the food supply of Great Britain itself; a hardy and well-trained army was needed to sustain the imperial peace that would allow Britain to mobilize her vast human and material resources to wage global war. The creation of a mass army had to take third place to these considerations.

The United States, 1950–1971

From 1950 to the present day the United States has faced a dilemma similar to Great Britain's in 1904, namely, how to order its system of military service to cope with two completely different kinds of threats. The tension between the kinds of armed forces required for a massive commitment to the conventional, land-based defense of Europe and those needed to fight small wars on the Eurasian periphery became particularly clear during the Korean and Vietnam wars. As we shall see, these limited wars placed immense burdens on the system of military service that the United States inherited from the World Wars, Selective Service.

Korea was the first small war the United States took on as guarantor of the postwar order. Although it was officially a United Nations effort, the American role predominated from the first. American battle deaths outnumbered those of her non-Korean allies by two to one, and her level of troop commitment (a quarter of a million men) by an even greater ratio. It was a war limited in geographical terms (both sides maintained sanctuaries, the one in Manchuria, the other in Japan), in terms of force applied by the United States, in terms of domestic mobilization (there were no blackouts, rationing, or other measures of total war on the home front), and eventually in political aim, as the object became to restore the border along the 38th parallel. For a country that had just undertaken such extraordinary efforts—and achieved such extraordinary successes—in World War II, it was, as one author called it, "a peculiar kind of war."

The war opened on 25 June 1950 with a conventional assault by the North Korean People's Army (NKPA) against the embryonic forces of the Republic of Korea (ROK). The remnants of the ROK Army, reinforced by American troops (which began arriving in Korea on 5 July 1950), established a defensive perimeter around the southeastern port of Pusan. On 15 September 1950 the United Nations forces under General Douglas MacArthur counterattacked, spearheaded by marines and soldiers in an amphibious assault on Inchon harbor. This force (X Corps), together with the Eighty Army, crushed the NKPA and drove north of the 38th parallel toward the Chinese border. In November the Chinese attacked and drove the United Nations forces back below the 38th parallel; in the spring of 1951 the line of battle again moved up, spurred by a series of local counterattacks. From then until the ceasefire of 7 July 1953 the war was a stalemate punctuated by local attacks. Until late 1952, when an effective ROK Army began to emerge, the U.S. Army bore the brunt of the fighting.

When the United States entered this war it had an army of 600,000 men scattered around the world, enervated by the precipitate postwar demobilization, the temporary suspension of the draft, and the labors of occupation duty. The quality of personnel was poor (40 percent of the army's personnel were in Categories IV and V—the lowest mental categories in the evaluation system); units were undertrained and undermanned; equipment was short (the first troops went to Korea without bazookas that could stop the Soviet T-34 tanks used by the NKPA).[38]

Because President Truman and his advisers saw the NKPA attack as but a diversion from an impending war in Europe, some of the country's best troops (for example, the 82nd Airborne Division) were retained as a strategic reserve. The draft was quickly extended and the reserves and National Guard mobilized, with Congressional approval. Within four months, 130,000 soldiers and 20,000 marines were fighting in Korea, and eight months after that their numbers had expanded to fully seven divisions, or a quarter of a million men. Initially the war was fought by reservists, because although Selective Service had continued to register men, none had been called since January 1949. By September 1950, however, 50,000 men per month were being drafted, and it was this group that did most of the fighting in the static phase of the war; the draft also enabled the army to more than double its size (to 1,500,000 men by June 1952).[39]

The mobilization of virtually the entire organized Army Reserve (130,000 men were recalled), many of the 415,000 individual reservists (those without organized units but with a residual reserve obligation), and almost all of the organized and individual Marine Reserve (about 100,000 men all told) created numerous hardships. Many World War II veterans with families and jobs found themselves fighting in the hills of Korea while twenty-year-olds back home awaited their draft notices. On the other hand, these men provided the improvised forces of the Eighth Army and X Corps with a solid cadre of experienced soldiers: in June 1951, for example, fully half of the Marines in Korea were reservists.[40]

By 1952, however, the burden of the war had shifted to the conscripts, some twenty or thirty thousand of whom went to Korea each month as replacements. This personnel turbulence raised front-line troop morale, because service on the front was brief; it played havoc, however, with the development of cohesive and effective units. The Chinese, who stayed on the front more or less for the duration, learned the arts of camouflage, patrolling, and the construction of defensive positions; American units did not. When an American general asked S. L. A. Marshall what could be done, he replied:

Nothing. They [the Chinese] sit there year after year. The longer they stay the smarter they get. Our youngsters keep moving in and out.

They're smart and they've got guts, but they don't stay long enough to learn. You can't beat Davy Crockett with a boy scout.[41]

A point system (awarded to men as individuals) controlled when a man would be rotated out of Korea. This system—a fair one in many respects—was at once militarily unsound and politically inevitable in a small war fought by conscripts.

It is interesting that, to judge strictly by the opinion polls, U.S. involvement in Korea was almost as unpopular as in Vietnam; although initially most Americans supported it, by November 1950 more than half of respondents to one poll thought the war "utterly useless." Polls of male college students in April and May of 1952 found that approximately two-thirds wished to avoid military service if possible, and close to a quarter wanted to avoid it at almost any cost.[42] Nonetheless, the Korean conflict, despite its length (three years) and the widespread disgust with it, occasioned no social disruption of the kind caused by the Vietnam war.

This is attributable to a number of factors: memories of capitulation to the dictators in the 1930s, and of the consequences; the intensity of the Cold War; the endorsement of the cause by the United Nations, which was still a name to conjure with, and the visible presence of other allies; the clarity of the *casus belli*—an open invasion, unquestionably abhorred by the population of South Korea. In addition, the war was, initially, a conventional one with a moving battlefield, a war intelligible on a map. The reserve mobilization probably defused some opposition to the draft; after all, the younger brothers of those who had fought World War II and then been recalled to fight another war could hardly consider themselves singled out for harsh treatment. Moreover, general acceptance of a draft was probably higher at this time than at any other period in American history, as sustained popular endorsement of Universal Military Training (UMT) indicated. Thus, an unusual confluence of factors inhibited the kind of social turmoil that war incited. The military inefficiency of an individual replacement system was redeemed by the static nature of the fighting along the 38th parallel, and the use of overwhelming firepower (delivered by artillery and airpower) against a poorly equipped, if resourceful, peasant army. Although some observers (notably many of the army's senior generals) drew cautionary lessons from Korea, most Americans were only too glad to forget an unfamiliar and thoroughly frustrating war.

The Vietnam war, America's next small war (putting aside the Dominican Republic episode—a fairly successful application of force consummated, interestingly enough, by predominantly volunteer units of paratroopers,[43] engendered more civil strife than any war since that which nearly destroyed the Union. It destroyed two presidents and embittered American politics for a decade. Even after the surface disturbances had ceased, a profound sense of resentment and bitterness lingered, among those who had opposed the war, those who had supported it, and those who fought it. Since then, no use of American military power in any corner of the world—from the Mayaguez incident of 1975 to the dispatch of a few dozen advisors to El Salvador in 1983—has escaped comparisons with Vietnam.

This is not the place to review the tangled history of the Vietnam war; rather, my purpose is to inquire how the manpower system used by the United States shaped the outcome of the war abroad and at home. Only a few milestones need be mentioned. In the spring and summer of 1965 the first American fighting (as opposed to advisory) units were deployed in Vietnam, and embarked on combat missions; by the end of that year, 184,000 were serving there. Thereafter, a steady buildup occurred until 1968, when troop strength peaked at over a half million, the largest number sustainable without the reserve mobilization the military had long requested. Withdrawals from Vietnam began in June 1969, and by January 1972 U.S. troops there numbered 133,000. Within a year, the American military presence was virtually over.[44]

The United States fought the war with an army composed of conscripts and volunteers (many of these draft-motivated) led by a cadre of professional officers, although many junior officers and NCOs had also been swept into the military by the draft. Unlike in Korea, there was no substantial reserve mobilization; each time the Joint Chiefs of Staff or the commander of U.S. forces in Vietnam, General William Westmoreland, suggested this course (particularly in April 1967 and again in April 1968, after the Tet offensive), the president rejected it. To be sure, after Tet and the *Pueblo* affair (1968) President Johnson mobilized some 23,000 reservists in specialist units, and dispatched 11,000 of these to Vietnam; nonetheless, the government was unwilling to accept the political costs of such an action on anything like the scale to which it rose in Korea. Curiously enough, many of the president's advisers (John Mc-Naughton, for example, the assistant secretary of defense for international security affairs) feared that a massive call-up would create pressure to *expand* the war, perhaps with the use of nuclear weapons. Secretary of State Dean Rusk put the matter this way after the war: "We never made any effort to create a war psychology in the United States during the Vietnam affair. . . . We tried to do in cold blood perhaps what can only be done in hot blood, when sacrifices of this order are involved."[45]

Draftees, therefore, bore the brunt of the war; 70 percent of the fatal casualties fell on them. Inductions, which had ranged between 60,000 and 150,000 a year in the early 1960s, increased to over 340,000 in 1966 and were still as high as 200,000 in 1970. In addition, between 60 and 90 percent of the voluntary enlistments in the Vietnam period resulted from the draft—the desire of potential draftees to pick their service or to anticipate the inevitable. Conscripts served in Vietnam for no more than a year. As in Korea, the army felt it necessary to maintain morale and spread the burden of fighting across the population—in short, to "extend the nation's staying power by forestalling premature public pressure to 'bring the boys home.' "[46] As in Korea, individual rotation undermined unit integrity. During the last two months of these short tours, combat efficiency declined because of the soldier's understandable desire to leave Vietnam in one piece; and the fresh soldier, of course, took several months to adapt to the climate, terrain, and battlefield. The high turnover forced the army, in the absence of a reserve mobilization, to promote large numbers of unqualified NCOs and junior officers (for instance, Lieutenant Calley of My Lai infamy) while inflicting upon professional officers as many as three tours to Vietnam. The short tour policy (six months per position for officers, or two jobs in the course of one one-year tour) prevented enlisted men and officers from becoming familiar with the country's culture, geography, and peculiar military problems. As John Paul Vann, one of the more successful American advisers, put it, "We don't have twelve years' experience in Vietnam. We have one year's experience twelve times over."[47]

The American forces in the period 1965–1968 adopted a high-firepower "search and destroy" system of operations, which inflicted heavy casualties (almost a quarter of a million dead) on the enemy but failed to uproot the enemy's organization in the villages or create an effective indigenous force. In the words of Sir Robert Thompson, "In Vietnam resources were constantly substituted for efficiency and organization."[48] Historian Guenter Lewy points out that the Americans actually suffered because of the availability of massive numbers of their own troops and massive quantities of ordnance. Simply put, the American military used all the human and technological resources it could draw on to fight the war, even when they were unnecessary or downright detrimental to the basic objective, the creation of a South Vietnam capable of resisting the Viet Cong and North Vietnamese Army (NVA) more or less on its own. More sophisticated (and more difficult) strategies of Army of the Republic of Vietnam (ARVN) development and pacification, (including the Phoenix and CORDS (Civil Operations and Rural Development Support) programs, were eventually imposed on the army by the necessity to reduce casualties and the number of soldiers in Vietnam. Despite the swiftly deteriorating morale of the conscript army in Vietnam (soldiers absenting themselves without leave numbered fifteen per thousand in 1966 but seventy per thousand in 1970, as opposed to a Korean Conflict figure of twenty-five per thousand), these measures achieved considerable success.[49]

In retrospect, it is clear that the dispatch of over two and a half million troops to Vietnam in the course of a decade was a ghastly military mistake. Inevitably, this gargantuan force distorted the society of South Vietnam, for forces of such size invariably bring with them prostitution, black marketeering, and racial hostility, in addition to inflation and other economic troubles. In addition, this huge force led American commanders to look for straightforward ways of doing a most difficult and complicated job. Vietnam was not Korea, where brute firepower could halt an enemy and bring him to terms. It was a much more highly political conflict, and as such more typical of postwar conflicts than the earlier war. It is interesting to note that only when Washington imposed strict manpower constraints (as had occurred from the very beginning in the Philippines in 1899, and after a year in Korea, when additional American forces went to Europe rather than the front) did the Army buckle down to the crucial task of constructing effective local forces.

The use of large numbers of draftees did not merely undermine the Army's efforts in Vietnam; it inflicted grievous wounds on American society as well. Only a tenth of the eligible pool of men served in Vietnam, although fully two-fifths served in the armed forces during the war. Nonetheless, the draft hung over the heads of all able-bodied young men. Fully 30,000 fled the country and as many as half a million evaded the draft through various illegal means. College students in particular evaded the draft until 1970. Of this group, only 23 percent served in the armed forces and 12 percent went to Vietnam, as opposed to figures of 45 percent and 21 percent for high school graduates.[50]

College students menaced by the draft provided the elite that led the antiwar movement and much of its rank and file strength. Sam Brown, the coordinator of the Vietnam Moratorium Committee between 1969 and 1970, reluctantly conceded after the war: "A fundamental reason for the failure of the antiwar movement was overdependence on upper-middle class draftable young men."[51] Similarly, Eugene McCarthy, the antiwar senator whose surprisingly strong showing in the New Hampshire primaries triggered President Johnson's decision not to run for reelection in 1968, remarked the correlation between the draft and the antiwar movement.[52] As many have noted, the peak of the antiwar movement coincided with the height of American involvement, from 1968 through 1970. By contrast, the renewal of heavy bombing of North Vietnam in 1972 did not cause much of a stir.

To be sure, opposition to the war was widespread, as in the case of Korea, but working-class opposition to the war differed from that of the college elite. As John P. Roche put it, the two working-class slogans were "Let the gooks fight it out" and "End the ——ing war and shoot the ——ing draft dodgers."[53] Not only was middle- and upper-middle-class opposition to the war, particularly among the young, more vociferous than that during the war in Korea; it was far more durable. Whereas support for the draft remained strong throughout the Korean Conflict, support for any kind of draft plummeted during the Vietnam was and has remained low until today.[54]

Polling data indicate that until 1967 the Vietnam war was not particularly unpopular. This was particularly true in the early 1960s, when the troops stationed there were primarily volunteers and officers. Whether it was an unwinnable war is far from clear. What does seem certain is that the way it *was* fought, and in particular the open-ended manpower policy used to fight it, doomed the effort to military stalemate and domestic revulsion. One may wonder whether a policy such as that followed in the Philippines in 1900—of sending only volunteers, in whole units rather than as individuals, and for two years at a stretch—would have forced upon the American military a more intelligent strategy and provided it a more reliable tool to pursue that strategy. At the very least, we can conclude that if a decision to send draftees had required the same political effort as would have been required for a mobilization of the reserves, decisions to escalate would have been made far more cautiously.

POSTCOLONIAL CAMPAIGNS

As noted in the discussion of British manpower policy during the height of the imperial period, the British, like most other colonial powers, relied on a volunteer professional army to police their Empire. After World War II, however, Great Britain continued its policy of relying on a draft (National Service), a system that was not fully abolished until the early 1960s, although the White Paper of 1958 announced a return to an all-volunteer army. Thus, many of Britain's post-1945 imperial campaigns were fought, in part, by conscripts.

The relative success of British National Service troops in postcolonial war requires some explanation. As in the United States and Australia, in Great Britain a draft was popularly accepted after 1945 in large part because of the legacy of World War II. The National Servicemen of the 1950s could not very easily object to a burden that, they very well knew, was far lighter than that borne by their fathers and elder brothers.[55] More important, however, was the fact that most National Servicemen did not serve in a colonial theater of war. Whereas draftees bore the bulk of the burden of the fighting in Vietnam, most British infantrymen ouside Europe were regulars. In Malaya in 1957, for example, the British deployed some thirteen battalions, of which five were British, one Australian, one from New Zealand, and fully six, or nearly half, Gurkha mercenaries. The British relied on large indigenous police forces for local security, and used small groups of their troops— primarily the Gurkhas and the elite Special Air Service regiment— to fight a small-scale war of patrol and ambush in the jungle.[56]

One lesson of Malaya, as of virtually every other post-1945 war waged by Britain, France, and the United States, is that small wars continue to pose peculiar military problems, in terms of both individual prowess and tactics. As in Callwell's time, they demand physical stamina. This was even true in the case of Korea, an atypically conventional conflict. One of General Matthew Ridgway's major complaints when he took over the Eighth Army in Korea was that its men were reluctant to sacrifice their comfort by hiking along the hills rather than traveling in motorized columns.[57] The latter practice was the product of World War II experience, when there was little point in exhausting troops before they closed with the enemy.

As with means of movement, so with tactics. World Powers always face a standard challenge of small war, the necessity of unlearning tactics methods of operation, and above all modes of thought suited to European warfare but useless in small war. A British officer writes of Malaya:

> Initially, because of their previous training and experience, senior army officers were inclined to launch their units into the jungle in battalion strength—either in giant encirclement operations when a camp was known to be in the area, or in wide sweeps based on no information at all. Neither of these types of operation had any success.[58]

As in the late nineteenth and early twentieth centuries, small wars remained preeminently light infantry wars, won by small groups of men moving by foot for long periods of time over rough terrain.[59] In Malaya and elsewhere air transport (helicopters and small cargo planes) was useful for supporting troops operating for long periods in the jungle or the mountains, not for replacing their legs. In guerrilla-type warfare the enormous technological superiority of the World Power could not be brought to bear; as the British (unlike the Americans in Vietnam) realized, indiscriminate use of artillery and close air support would only lead to civilian casualties, and thereby alienate the population that was intended to be won over. The need for carefully controlled use of force was reinforced by the revolutionary character of these wars. The opposing forces could be relied upon to make clever use of opportunities for agitation and propaganda, as could their allies on the outside.

Finally, the British campaign in Malaya, like many other British colonial and postcolonial campaigns, revealed the importance of developing local levies in the form of rural police, militia, and guides. Such forces served as the first line of defense against insurgents, were a ready source of intelligence, and in addition could relieve the professional troops of all tasks save the most difficult one—finding and fighting enemy units in the jungle. Here, too, the Americans in Vietnam failed to profit as much as they should have from the British example.

Britain's involvement in small wars did not end with the British draft. British advisers—and troops—engaged in a small, undeclared war against Indonesia and in counterinsurgency campaigns throughout the Arab world. The Falklands war of 1982 showed the tremendous advantage of highly professional volunteer forces in fighting sudden, small campaigns in remote parts of the world. Nor were the advantages solely military: the professional and volunteer nature of the British forces lowered public resistance to the use of force, and helped the nation absorb the inevitable losses.[60]

Other European states have, of course, fought numerous conflicts overseas in the nineteenth and twentieth centuries. As a rule, they discovered empirically what the British knew by instinct, namely that conscripts were both militarily inept and politically dangerous to send overseas.[61] After a bad experience in Tonkin in the 1880s the French refrained from sending conscripts overseas. In fact, throughout their involvement in Indochina from 1946 to 1954 the French used a polyglot force of North Africans, sub-Saharan Africans, and tens of thousands of Foreign Legionnaires. That war is proof, if proof is needed, that mere use of a professional army to fight a small war is no guarantee of success. If the strategy and tactics it adopts are poor, and, above all, if country waging it fails to understand the war it is fighting, it cannot hope to win. The French lost the Indochina war for a number of reasons, including Viet Minh skill and tenacity, Communist Chinese support for the insurgents, and the extraordinary difficulty of the terrain. Perhaps the most important factor was French reliance on conventional operations aimed at the establishment or relief of fortified bases, such as Hoa Binh (1951). Dienbienphu was merely the least successful of such enterprises. In short, a professional, or at least a volunteer, army might be a prerequisite for success in such wars; neither, however, is a guarantee of success.[62]

Once the army turned to the government requesting draftees for service in Indochina, the French government knew that it could no longer continue the war.[63] The political necessity of not using conscripts of reservists meant that the French government fought the war not only with professional soldiers, but with professional officers as well. As a result, the French officer corps took losses that, though numerically small (2,000 killed), were the equivalent of losing seven complete classes from St. Cyr (the French West Point). In addition, French officers served at least one and frequently more tours of roughly twenty-seven months in Indochina, an ordeal which contributed to their isolation from, and bitterness toward, French society.

France's next and last major colonial war was waged in Algeria.

There conscripts were used, and in large numbers. By the late 1950s some three hundred thousand troops were engaged in suppressing a rebellion in what was, in theory, an integral part of France, not a colony. The conscripts held the outposts, or *quadrillage*, while the professional troops, including paratroops, Foreign Legionnaires, and *chasseurs* (commando-type forces), swept the countryside. These units provided the shock troops that helped install de Gaulle in power in 1958, and attempted to overthrow him in 1961. Despite France's historic ties to Algeria, and despite some dearly bought military successes, the French government gave it up, in large part because French opinion would no longer tolerate the expenditures of blood and money required to keep it. Even the putschists of 1961 realized this; part of their program was the return of conscripts to France and a pledge to win the war with professionals and settler volunteers.[64]

The experience of the French Army in Algeria was paralleled some fifteen years later by that of the Portuguese Army in southeastern and southwestern Africa. There too a demoralized conscript army led by conscript junior officers occupied a network of strongpoints and outposts; there too an elite professional force of paratroops, radicalized by a counterrevolutionary war, turned on a government shaken by the discontent consequent upon fighting a long colonial campaign with conscripts.[65]

Although the Portuguese and French made use of local troops, they did not do so nearly as much as the British, or even in the latter stages of the Vietnam war, the Americans. In Algeria and sub-Saharan Africa they relied on large masses of conscripts led by disgruntled middle-class reserve officers to perform tasks ot static security filled in Malaya by rural police and in Vietnam (at the end of the war, at least) by the Regional Forces/Popular Forces (the two militia forces) and the ARVN. In Indochina the French had neither conscripts nor substantial bodies of effective local troops, save where they could arm religious or ethnic minorities (such as tribesmen). As a result of these practices, the burden of fighting fell on an extremely small, and soon a radicalized, professional officer corps. When France and Portugal used masses of draftees in North and South Africa (respectively), they found domestic opposition mounting sharply because conscription affected the literate and politically active middle class, members of whom were needed as reserve officers.

From a purely military point of view one can argue that a cadre/conscript army such as the French Army in Algeria, the Portuguese

Army in Africa, and the U.S. Army in Vietnam can wage counterinsurgency warfare and succeed. At the end of each conflict the
commanding generals could claim, with some justification, to have
killed or driven back most enemy guerrillas and to have regained
control of territory and population. Such a claim, however, would
be disingenuous, for in all three cases the territories and populations fell to the enemy in short order. This occurred for two reasons. First, the large-scale use of conscripts removed the pressure
for the creation of effective indigenous forces, which alone could
hope to win the war in the long run. Second, the extensive use of
drafted manpower ensured rising domestic discontent with the
war, and even violent social disorder. Given these facts, it is mean-
ingless to speak, as some have, of military victory *but* political
defeat, for the one was purchased at the expense of the other.

SMALL WARS AND DEMOCRATIC POWERS

The domestic politics of small wars pose peculiar problems for
democratic countries. Tocqueville argued that when thoroughly
aroused, democratic nations can sustain great efforts and thereby
overcome their enemies. At other times, however, "No kind of
greatness is more pleasing to the imagination of a democratic people than military greatness which is brilliant and sudden, won
without hard work, by risking nothing but one's life."[66] Small wars
offer few such prospects. They are long and won by the persistent
application of intelligent methods. To take one final example, consider the extremely successful U.S. Marine Corps Combined Action Platoon program of 1965–1966, which inserted a squad of
Marines (fifteen men) into a village together with thirty-five or
forty Vietnamese militia, and kept them there to protect the population.[67] For such programs to work, soldiers must know a country
well, both its culture and its terrains. Junior leaders must be proficient and sensible, their men highly disciplined and hardy.

Progress in small war is not, as in conventional war, measured
by the movement of a front line. The large-scale use of conscripts, a
workable practice in large wars, merely exacerbates the problems
faced in small wars. A liberal democracy cannot, however, send a
few draftees to fight overseas for long periods of time—considerations of humanity and equity prohibit it, so that rotation policies
such as those used in Korea and Vietnam are likely. The resulting
use of large numbers of conscripts defeats the purpose of waging

such a war, which is usually the creation of a stable and decent government supported by indigenous armed forces.

By definition, a small war is not fought over issues vital to the intervening power, and this means that it cannot be waged with that power's full resources. A democracy can indeed sustain the human and material costs of total conflicts, as we have seen in this century, but in each small war that a World Power wages it must set a limit for itself, the point at which the effort and the costs it engenders are deemed no longer commensurate with the rewards of success. The French gave up in Indochina once it became clear that they would need draftees to continue the war; the Americans drew the line at mobilization of the reserves and National Guard. *In each case it was a change in the system of military service used to fight the war that was identified as an unacceptable change in the level of military commitment.*[68]

Britain (and, for the most part, France) refrained from using conscripts to fight imperial wars, and was often willing to accept temporary defeat, at least, rather than do so. The United States attempted to use conscripts in Vietnam and suffered the military and political consequences. To be sure, in those cases where victory seems quickly achievable, and against an unambiguously malevolent enemy, conscripts can be used. Such was the case in the opening stages of the war in Korea. But these conditions—universal hatred of the enemy and an opportunity to win swiftly—are rarely present. As Adolphe Thiers told French parliamentarians in 1848: "But when it will be necessary to support what I will call political wars, wars in which enthusiasm does not play the major role, such a [conscript] army will be inadequate."[69]

Both the military and political requirements of small wars (if one uses such a suspect distinction) mandate the use of professional soldiers. In this century as in the nineteenth century, small wars have usually been light infantry wars won by resourceful and rugged footsoldiers operating in inhospitable places—conditions enacted as recently as 1982, in the Falklands war. As in the past, they do not engage the full attention or energies of the World Power that wages them.

Small wars are low in intensity but long in duration. A cadre/conscript system waging such a conflict finds itself facing either a shortage of capable junior leaders or the politically unpalatable prospect of mobilizing settled reservists. The solution, it would seem, is to use from the very beginning an augmented professional army, that is, a professional army backed either by indigenous

Table 2. Types of Military Service Appropriate for Different Types of War

Intensity	Duration	
	Short (months)	Long (years)
high	cadre/conscript	expansible selective service *or* militia *or* cadre/conscript
low	professional	augmented professional

forces or specially raised corps of volunteers. During short, sharp conflicts, of course, a completely professional force will likely be the most effective and politically usable tool of a World Power.

The political-military dilemma that Great Britain faced at the turn of the century, and that the United States has faced since World War II, can be summed up schematically (see Table 2). Whether a workable (if uneasy) compromise to meet the requirements of long and short, high-intensity and low-intensity wars is possible is a question I address in Chapter 9.

[5]

Military Service and Republican Ideology: Civic Obligations and the Citizen-Soldier

Since the end of the eighteenth century, most European and many American democrats have instinctively identified universal and compulsory military service with democratic forms of government. This view derived much of its force from the experience and thought of the French Revolution, which, as we have seen, seemed to provide an enduring lesson concerning the merits of mass conscription conjoined with the pursuit of republican ideals. Here, as in other respects, the French revolutionaries and their sympathizers indulged in a self-conscious classicism, which shaped even their choice of political-military titles (for instance, "Consul"). Following Rousseau, they identified republican virtue with military service: "As soon as public service ceases to be the main business of the citizens, and they prefer to serve with their pocketbooks rather than with their persons, the State is already close to ruin."[1]

The relationship between military service and free government is much more complicated in the Anglo-Saxon states. The peculiarities of the relationship between military service and liberal-democratic ideology form the subject matter of this and the next chapter. In this chapter I look at how compulsory military service generally fits in with Anglo-American conceptions of obligation. In particular, I examine the concept of the citizen-soldier, a figure with whom republicans of all stripes seem comfortable. In the next chapter I take a rather different point of view, seeking there to analyze the many ambivalences afflicting the liberal-democratic view of military service. This chapter is concerned primarily with an ideal type of military service; the next chapter, with military service as it is shaped in practice by often contradictory aspects of republican thought.

The views of Adam Smith on the nature and effects of military service remain of special interest to the contemporary student of conscription, for they combine an understanding of military and economic necessity with an appreciation for the philosophical appeal of compulsory military service. In addition, a study of Adam Smith's though on this matter is peculiarly appropriate because so many contemporary students of conscription are also advocates of the free market system, avowed followers of Adam Smith.

Smith's economic thought rests on several propositions, among them the notion of a commercial society acquiring wealth by way of specialization (the division of labor) and the pursuit of private interest. At the heart of Smith's philosophy is his endorsement of self-interest, rather than communal endeavor, as the source of prosperity and progress. Where Rousseau speaks of a general will that is greater and more dignified than the mass of particular wills of the citizens, Smith celebrates the invisible hand of self-interest. It is in large part as a result of Smith's doctrines—his writings and their wide acceptance—that first Great Britain and then the United States became the wealthiest states on the globe.

Smith's *Wealth of Nations* covers much more than economics, however: in it he treats jurisprudence, education, and a host of other subjects, including foreign policy and defense. How does he reconcile the nature of military organizations, which require self-abnegation for their effectiveness, with a doctrine that rests on an enlightened selfishness? Smith did explicitly treat this matter, presenting a strong case for the ancien regime system of military service described in Chapter 2. In former ages, he argued, the everyday life of hunters and nomads prepared them for the rigors of war, but during an age of commerce and manufacture the populace had neither the leisure nor the aptitude for war.[2] Smith did not believe this a morally desirable development, although he did believe it an inevitable one: "Another bad effect of commerce is that it sinks the courage of mankind, and tends to extinguish the martial spirit." Civilized and prosperous peoples become soft and unwarlike: "By having their minds constantly employed on the arts of luxury, they grow effeminate and dastardly."[3] Smith conceded that aristocrats might fight for love of honor and loyalty, emotions that made them suitable to serve as officers if not entrepreneurs.[4] All others, however, would fight only out of fear or habit.

Smith thought highly, however, of the discipline produced by the draconian means associated with ancien regime military training:

> In the late war [the Seven Years' War] eight hundred Prussians defended a pass a whole day against several thousands of Austrians, and at night in their retreat deserted almost to a man. What could be at the foundation of this courage? It was not a principle of honour, nor love to their country, nor a regard to their officers, for these would scarce have detained them; it was nothing but the dread of their officers, who were hanging as it were over their heads, and whom they durst not disobey. This, by the bye, shows the governableness of our nature, and may also shew how much that manly courage we so much boast of depends upon external circumstance.[5]

Modern armies, he argued, require individual bravery far less than "regularity, order, and prompt obedience to command"; thus, a "well-disciplined and well-exercised standing army" will always be superior to a militia composed of men accustomed to liberty, and therefore resistant to good discipline. When a militia remains in the field for several campaigns, however, it becomes in effect a standing army, with all the advantages in skill that accrue thereto. Furthermore, although generals may forget their skill during peacetime, professional soldiers do not lose their courage, because their bravery is rooted in habit.[6]

Smith held that the courage of habit could prove superior to that produced by patriotic enthusiasm, although he freely conceded the moral superiority of the latter. The strength of such disciplined bravery suggested the need for armies composed of long-service volunteers. Moreover, the laws of progress pointed in the same direction. The art of war, like any other art, advances only through a division of labor, that is, specialization. "The art of war, as it is certainly the noblest of all arts, so in the progress of improvement it necessarily becomes one of the most complicated among them."[7] The skill required by the use of contemporary firearms put an additional premium on regularity of mechanical operation rather than individual skill.

In addition, said Smith, universal military service imposes too heavy a burden on civilized peoples: "No state can impose very great and intolerable hardships, as the military service would be, in a refined state."[8] Smith held with Frederick the Great that in commercially active countries only 1 percent of the population could be spared for military duty without inflicting harm on the economy of the state. In ancient Greece, Smith observed, one quarter of the population could serve as soldiers, albeit only in certain seasons of the year. States could not require more than militia service (muster once or twice a month, plus several days' camp in spring or fall) without ruining their economies.

Finally, Smith argued, the ancien regime system produced the healthiest state of civil-military relations. "That degree of liberty which approaches to licentiousness can be tolerated only in countries where the sovereign is secured by a well-regulated standing army."[9] If the sovereign is commander-in-chief and the nobility and gentry of a country make up the officer corps, a country need have little fear of military dictatorship.

Smith's defense of the ancien regime system differed greatly from the argument of present-day free-market economists who support an all-volunteer army. The latter agree that defense and foreign policy are prime duties of the sovereign or government, but they fail to distinguish between the dignity attaching to those areas and that attaching to (for instance) fire or police protection. Smith, on the other hand, referred to war as "the noblest of all arts," and if he supported the voluntary system it was almost as much because of his belief that commercial peoples would be too effeminate to fight as for technological or economic reasons. He refers to Rome and Greece with admiration, even with a certain wistfulness.

Smith's view paralleled that of his contemporary Edward Gibbon, who said, when comparing Rome's imperial armies with the republican militia of earlier days, "In proportion as the public freedom was lost in extent of conquest, war was gradually improved into an art, and degraded into a trade."[10] Like Smith, Gibbon believed that patriotism, "which had rendered the legions of the republic almost invincible, could make but a very feeble impression on the mercenary servants of a despotic prince." But according to Gibbon, other emotions—honor, superstition, fear, and greed—were "motives of a different, but not less forcible nature." Neither the political economist nor the historian thought that a conscript army animated by patriotism and republican virtue possessed an intrinsic superiority to a well-regulated mercenary force. On the other hand, both admired the examples of ancient Greece and Rome, and accorded military service a status higher than that of

[120]

any other kind of occupation. This curious combination of rationalist disbelief in the utility of conscription with an attraction to military service for its moral virtues embodies an ambivalence that remains with us today.

THE CONCEPT OF THE CITIZEN-SOLDIER

Smith's mixed attitude toward war, his respect for patriotic martial virtues coupled with a belief that free and prosperous peoples were incapable of cultivating them, suggests that we should examine carefully our usual understanding of Anglo-American attitudes toward military service. It is a commonplace that the Anglo-Saxon states, including the United States, have long regarded soldiers and soldiering with profound suspicion. In Samuel Huntington's words, "liberalism does not understand and is hostile to military institutions and the military function."[11] As we see from the example of Adam Smith, this is at best only a half-truth. Liberals have, from time to time, praised the courage and self-sacrifice that dignify military service. Woodrow Wilson summed up this unique aspect of military service in a speech made in 1919:

> A friend of mine made a very poignant remark to me one day. He said: "Did you ever see a family that hung its son's yardstick or ledger or spade up over the mantelpiece?" But how many of you have seen the lad's rifle, his musket, hung up! Well, why? A musket is a barbarous thing. The spade and yardstick and the ledger are the symbols of peace and steady business; why not hang them up? Because they do not represent self-sacrifice. They do not glorify you in the same sense that the musket does, because when you took that musket at the call of your country you risked everything and knew you could not get anything. The most that you could do was to come back alive, but after you came back alive there was a halo about you.[12]

Wilson did not delight in the imagined glories of conquest or thrill of battle. He did, however, reveal in this and other speeches a deep admiration for the selflessness of military life and, almost as important, for its element of risk or hazard. One might even suggest that the metaphor of the gamble attracts democratic peoples to military service as much as any other aspect of it, that the heady alternatives of death or glory appeal to members of a society that respects the entrepreneur as much for his audacity as for his wealth. The perennial popularity of military heroes from George Washington to George Patton suggests a culture appreciative, in some measure, of military prowess. No less a pacifist than William James once remarked: "The war party is assuredly right in affirming and reaffirming that the martial virtues, although originally gained by the race through war, are absolute and permanent human goods."[13]

Americans' approval of martial virtues goes beyond a lurking admiration for courage and daring, however, for we also find long-standing support for the citizen-soldier. This label has been affixed to soldiers from the Minutemen of Lexington Green to the volunteers of the All-Volunteer Force. But what precisely does it mean? In ancient Greece the relationship between military service and citizenship was clearly established: the citizen of Athens or Sparta was also a hoplite or other kind of soldier. This has remained true in a few countries, such as Switzerland and Singapore, which utilize an extraordinarily comprehensive militia. The political significance of such a system lies in the fact that it incorporates the bulk of a country's male citizens (and in some cases female citizens as well), the mature as well as the young, the heads of families as well as their sons. In countries that draft young men for a year or two of military service, however, the identity of soldier and citizen is less obvious. In both Australia and the United States during the 1960s, for example, there was considerable opposition to the drafting of young men who, inasmuch as they lacked the right to vote, clearly were not full citizens.[14]

One might argue that the concept of the citizen-soldier embraces military service as a rite of passage by which one both learns and earns citizenship:

> Military training brings a man into contact with his fellows solely upon the basis of fellow-citizenship. For the time, at least, the differences of wealth, education, locality, taste, occupation, and social rank, which divide Americans as effectively as though they lived on different continents or in different centuries, are lost sight of. Men are brought face to face with the elemental fact of nationality.[15]

Yet such an understanding of military service, as either a prerequisite for citizenship or an essential transmitter of civic virtue, would disenfranchise women (in most cases), the disabled, and those who become citizens when over military age. This would not have presented many difficulties for ancient republics, or even for such small and exclusive republics as Switzerland. For the Anglo-Saxon states, however, particularly the United States, such an under-standing would be intolerable.

William Blackstone, the English legal theorist, held that a man "put not off the citizen when he enters the camp; but it is because he is a citizen, and would wish to continue so, that he makes himself for a while a soldier."[16] In the liberal state, a man is a citizen prior to military service, not because of it. In addition, arguments about the identification of citizenship with military service neglect the forbearance and respect that have long been shown conscientious objectors in Anglo-Saxon countries. Indeed, the Virginia convention held before the ratification of the American Constitution proposed that the Bill of Rights include the statement "that any person religiously scrupulous of bearing arms ought to be exempted, upon payment of an equivalent to employ another to bear arms in his stead."[17]

The case for the citizen-soldier, therefore, rests on other grounds than a crude equation of citizenship and military service. One argument turns on the question of civil-military relations—more specifically, on the issue of civilian control of the military. Blackstone prefaced the remark quoted above with the assertion that "in free states the profession of a soldier, taken singly and merely as a profession, is justly an object of jealousy." He continued by saying that in liberal states "no man should take up arms, but with a view to defend his country and its laws."[18] Even if soldiers are nominally citizens, a professional army is one separated from the nation and thus a possible threat to it. Professional soldiers, in this view, conceive of themselves less as citizens than as soldiers, though they may in theory be both. Professional armies pose threats to the polity because they might seize power for their own purposes or serve as the compliant tools of tyrants. At the heart of democratic civil-military relations lies the subconscious but chilling fear of a Cromwell or King George III using professional soldiers to crush popular liberties.

This understanding of the value of the citizen-soldier as a brake on tyranny suggests that what we speak of is not merely a soldier who can vote, but a sort of civilian-soldier. According to this argument, it is necessary that the bulk of the armed forces consist of men whose main pursuits are pacific, who are fresh from their civilian lives and look forward to their swift return to those lives, whose main identity is as citizens and not as soldiers, whose loyalty lies with home and community, and not with the military as a corporate body. In Woodrow Wilson's words, "We must depend in every time of national peril, in the future as in the past, not upon a standing army, nor yet a reserve army, but upon a citizenry trained and accustomed to arms."[19]

In nineteenth-century Europe it was a commonplace on both Left and Right that "it is impossible to rule for long against the will of the nation in a country where universal military service is established."[20] Such episodes as the abortive coup by French professional soldiers in 1961—a coup quashed in large part by the opposition of conscripts—seems to confirm this view. The advent of totalitarianism, however, which always bears in its train universal military service, would seem to cast doubt on this view. Soldiers may become disaffected, but unless they have some means of organization independent of their officers they are impotent to defend democratic governments. Moreover, as we have seen (Chapter 2), the advent of the modern cadre/conscript army in Germany was in no way coupled with political liberalism; indeed, the introduction of military service allowed the Prussian monarchy to subvert and eventually abolish the real military bulwark of Prussian liberalism, the voluntary Landwehr.

It is also true that the large-scale incorporation of citizens into the military can open opportunities for the destruction of civilian rights through martial law, as when the French government broke a railroad strike in 1910 by calling railroad workers to the colors in their capacity as reservists. Moreover, in countries such as the United States and Great Britain the tradition of military subordination is well-established and fears of a putsch minimal, professional army or no. Thus, this understanding of the value of the citizen-soldier also seems inadequate.

In liberal-democratic states the true political argument for the use of citizen-soldiers is more subtle. It rests on the political counterpart of John McAuley Palmer's dictum that the militia system used the brain as well as the brawn of a country, and is the view that war ought to be *directed*, not merely fought, by citizens. Those holding this position see little merit in the cadre/conscript system. In the Prussian system, they would argue, the conscripted mass provided the raw strength of the military, but not its guiding intelligence. To use a metaphor from business, in a cadre/conscript system the citizenry are day-laborers, not stockholders, persons whose services are needed and used, but who have no control over the enterprise of which they are part.

According to this view the most proper as well as the most

effective defense of a country rests with those who have the largest stake in it; there is something mean or degenerate in a community that relies on hired members of the lower classes to fight its great battles. "The spirit of every profession is different from the spirit of the country," said Woodrow Wilson in 1915, even as he praised the devotion and intelligence of America's professional soldiers. Therefore, he continued, "we want men whose occupation is peace, because they are the only men who can carry into the field the spirit of America as contrasted with the spirit of the professional soldier."[21] It is essential, he said, that "the forces of the nation should indeed be part of the nation and not a separate professional force."[22] According to this view it would be as wrong to delegate the defense of a country to paid professionals as it would be to let elections be handled by hired professional electors; in the saltier words of General George S. Patton, "even the jackal does not hire someone to defend its young." In time of war, in particular, the distinction between the civil and the military is artificial—"it is for the happiness of both to obliterate it," according to Jefferson.[23]

THE MILITIA CONCEPT

The type of military service that most closely matches the ideal of the citizen-soldier is that of militia duty. We shall see (in Chapter 6) that this system also neatly resolves some of the tensions between a liberal desire to minimize enforced service and an egalitarian desire to spread it evenly. The militia obligation is a form of compulsory service that, in the United States by mid-twentieth century, was imperfectly understood. General Lewis Hershey, the head of Selective Service from the beginning of World War II through 1970, disingenuously claimed that "the militia system . . . is the ancestor of the Selective Service System and the direct descendant bears a very close resemblance to its illustrious forefather."[24] Nothing could have been farther from the truth.

The drafts of the Civil War and afterward rested on Congressional authority to raise armies, not on the liability of citizens to do militia service. Indeed, American opponents of conscription have often made their legal assaults on the draft in the name of militia service, a form of obligation held by some (including Chief Justice Roger Taney during the Civil War) to be legitimate even if a draft per se is not.[25] The Selective Draft Law Cases (1918), in which the constitutionality of Selective Service was finally established, reasserted the reliance of the draft law on Congressional power to raise armies rather than on citizens' obligation to perform militia duty.[26]

What are the distinguishing characteristics of the militia concept? First, it is a form of near-universal service. "Each and every free able bodied white male citizen . . . who is or shall be of the age of eighteen years [or older] . . . shall severally and respectively be enrolled in the militia," read the American Militia Act of 8 May 1792.[27] In Switzerland, the exemplar of such a system, those who have not served for whatever reason pay additional taxes. Unlike cadre/conscript or selective service systems operating in peacetime, the militia system does not titrate its induction of new soldiers to meet purely military needs for a fixed quantity of manpower. Rather, as many men as are physically able serve.

Second, under the militia system active military duty is required primarily if not exclusively for the purpose of training, the only exception being when the militia is called out to support the public order. By contrast, in cadre/conscript systems military service is required to provide a standing force of soldiers. National training and national service schemes envision the performance of nonmilitary work by conscripts. Additionally (and unlike either the cadre/conscript system or national service), militia duty implies a military commitment of as many as thirty years, rather than only two or three. Militia service therefore entails membership in an organized unit that meets regularly for drills and maneuvers. For these reasons and others, a third distinguishing characteristic of militia service is its basis in local units. Whereas virtually every other system provides for the mixing together of young men from all over the country (indeed, that was one of the primary purposes of the Universal Military Training proposals advanced in the late 1940s), militias are local. Not mentioned in the earlier discussion of the relative advantages and disadvantages of localized recruiting is its effect of reinforcing the notion of military service as an obligation to protect one's home and community.

Fourth, and perhaps most important, the militia obligation usually entails a limited obligation to actually fight. In the United States one of the major differences between Reserve and National Guard units is that the latter require a Congressional proclamation to be mobilized. In all of the Anglo-Saxon countries the question whether or not militiamen can be compelled to serve overseas has been a delicate one. The Canadian Militia Act of 1904, for example, allowed the Governor in Council to dispatch the Canadian Militia overseas if necessary; in practice, however, the Canadian government refrained from dispatching unwilling militia conscripts to serve overseas. During World War II Australian militiamen could only be obliged to serve in the Pacific theater, not in North Africa or Europe. In the United States some National Guardsmen attempted (albeit unsuccessfully) to resist military service overseas. On the other hand, presidents have been increasingly reluctant to mobilize reservists of any kind, including Guardsmen, for any but the gravest emergencies (the National Guard mobilization of 1950, for example, occurred in the context of a general national mobilization).

These four traits of the militia obligation—universality, limited active service, local recruiting and service, and limited obligation to fight—should make this system of military service most ideologically attractive to liberal-democratic states. In fact, variants of compulsory militia service have flourished for varying periods of time in all of the major Anglo-Saxon states. In all cases, lack of a compelling need for such a system has inhibited its growth, and the instrumental or temporary ideological attractiveness of other systems has led to their adoption on an equally tentative basis.

In the United States, understanding of the militia system as a *concept* has been distorted by the militia system as *practiced*, primarily because of the seemingly indissoluble connection between the militia and the states. The variation in training and equipment and the corrupting effects of state control (particularly as it has affected officer promotion) have led to regular officers' long-standing scorn and mistrust toward the militia.[28] The continuance of the contemporary National Guard as a part-state, part-federal institution has not alleviated this.

The founders of the United States argued that "a well-regulated militia is *the most natural* defense of a free country" (emphasis mine).[29] Washington's unhappy experience with militia units in the War of Independence inclined neither him nor his advisers against the militia system as such; rather, their insistence on the phrase "well-regulated" was translated into an insistence on federal control. Indeed, after the war Washington (aided by Alexander Hamilton and General Henry Knox) submitted a proposal for a federal militia filled by compulsory service (although its members would not be obliged to serve in small foreign wars). Similarly, the only thoroughgoing militia proposal in the United States in this century—General Palmer's in 1916–1920—envisaged the creation of Reserve divisions that would not be part of the National Guard.[30]

Three types of compulsory service have been advocated in the United States on the basis of their ideological appeal. The first is the militia system, the second Universal Military Training (UMT), and the last universal national service. I will consider here the arguments for these last two schemes, as opposed to proposals for pure military service aimed solely at creating effective armed forces. Universal Military Training was advocated in the United States briefly at the end of both World Wars, and indeed was nearly adopted. Proposals for national service have had a much longer life, dating back to William James at the turn of the century and enduring to the present day. Both kinds of proposals remain perennial favorites of a majority of Americans, if public opinion polls are to be believed.

One appeal of UMT and national service rests in the supposed ability of such programs to foster national unity by mixing together young men (and in some versions, women) from all parts of the country. Indeed, military service itself has often been supported by developing countries on just such grounds. National unity was one aim of conscription in France during the early years of the Third Republic, and as one French historian observes, "By the 1890's there is persuasive evidence that the army was no longer 'theirs' but 'ours.'" By then the army had become "as potent an agency for acculturation and civilization as the schools."[31] Similarly, many American advocates of UMT during and after World War I hoped that UMT would help create a unified American people out of a mass of immigrants.[32] But in France such acculturation meant, in practice, little more than teaching provincial recruits French. By and large,

> The army was too complex a body to leave a distinct imprint on those who passed through it . . . the interest of the army to the historian is rather that it acts as a magnifying lens revealing aspects of national problems and of personal tensions, more clearly than they can be seen in civil society.[33]

[128]

It seems that compulsory service is most likely to enhance national unity when it is for a vital military purpose, as in Israel, for example. This is not surprising, perhaps, for unity in any group is likely to come about from a sense of working toward an important goal, rather than from striving for unity for unity's sake. A program with the purpose of fostering unity, moreover, can make sense only when a country requires national unification—a process well advanced in late twentieth-century America without such measures.

A more serious argument for UMT and national service—again, one that has been advanced for military service as well—is its value as education. Indeed, in all countries that conscript young men for some form of military service there seems to be consistent pressure for the use of military service as a form of post-secondary or remedial education. "Our Army furnishes us with a peculiar and logical extension of our school system," wrote Heinrich von Treitschke before World War I.[34] In a similar vein, the civilian leadership of the Defense Department during the 1960s pressured the military to take below-standard inductees and provide them with remedial education (Project 100,000).[35]

As early as 1786 arguments were advanced for universal military service or training that relied heavily on the supposed moral educational value of such experiences. General Henry Knox argued for the adoption of universal militia service in the following words:

> A glorious national spirit will be introduced with its extensive train of political consequences. The youth will imbibe a love of their country; reverence and obedience to its laws; courage and elevation of mind; openness and liberality of character; accompanied by a just spirit of honor; in addition to which their bodies will acquire a robustness, greatly conducive to their personal happiness, as well as the defence of their country; while habit, with its silent but efficacious operations will durably cement the system.[36]

Most of the proposals for compulsory military training in the British Dominions at the beginning of the twentieth century concentrated on military training for students. In Australia, for example, military training began at age fourteen, although this met with frequent opposition. The war correspondent of the Melbourne *Argus* called it "a broad shirk on the part of the man and an imposition on the boy."[37] In the United States during and after both World Wars, programs of universal training were advocated in large part as supplements to vocational training programs.[38] In 1966 General Eisenhower wrote, "This year [of military service at age nineteen] should be considered not only as their contribution to the country but as part of their education," and as for its purposes, "If UMT accomplishes nothing more than to produce cleanliness and decent grooming, it might be worth the price tag."[39]

These kinds of arguments, however, have always met—and in the end succumbed to—several rebuttals. First, even advocates of UMT have conceded that the externally imposed orderliness of military life does not always—or even usually—carry over into civilian life: "We have seen the orderly, neat arrangements of the West Pointers, and we have seen the chaos of their rooms when they returned home."[40] Military discipline is not the same as self-discipline, as educators throughout the century have argued, for military discipline rests on a peculiar set of externally created sanctions and pressures unlikely to be found in civilian life.[41] The effectiveness of military inculcation of social values is also open to question. The German Army, which made intensive efforts to wean young recruits away from socialism during the late nineteenth century, failed to do so and, in fact, by 1910 gave up the attempt entirely. The clumsy efforts of sergeants and junior officers only evoked scorn and resistance, and they themselves were more interested in the military training of recruits than in their indoctrination.[42]

An obvious objection to emphasis on the educational aspect of military training is the effect that such use of the military has on its primary mission, preparation for war. Educational programs obviously take time and resources away from the main task of military training; moreover, an educational program is likely to bring in recruits who are unusually troublesome to educate. Less than half of the servicemen brought into the American armed services for academic remedial training between 1967 and 1972, for example, performed acceptably at their jobs. Professional officers and sergeants resent—as their counterparts in other countries and at other times have resented—being used as teachers and social workers.[43]

One finds, in addition, a principled insistence among many advocates of UMT that the sole purpose of military training must be preparation for defense, that the deliberate inculcation of military habits and virtues for their own sake is simply militarism. One of the main proponents of UMT in the late 1940s insisted:

> The program is one of military training and not one of general educational or sociological experimentation; any educational, social, and

physical benefits are incidental and only byproducts of the military training. The justification of the military training program is based solely on military considerations. . . . No other justification is valid.[44]

Herein lies the great difference between UMT and national service. The one has as its primary rationale national defense and military utility, the other does not.

National service schemes present huge practical problems, among them how staffing would be handled, how the millions of participants would be controlled in the absence of military discipline, and what projects would be found that would not throw adults out of work. Far more important than these questions of efficacy and efficiency, however, is the larger question of legitimacy. To adequately measure legitimacy, in the sense of congruence with fundamental beliefs, we have to look beyond opinion polls to the core beliefs that inform the entire structure of a liberal-democratic republic.

The problem is fundamentally one of the appropriateness of compulsion in such societies, and more specifically, compulsion directed at those who have done no harm to others. Compulsory military training may be accepted in peacetime by a liberal state as the price it must pay for remaining free. Compulsory high school education can be justified on a number of grounds—it ensures that all citizens have the wherewithal to earn a living, it ensures minimum standards of literacy, it helps prevent the appearance of masses of unemployable youngsters. None of these justifications, however, can be applied to compulsory military/industrial training or to national service programs, under which all young men (or all young men and women) are obliged to do a year or more of low-paid national service, not necessarily military. Such programs cannot be said to be necessary to create good citizens, for the long history of the United States and Great Britain shows that a patriotic and well-educated citizenry can flourish without military service.

There remain two possible rationales for universal and compulsory national service. The one most popular today is the notion that the citizen owes a year of labor to the state. The idea is that those who have benefited from the protection of the state (defined, rather questionably, as the federal rather than state or local government) owe a debt that they must repay with personal service. The theoretical grounds for this assertion, however, would seem to run counter to the liberal political philosophy that underlies American politics.

[131]

The two elements that comprise national service—compulsion and personal service—make it quite different from obligations that partake of only one element. Liberal states regularly demand of their citizens only one form of personal service other than military—jury duty, which offers an instructive analogy. Jury service is limited in time and location, and is deeply rooted in tradition. Through it, citizens participate directly in the administration of justice, a concern as vital as defense. Conscription for nonmilitary service, however, has no such dignifying goal; it is based simply on the notion that the young owe the state a year of labor. National service is thus more akin to *corvée* than either jury duty or military service, a conscription of labor such as was not even adopted during America's greatest military struggle, World War II. Nor would tradition alone run counter to such a program: in the United States it might well run afoul of the Thirteenth Amendment, which prohibits involuntary servitude.

The other major rationale for national service was advanced by William James in his essay "The Morale Equivalent of War." James advocated national service that would be pacific, yet cultivate "manly virtues": "Martial virtues must be the enduring cement; intrepidity, contempt of softness, surrender of private interest, obedience to command, must still remain the rock upon which states are built."[45] James's goal was not only to channel martial energies into peaceful projects including coal-mining, road-building, and "fishing fleets in December," but to secure the permanence of martial virtues.[46]

James's argument differs from that of current national service advocates in important ways. Whereas they are willing to see national servicemen volunteer for military duty, James spoke as a self-confessed pacifist and utopian; and whereas they speak of the goal of a young man's or young woman's service being fulfillment of an obligation, James expressed a desire to see "the childishness knocked out of them." James's argument, therefore, is similar to that of those who pressed for military training as a form of education, and in the end succumbs to similar objections.

From the largest political point of view, the sole purpose of military training or compulsory service must be the strengthening of the armed forces. When the governments of liberal states stray into other purposes they find themselves subjected to furious criticism. The revelation in the late 1960s of the Selective Service System's "channeling" policy—the use of draft exemptions to pressure young men into such fields as teaching, science, and defense-related industrial specialties—was a major cause of the drastic overhaul of Selective Service in 1970, and its replacement by a strict lottery system.[47] When the issue was one of practice rather than mere opinion, the American public vehemently rejected a military service program that attempted to shape nonmilitary behaviors. In a society in which any governmental coercion of individuals is automatically suspect, a nonmilitary draft, or quasi-military draft, can be expected, in the long run, to excite derision and opposition.

Perhaps the best proof that the replacement of conscription for military service by compulsory national service or vocational education is widely deemed illegitimate is that in recent years it has never been proposed independently, but rather as a way of sweetening a proposed military conscription. Universal military training, on the other hand, with its somewhat narrower goal, and other forms of military conscription have been proposed frequently in the past century and have gained substantial if not decisive public support in times of peace.

[6]

Military Service and
Republican Ideology:
Liberalism and Egalitarianism

In the last chapter I examined the connection between re-publican institutions of government and obligatory service gener-ally, be it military or in the form of national service. In this chapter I look more closely at two opposing strands of republican thought, the liberal and the egalitarian. These two traditions have not mere-ly favored or opposed conscription, but have shaped the imple-mentation of different types of military service. Their uneasy coex-istence is revealing of a philosophical ambivalence toward conscription quite as profound as the geopolitical ambivalence dis-cussed in Chapters 2 and 3.

THE LIBERAL ARGUMENT

In general it is difficult to reconcile compulsory military service with the liberal conception of the ends of politics. Hobbes and Locke argued that the goals of the polity are the preservation of life and property:

> The final cause, end, or design of men, who naturally love liberty and dominion over others, in the introduction of that restraint upon themselves in which we see them live in commonwealths, is the foresight of their own preservation, and of a more contented life thereby.[1]

> The great and *chief end* therefore, of Mens uniting into Common-wealths, and putting themselves under Government, *is the Preserva-tion of their Property.*[2]

[134]

Because man's chief goal is the preservation of life (and, if possible, property), he cannot be expected to willingly die for the state. True, it is just for a man to be required to pay taxes and even render military service, but when ordered actually to *die* for the state the citizen may justly refuse:

> When armies fight, there is on one side, or both, a running away; yet when they do it not out of treachery, but fear, they are not esteemed to do it unjustly but dishonorably. For the same reason, to avoid battle, is not injustice, but cowardice.[3]

The sovereign, it would seem, has the right to contrive situations in which death is more certain if one flees the enemy than if one attacks, and indeed, armies in Hobbe's and Locke's time paid great attention to the problem of coercing soldiers to stay in the battle line.

Hobbes and Locke wrestled with the problem of military service in similar ways. They recognized the desirability of military obedience and of a state powerful enough to exact it, yet their conception of the ends of politcs gave no compelling reason for the citizen to risk his life for the state. Hobbes sought a way out by drawing a distinction between those who enlist voluntarily and those who do not:

> But he that enrolleth himself a soldier or taketh imprest money, taketh away the excuse of a timorous nature; and is obliged, not only to go to the battle, but also not to run from it, without his captain's leave.[4]

Yet, according to Hobbes, no man can forfeit his right to self-preservation. Locke attempted an equally arbitrary assertion:

> For the Preservation of the Army, and in it of the whole Commonwealth, requires an *absolute Obedience* to the Command of every Superior Officer . . . . But yet we see, that . . . the Serjeant, that could command a Souldier to march up to the mouth of a Cannon, or stand in a Breach, where he is almost sure to perish . . . can not command that soldier to give him one penny of his money . . .[5]

Both Hobbes and Locke insisted that such orders are legitimate because the preservation of the state requires it, and neither goes any further. (Notice also Locke's use of the qualifier "almost" in the last sentence.)

[135]

Neither philosopher doubted that conscription was legitimate:

> When the defense of the commonwealth requireth at once the help of
> all that are able to bear arms, every one is obliged; because otherwise
> the institution of the commonwealth, which they have not the pur-
> pose, or courage to preserve, was in vain.[6]

However, two limits on compulsory military service would seem to
stem from this philosophy. First, such forced service must be for
the purpose of defending the commonwealth, not merely aggran-
dizing it. The peril to a society must be a grave and visible one for
the citizens to accept the risk (not to mention the certainty) of death
to preserve it. Second, the soldiers of a Hobbesian or Lockean state
cannot be ordered to die for their country. As Michael Walzer
observes, "Indeed, the great advantage of liberal society may simply be this: that no one can be asked to die for public reasons or on
behalf of the state."[7] True, this doctrine presents no insuperable
obstacle to conscription and the use of conscripts in war, for rare
indeed are the times when men must be ordered to *certain* deaths.
It does, however, put tacit limits on conscription: it precludes acceptance, whether passionate or a fatalistic, of orders to risk one's
life for one's country. It suggests that conscription for military
service will be acceptable only when the need for it is clear, the
danger immediate, the peril mortal:

> Conscription, then, is morally appropriate only when it is used on
> behalf of, and is necessary to the safety of, society as a whole, for
> then the nature of the obligation and the identity of the obligated
> persons are both reasonably clear.[8]

The proof of this contention, namely, that compulsory military
service (not training, but service) is fundamentally incompatible
with, or at least antagonistic to, liberal doctrine is borne out by the
history of conscription in the liberal Anglo-American states, those
states most influenced by the views of Hobbes and Locke. Even in
the midst of World War I, conscription for overseas service was
voted down in Australia, albeit by a slender margin.[9] None of
these countries has maintained peacetime conscription for military
service for more than a decade or two. Furthermore, in the case of
Britain and the United States, peacetime conscription followed
World War II and required merely the continuance of wartime
practice rather than peacetime innovation. The case of France,
where for nearly a century peacetime conscription for military ser-

[136]

vice has been considered a keystone of national security and republican institutions, provides a striking contrast.[10]

The liberal states find military compulsion repugnant but at the same time they elevate the virtues of military voluntarism and see in widespread willingness to join the armed forces in time of need an evidence of the superiority of the free state. Paradoxical though it may be, the liberal theory stemming from a limited conception of the ends of the state, and which initially would seem to expect so little from the citizen, eventually requires more.

> The voluntary theory implies that men *shall* volunteer. It does not mean that men shall freely choose to serve or not to serve, according to taste or aptitude, but that they shall choose *service* according as national exigencies shall dictate.[11]

Thus, grafted on to the unromantic conceptions of Hobbes and Locke are the virtues of Athens in her heyday, as illustrated in Pericles' Funeral Speech:

> There are certain advantages, I think, in our way of meeting danger voluntarily, with an easy mind, instead of with a laborious training, with natural rather than with state-induced courage. We do not have to spend our time practicing to meet sufferings which are still in the future; and when they are actually upon us we show ourselves just as brave as those others who are always in strict training.[12]

The strength of this ideal was born out by the mass voluntary enlistments of the Civil War, the Boer War, and World War I. For many hardheaded soldiers and strategists as well as politicians and journalists, these conflicts (or at least their early stages) bore out the view that the urge to volunteer was a unique and precious heritage of the Anglo-Saxon states. Colonel G. F. R. Henderson, for example, the foremost English-speaking military thinker of the nineteenth century, made this one of the themes of his magistral biography of Stonewall Jackson. Shortly before his death he again declared: "What foreign soldiers cannot, or perhaps will not, see is that the war in South Africa, like the war in the Peninsula, and the Civil War in America, is a triumph for the principle of voluntary service."[13] So powerful was the voluntary ethic that when during World War I the United States created its first systematic draft, Selective Service, President Wilson defined it in terms of the voluntary ideal. "It is in no sense a conscription of the unwilling; it is, rather, selection from a nation which has volunteered in mass."[14]

Moreover, this faith in voluntarism, even on the part of doctrinaire liberals, does not preclude a draft although it does shape the nature of such a draft. In 1940, for example, Senator Robert Taft freely conceded the legitimacy of a draft as a last resort.[15] When Prime Minister William M. Hughes of Australia proposed a draft for overseas service in 1916, he said, "The proposals of the Government do not destroy voluntaryism—rather do they stimulate it to nobler effort. If it proves itself worthy, then the need for compulsion ceases."[16] Similarly, during the Civil War the Union used its draft to spur enlistments—it obtained only 8 percent of its manpower through use of the draft, and most of those in the form of substitutes. The use of the draft as a spur to enlistment for patriotic or psychological reasons (as during the Civil War in the United States and World War I in Australia and Canada) or for prudential ones (as in the United States during the period 1950–1970) is obviously at variance with notions of either universal obligation or pure selective service, as described by Enoch Crowder (Chapter 3).

The most interesting exposition of the problems a draft poses for a liberal society is Lincoln's "Opinion on the Draft." It too conceives of the draft as an unsatisfactory but necessary substitute for a strong volunteer effort:

> There can be no army without men. Men can be had only voluntarily, or involuntarily. We have ceased to obtain them voluntarily; and to obtain them involuntarily is the draft—the conscription. If you dispute the fact, and declare that men can still be had voluntarily or in sufficient numbers prove the assertion by yourselves volunteering in such numbers, *and I shall gladly give up the draft.* [emphasis mine][17]

Lincoln never published his "Opinion on the Draft." Some historians have argued that he felt it unnecessary; another reason, however, might have been Lincoln's awareness of his own less than romantic conception of the voluntary spirit, coupled with a surprising understanding of the predicament of those who opposed the draft. His was a position that, however reasonable, had little rhetorical appeal. He said that men decide whether to volunteer or not after a weighing of motivations. "Among these motives would be patriotism, political bias, ambition, personal courage, love of adventure, want of employment, and convenience, or the opposites of some of these." Later he frankly says, "You who do not wish to be soldiers, do not like this law. This is natural; nor does it imply want of patriotism."[18] Lincoln did not attempt to dignify the draft;

rather, he called it "involuntary, or enforced service," and justified it simply on the grounds of military necessity.[19] He raised no principled objections to substitution or commutation (payment of three hundred dollars in lieu of service), and indeed, he defended the latter as a method of enabling the poorer classes to avoid service, as the price of substitutes occasionally reached several thousand dollars or more. That voluntary motives—be they noble or not—were insufficient, Lincoln realized. Similarly, in Britain, Canada, and Australia during World War I (through 1915, at least) the voluntary sprit was supplemented by social pressure of an overwhelming and occasionally brutal kind.[20]

Thus, the liberal position proclaims an ideal—voluntarism—in which it cannot wholeheartedly believe, and which historically has not succeeded, at least not in time of large-scale war. It is equally true, however, that as an ideal it remains powerful, if only because it corresponds to the voluntarism generally characteristic of Anglo-American political culture, as described by Tocqueville. In more practical terms, the legacy of the ideal—the use of small-scale conscription as a spur to enlistment—has remained part of the Selective Service System throughout its peacetime operation.

Conscriptionists in liberal societies often argue that compulsion is not antithetical to the political ideals of such societies. If military service is compulsory, so are taxes and high school attendance.[21] These analogies, however, are inapplicable, for only in the case of military service does the state demand of the citizen that he risk his life. Military service means forfeiture of normal rights and submission to martial law. It subjects those who undergo it to a discipline far more stringent than that of school. Far from being a preparation for a productive career—as high school is or should be—it may well be an interruption of it. One must pay one's taxes but can make the money to do so in a host of ways; military obligations, however, must be met by personal service. One can select a high school by kind and location—not so the locus and type of military service. Only in the case of jury duty do we find society making such direct claims on the individual, and only for a short period of time, near one's home, and without the often harsh instruction that characterizes the indoctrination of a young soldier.

There are further liberal objections to military service or even training in peacetime, beyond the involuntary exposure to risk and the sheer fact of compulsion. These are the disruption of a draftee's life caused by conscription, the regimentation required by military life, and the moral threat posed by military service. The first of

[139]

these requires little explanation and is probably less important than the others. The problem of interrupting a young man's education or work is usually dealt with by arranging for induction at age eighteen, that is, before college and immediately after secondary education, at a natural break in a young man's life. A further expedient has been the granting of deferments until the completion of higher education, which was generally the practice in the United States during the 1950s and 1960s, although it gradually became a means for the more privileged classes to escape military service altogether. During the nineteenth century, Germany and (briefly) France instituted a program of one-year unpaid service as a reserve officer (*Einjaehrig-Freiwillige*) in lieu of the full term of service. In France, another device that stemmed in large part from the desire to preserve sons of the bourgeoisie from the interruption caused by military service was the practice of substitution.

A more serious criticism of military service has been that it imposes habits and doctrines repugnant to free and civilized men. The essence of a soldier's training is that he learn to kill. When, in 1945, Colonel Edward Fitzpatrick argued for universal military training, he warned his readers of this fact:

> Military training is not a dilettante business. It is not keeping formation in unmartial parades to martial music. It is not physical training. It is not vocational training for peacetime pursuits. The central lesson to be learned is that one must kill or be killed. The "fine art" of killing must be learned. War is violence. The battle is the payoff. . . . This determines the character of military training, and such objectives and strategy must be understood by the trainee. Such statements are not ordinarily made, but it is important that they be understood.[22]

That such training is open to morally principled objection has long been recognized through the practice (in most liberal states) of allowing conscientious objection.

Even if we leave aside the instruction in killing, we find that the necessary regimentation and military discipline contradict liberal theories of education. According to this view, the instinctive obedience required to some extent in every soldier, obedience induced by drill and petty harassment, produces no beneficial effects on the recruit. George Nasmyth argued in 1917 that

> The whole object of military training is to secure instantaneous obedience without thought, to make men a part of an autocratic military machine, so that if he is ordered to sink the *Lusitania* or destroy the

city of Louvain, he will obey instantly and unquestioningly. Surely unthinking obedience is far removed from the self-imposed discipline, that respect for laws because they have been enacted by common consent and for the welfare of the people.[23]

On the other side, it was held by military men that free citizens could not be made into reliable soldiers without years of patiently imposed discipline. George Washington told Congress:

Men accustomed to unbounded freedom, and no control, cannot brook the Restraint which is indispensably necessary to the good order and Government of an Army. . . . To bring men to a proper degree of Subordination, is not the work of a day, a month, or even a year.[24]

The final profound objection to military service, one which may have less urgency today than in the past, concerns the moral consequences of military service. As the advocates of universal military training declared in 1947:

We must admit at once that a serious moral problem is presented by the very removal of a boy of eighteen from the normal influences of his home, church, school, and local community and his comparative isolation in a group with large numbers of other men under an entirely new and different environment.[25]

Daniel Webster declared in 1814:

But this father, or this son, or this husband, goes to camp. With whom do you associate him? With those only who are sober and virtuous and respectable like himself? No, Sir. But you propose to find him companions in the worst men of the worst sort.[26]

The fear of unregulated sexual indulgence by draftees exercised a considerable influence over critics of various compulsory service plans in the years after 1918. They could point to the virtual epidemic of venereal disease that struck America's newly raised armies before World War I. In 1916, when expansion was already under way, the noneffective rate due to VD alone was over 5.5 percent, although this was subsequently reduced by prophylaxis and harsh but effective discipline (soldiers with VD were court-martialed and freedom from VD became a prerequisite for a return to the states).[27]

[141]

Even without the horror of VD, Americans were disturbed by the necessarily realistic and even tolerant attitude of the armed forces toward sexual activity. One World War I veteran wrote to the commission studying universal military service during World War II:

> In its [the Army's] concern not to appear Sunday-schoolish it actually exerted a profound influence in the direction of antiseptic license. There was the rather embarrassed lecture of the company commander (copy from GHQ), which mentioned the possibility of chastity (a suggestion rather hilariously received by the company) but went on to give specific suggestions as to what to do if and when the soldier followed other lines. . . . Understandable is the feeling of many that army life is an interlude which isn't to be judged by ordinary standards.[28]

Indeed, the minority report of the House Committee on Armed Services opposed Universal Military Training in 1948 on such moral grounds, among others.[29]

A liberal society that hopes to shape the sexual morality of its young along traditional lines relies primarily on the influence of religion, family, and local community. Military service inevitably removes these influences and creates pressures for conduct not otherwise accepted and opportunities not otherwise available. Moreover, because an army's main concern vis-á-vis sexual activity is to avoid medical casualties from venereal disease, it will place more emphasis on prophylaxis than on moral exhortation. The problem is perhaps exacerbated by the fact that peacetime military training falls on young, nearly adolescent single males, unleavened by older married men. As a result, one sober advocate of UMT said:

> These youngsters are still immature and should have, but may not welcome, guidance. The inhibitions and taboos of their normal life are gone. The protective mantle of family and home life have gone too. The old associations on which one relies are not there.[30]

In addition, critics of compulsory service have pointed to the reliance of any armed force on the cult of masculinity to instill in new soldiers toughness and esprit de corps. This exaggerated appeal to virility (evidenced in the invariably lewd marching ditties of the U.S. Army) further undoes the restraining and moderating influences of home and community life. On the other hand—and this is a major point—the revolutionary changes in sexual mores since World War II (although perhaps originating earlier) have probably gravely weakened the force of such arguments in the future.

Given these principled objections to compulsory military service and, in particular, peacetime military service, the liberal state has two choices. Either it can rely exclusively on inadequate volunteer forces, or it can attempt to minimize any form of compulsory service. It may use a draft as a spur to enlistment, or it may turn to another device, substitution, which was last used in the nineteenth century. Substitution and commutation (a close relative) have fallen into disuse primarily because of egalitarian arguments (discussed in the next section of this chapter); they are practices to which liberals should have few theoretical objections, and yet which are clearly unacceptable today.

Substitution, the provision of a recruit in place of a drafted man, and commutation, the payment of a fixed sum of money in lieu of service, were practiced in England throughout the eighteenth and early nineteenth centuries, when the militia was raised by lot, or "ballot." During the Civil War, both North and South used it widely: in the North, of 2,100,000 raised in the course of the war, 52,000 were drafted, some 87,000 paid commutation, and over 118,000 furnished substitutes. Thus, some four-fifths of the men held to service did not personally perform it.[31] The practice was not at first regarded as dishonorable in principle, and communities often made collective patriotic efforts to raise funds for bounties for substitutes. Lincoln defended the commutation provision (which for some reason was less popular than substitution), saying that its abolition would logically suggest the abolition of substitution altogether, and remarked, "This being a great innovation, would probably leave the law more distasteful than it now is."[32] The postwar report of draft administrator Brigadier General James Oakes of Illinois, a document that exercised considerable influence on Enoch Crowder and other founders of Selective Service during World War I, condemned substitution on practical quite as much as on theoretical grounds:

> In my judgement, the strong hand of the government should be laid upon the whole heartless crew of substitute brokers, whether as principals or subordinates, and all others who would make merchandise of the necessities and calamities of the country. The whole business is founded upon a supreme and sordid selfishness and profligacy unparalleled in the annals of corruption and fraud. . . . It presses into

[143]

the service, by devices which no vigilance can wholly prevent, great numbers of men wholly unfit for military duty.[33]

Peacetime substitution was commonplace in France throughout the late nineteenth century. In order to create a long-service force, the French Army took half or less of the group eligible young men selected by lot for five to seven years' service, but allowed—in fact, encouraged—substitution. Thus, in 1848 the army was one-quarter draftees, one-quarter substitutes (two-fifths of these former soldiers), and one-half volunteers.[34] In theory the Niel Law of 1868 obligated those not undergoing the full period of service to perform six months of training for reserve duty, but this was not implemented.

The market for substitutes was well developed, and included insurance against the drawing of an unlucky number in the lottery. Substitutes had to be free of any military obligation of their own, suitable for service, and aged twenty to thirty (unless they were veterans, in which case the age limit was thirty-five). The result was a free market along classical liberal lines for substitutes.[35] One beneficial result, from the military point of view, was the considerable reenlistment rate induced by the bounties paid by substitute brokers.

The most eloquent defender of this system was Adolphe Thiers, the most durable French politician of the nineteenth century and an historian of some skill. Even after the defeat of France in 1870 he stoutly maintained that conscription for long service combined with substitution would provide at once the fairest and most effective defense of France.[36] He believed that a hardened long-service army would provide France with a force suitable for both colonial and European warfare, and he backed his contentions with the testimony of General Bugeaud and his own voluminous studies of the Napoleonic wars.[37]

Reliance on long service did not ipso facto require substitution. Thiers's argument for that practice rested on the contention that some men—perhaps most men, certainly most middle-class men—were fundamentally unsuited for war. The average *honnête homme* of bourgeois society was concerned with the small circle around him, that is, his family; he would defend his family or himself resolutely, no doubt, and hence should be liable for service in the event of dire emergency or invasion, but he lacked the willingness to face death for anything else.[38] Only in the primitive barbaric state would every man be a soldier; in modern times prosperous peasants and the bourgeoisie had no inclination and little aptitude for the peculiar requirements and rigors of war.[39] Substitution allowed those who *did* have the requisite physical and psychological characteristics to take the place of those who did not, and this in a free marketplace, without coercion.[40] Moreover, substitution meant that education would not be interrupted; hence future doctors, lawyers, teachers, and the sons of the most productive peasants would be able to enter their professions or trades without delay. In a way, substitution would serve the purposes of a long-range selective service, exempting the most productive members of society for the good of the whole.

Substitution in France died slowly: only in 1905 was universal two-year service finally adopted.[41] It was a liberal institution in its reliance on free markets and freely made contractual agreements, but it had long been under attack from egalitarian elements. In Germany, for example, the Assembly of Frankfurt in 1848 voted against the practice, and criticism of it mounted steadily, in France as elsewhere.[42]

To be sure, military considerations played a part in the abolition of substitution. Despite government attempts in both the United States and France to regulate the practice, there were considerable fraud and racketeering. In the United States in particular, substitutes often proved themselves poor soldiers, frequently deserting to reenlist elsewhere for the bounty. Furthermore, the popular interpretation of the outcome of both the American Civil War and the Franco-Prussian War was that the Prussian system of large-scale short service and extensive use of reservists had proven itself superior to the raising of smaller long-service armies. On the other hand, a good deal of the opposition to substitution and commutation stemmed from political conviction.

The Egalitarian Argument

The case for equality in military service lends itself easily to the coining of slogans. Perhaps the sharpest denunciation of substitution during the Civil War was the slogan, "A rich man's war and a poor man's fight."[43] The sentiment contained in these few words is what doomed substitution, for no regulation of the substitute market, strict though it might be, could disguise the fact that substitution allowed one to escape danger and hardship simply by virtue of wealth.

[145]

Tocqueville defined the essence of the problem in his discussion of why democracies find conscription at once necessary and desirable: "The government may do almost whatever it pleases, provided it appeals to the whole community at once; it is the unequal distribution of the weight, not the weight itself, that commonly occasions resistance."[44] One can compare this with the judgment of one historian of the Civil War draft that "when conscription is employed, even the appearance of injustice as among classes in society must be studiously avoided."[45] Indeed, the history of conscription systems in Europe, North America, and Oceania reveals the steady chipping away of inegalitarian provisions. In France in 1873, substitution was abolished and replaced by a system of one-year "voluntary" service along the lines of the German *Einjaehrig-Freiwillige*.[46] By the beginning of the twentieth century the practice was abolished in both France and Germany. Similarly, in the United States during the 1960s college and other educational deferments were gradually eroded. The principle that in peacetime, at least, superior wealth or education (or a combination of the two, which is often the case) should not affect one's liability to military service has been fully established.

Conversely, the sight of equity in practice, of the privileged and pampered performing the menial tasks their fellows often did, has a strange fascination for democratic peoples. Nor is this fascination confined to the laboring classes. One of the founders of the Plattsburg military camps of 1913–1916 recalled:

> That which most entertained and impressed the country was the spectacle of the rich man or the favored of fortune digging trenches with a pick or otherwise deliberately submitting to unaccustomed toil and strange hardships. People read about it because it was funny, but they saw what it meant. They saw that the spirit of service could redeem physical labor from ignominy, and sweep away the external differences and inequalities that divide a man from his fellows.[47]

Yet equity is more difficult to achieve than might at first be supposed: the possibility of evasion of service by commutation or substitution by no means exhausts the range of issues that have encountered egalitarian opposition.

There are egalitarian objections, for example, to purely voluntary systems, which are equal in the sense that no one is forced to serve. One type of criticism was advanced repeatedly during the Civil War and before World War I, and was most cogently expressed by Munroe Smith, a law professor at Columbia, in 1916:

It is the greatest evil of the volunteer system that it slays or maims those who are most energetic and enterprising, who have the highest courage and the warmest devotion to their country, while it spares the inert, the timid, and the selfish.[48]

A different kind of egalitarian complaint is advanced today by those who argue that the poor and ethnic minorities, particularly blacks, bear too much of the burden of national defense.[49]

The fairly recent provenance of these complaints suggests that the democratic desire for compulsory military service during wartime, at least, has increased over time. By World War II the previous patriotic celebration of voluntarism had diminished, although the liberal free-market preference for voluntarism had not. In the past ten years defenders of the all-volunteer armed forces have claimed that blacks and other minorities are not or will not be represented disproportionately in the armed forces. This contrasts with the public's acceptance during the nineteenth century of an army nearly 50 percent of whose soldiers were recent lower-class immigrants, primarily Irishmen and Germans.[50]

The egalitarian impulse as described by Tocqueville, therefore, would seem to tend toward universal military service. This tendency is vitiated in practice, however, by the fact that so much of military service is inevitably inegalitarian. Military society is, of course, highly structured. Even such revolutionary armies as the French, Russian, and Chinese have found the use of ranks and such military tokens of respect and subordination as saluting to be vital. The gap between officer and enlisted men is far wider than that between, let us say, plant manager and worker, for the foreman can hardly order the latter to risk his life or threaten him with court-martial. Moreover, within an army the risks to which one is subject are scarcely equal. The benefits of a college education, for example, may include becoming a clerk at divisional headquarters rather than an infantryman, with a very different risk of being wounded or killed. Similarly, the drafted infantryman stationed in Berlin in 1968 faced a far smaller chance of injury than his fellow sent to the central highlands of South Vietnam.

Moreover, compulsory military service has not fallen (in this country, at any rate) on women. Although the United States has recently witnessed attempts to change the law so that women would be drafted, the prospect appears unlikely. As Ralph Barton Perry (an advocate of suffrage and women's rights generally) wrote in 1916, women are exempted from military service because of the fundamental differences between men and women in physical strength and aptitude for war, and because of women's vital role of bearing and rearing children.[51]

The inequities of selective service have been mentioned above. The munitions worker or farmer exempted from service may, in the largest sense, be as useful to the nation as the soldier is, but he clearly runs fewer risks. The physically and mentally disabled have always been exempt from military service except, of course, in time of direst emergency. Peacetime military service falls on the young and hence is unequal, although if universal service is maintained through the decades eventually all eligible men pass through it. In almost all countries exemptions have been made on compassionate grounds—for the sole surviving son, or brothers of those killed in the service. Finally, there are exemptions on the basis of conscientious objection, which in the United States has become more widespread in recent decades.

Yet most of these obvious inequalities of treatment associated with compulsory military service represent either compromises with necessity or the triumph of pity over egalitarian fervor. Even the defenders of conscientious objection concede that there is something undemocratic about it, and that it can only be justified by a compelling higher good for society as a whole.[52] The best testimony to the power of egalitarianism is the insistence we see in virtually all peacetime conscription proposals that all young men of a certain age should serve.

Thus, Jefferson spoke of "the necessity of obliging *every* citizen to be a soldier; this was the case with the Greeks and Romans and must be that of every free state. . . . We must classify the *whole* of our male citizens" (emphasis mine).[53] The post–World War I schemes for conscription involved *universal* military training: the sole politically acceptable alternative was the return to voluntarism.[54] A primary reason for the popularity of the Swiss model of military service has been its seemingly all-encompassing nature; hence the Australian system as adopted before World War I and the efforts made by the National Service League to secure the adoption of universal service throughout the British Empire during that period. The military training schemes of the late 1940s emphasized universality to the point that defense planners were willing to accept military inefficiency and the costs of alternative training in order to induct all young men, even the physically and mentally handicapped.[55]

In practice as opposed to theory, however, it would appear that the semblance of universality or even its approximation was more important than its reality. In Switzerland, for example, before World War I less than three-fifths of the male population aged twenty were judged fit for service. In Germany during the same time, scarcely more than half of the eligible cohort was inducted.[56] In the United States the problem of equity became severe only during the mid-1960s. Until then, even though the system was theoretically one of selective service, in practice the bulk of the middle and lower middle classes served. A Department of Defense study showed that of men aged twenty-six to thirty-four in 1964 (that is, post–World War II eligible pool), 64 percent had undergone some sort of military service, 24 percent had been judged unfit for service, and only 12 percent had escaped being considered for military service. Of high school and college graduates, 74 percent and 70 percent respectively had served.[57] (Interestingly, of those with only eighth grade educations and those with graduate educations, only 41 percent and 27 percent respectively had served.)

For practical purposes, therefore, so long as most of the middle class serves, there is an effect of universal service, and a concomitant level of acceptance. In December 1965 a Harris poll showed that 90 percent of the American population favored "having *all* young men who are able-bodied and eligible drafted for military service" (emphasis mine).[58] The Defense Department study referred to above was properly subtitled, "Who Serves When Not All Serve?" for it described the dilemma of an induction system that needed most of the eligible young men when the cohort reaching age eighteen numbered one and a third million in the early 1960s, but would need less than half the pool when the size of that cohort rose to over two million in the 1970s.[59] Despite the increased draft calls occasioned by the Vietnam war, a declining proportion of the manpower pool would be needed if a selective service system remained in force. One may wonder whether that draft would have declined in popularity during the late 1960s and the 1970s even without Vietnam, because of the decreasing proportion of men required by the armed forces.

The resort suggested by the National Advisory Commission on Selective Service in its report, *In Pursuit of Equity*, was a lottery draft, rather than the local board system used by Selective Service since World War I.[60] Unknowingly, perhaps, they were harking back to ancient times, when the lot was regarded as a quintessentially democratic device. The underlying notion was that even if equality of service could not be obtained, equality of risk would suffice. In 1970 Selective Service officials took extraordinary measures to ensure that the lottery would produce random results— the barrel holding the capsules was churned for an hour before the first drawing and several times after each one thereafter.[61]

Equality of risk, however, does not satisfy the democratic urge in the way that equality of service or obligation does. To be sure, after the inequities of Selective Service as it operated during the period 1965–1969, a lottery draft seemed a considerable advance: as remarked in Chapter 4, the draft until 1969 passed over a disproportionate percentage of America's middle and upper middle class. A system that promised to fall equally on rich and poor was more popular than one that hit the lower classes exclusively. On the other hand, America's lottery system only operated for a period of three years (1970–1972); as such, the principle of a lottery draft in peacetime was not fairly tested.

It is probable, however, that such a system would not long endure in a democracy. In the late 1960s, Australian conscription was at a low level, and the opposition Labor Party denounced it.

> But when it is proposed, as the Government does now, to conscript one in thirty of the boys eligible each year, rank injustice will be piled upon utter folly. These boys, with not only their careers, but possibly their lives at stake, are to be selected by some form of lottery, or Russian roulette.[62]

In the United States Senator Robert Taft had used the same metaphor nearly three decades before: "To choose one man in ten by lot, and require him to leave his home against his will is more like roulette than it is like democracy."[63] Nor has this sentiment weakened over time. In September 1981 a majority conclusion of an American Assembly conference, a group that included conservatives and liberals, politicians, scholars, and soldiers, concluded that it would be wrong to compel some eighteen-year-old men to serve while others did not. In the words of one participant:

> There is no way you can have a fair draft that sends one young man to jog twenty miles a day, to train in the desert in the summer and the arctic in the winter, while three of his friends sit at home and drink beer.[64]

Even those who defend a lottery draft would not support a lottery draft of, let us say, one out of ten college graduates for five or six

[150]

years' service. As Tocqueville said one hundred years ago, it is equality of burden, not equality of risk, that makes a draft democratic.

The mixed liberal and democratic nature of the United States in particular, and the Anglo-Saxon republics in general, creates a variety of tensions in the choice and implementation of systems of military service. We may sum this up crudely by saying that liberals hope to minimize coercion and egalitarians to spread it evenly. The question, therefore, becomes not simply whether there should be conscription, but rather what kind of conscription there should be and under what circumstances.

Moreover, the tension in American ideals is such that a substantial, vocal, and philosophically coherent portion of American society will always be deeply troubled by whatever choice is made. This ambivalence is reinforced by the more narrowly military dilemmas described in Chapter 3 and 4. How the United States attempted in practice to cope with these multiple and cross-cutting tensions forms the subject of the next two chapters.

[7]

American Manpower Policy,
1940–1970

In previous chapters I have analyzed the difficulties that stand in the way of a sound American manpower policy: the strategic problem of having to prepare to fight two very different kinds of war; the philosophical problem of reconciling opposing notions of just obligation; and, overarching both, the practical difficulties imposed by the demands of war and normal political life. I have suggested that these contradictions and perplexities stymied the development of a durable system of military service. This and the following chapter trace the evolution of America's military manpower system from the end of World War II to the present day. It is only after World War II that the dilemmas discussed above began to operate fully.

Rather than attempt a full chronology of American conscription policy since World War II, I will look at turning points in that policy. Two such turning points (the subject of this chapter) were the Universal Military Training debate of 1948–1949 and the resumption of a modified selective service draft in 1950. The former was perhaps the last major attempt at an ideologically based system of military service; the latter was a decision taken by default, a decision that bore bitter fruit in the late 1960s. In Chapter 8 I will examine the third major turning point in America's postwar conscription history, the decision to adopt an All-Volunteer Force in the early 1970s.

FROM WORLD WAR TO DEMOBILIZATION

World War II was fought with the same Selective Service System that had served so well in World War I. The apparatus of local draft boards coordinated by a central Washington bureau coped as well as could be expected with the shock of a twenty-five-fold expansion of the prewar armed forces. This is not to say that the United States faced no manpower difficulties in the course of the war: it did, and these problems shaped the procedures and modes of thought of postwar manpower planners.

The most important problem was that of scarce manpower. Unlike any other combatant, the United States had to juggle five major manpower commitments—to the Army, Navy, Marines, Air Force (then the Army Air Force), and, above all, to industrial production in support not only of its own armed forces but those of its allies as well. Not only were these forces huge in and of themselves; their presence in distant theaters of war presented a need for logistical support forces unprecedented in the history of warfare. This problem was particularly acute because the United States, again unlike any other of the major combatants, fought an all-out war on two different global fronts.

The result was an acute manpower shortage, one that worsened sharply once the fighting in Europe began to exact heavy casualties from the U.S. Army there. Foreseeing this, army planners scaled down their original intention of raising a two-hundred-plus-division army, creating instead only ninety divisions. It was a gamble, as historians have pointed out, for it relied on American firepower and logistical support to substitute for strength in numbers of front-line troops.[1]

To sustain this force, the U.S. Army adopted a system of individual replacements to make up casualties. Whereas other armies, the German in particular, raised a large number of divisions and rotated them out of the line when they had suffered heavy casualties, the Americans kept their divisions at the front, sending individuals forward to replace men who had been killed, wounded, or captured. This policy made administrative sense for an army that suffered a chronic shortage of manpower; the rear and support troops of a division could remain constantly at work, and the relatively small pool of reserve manpower could be used to maximum efficiency.

From a social point of view, however, the policy was pernicious, and in some cases disastrous. Because individual replacements often had no time to become socially merged into units, battlefield cohesion suffered and casualty rates rose. The overwhelming majority of casualties were suffered in the real combat units, which often numbered only a quarter of a division's ration strength. As remarked earlier (Chapter 3), the average infantry division lost 100 percent casualties in its infantry regiments every three months. Many of those men were fresh replacements not yet integrated into their units. As one replacement put it, "We want to feel that we are a part of something. As a replacement we are apart from everything. . . . Being a replacement is just like being an orphan."[2] At the same time, those veterans who survived became demoralized, many suffering mental collapse. The surgeon-general reported during the summer of 1944 that "practically all men in rifle battalions who are not otherwise disabled ultimately become psychiatric casualties."[3] Two hundred to 280 days in the front lines—or as few as 40 days of continual intense combat—were enough to cause mental breakdown. The consequences for the veterans were reflected in the words of one man who told an investigator that the average GI "feels as long as he is able to keep going he will be kept over here, until he is a physical wreck or his body is buried with four or five more in some dark jungle or scattered over the ground by artillery shells or bombs."[4]

Nonetheless, it was the individual replacement system that saw the Selective Service System through the war; indeed, it is doubtful that alternative policies were available. And the legacy of Selective Service, its commitment to the scientific allotment of manpower between home and fighting fronts and its insensitivity to the social costs of its policies, lasted a long while—in fact, until the 1970s. Like many other successful organizations, it was eventually ruined by its own accomplishments.

At the end of the second World War the victorious armies of the United States underwent the same kind of precipitate demobilization that had occurred after World War I. In 1945–1946, as in 1918–1919, the politics of demobilization—the desire to return as many men as fast as possible to civilian life, and in accordance with some elementary rules of fairness—left the army debilitated and disorganized. This problem was compounded by the fact that some 40 percent of the Army was tied down overseas by the need for occupation troops.

The draft was extended, briefly, in order to supply replacements for the men being released from service. Over 180,000 men were inducted in 1946 and some 570,000 volunteered, although many of these enlistments were draft-induced. All inductees entered the Army; after 1945 the Navy, Marine Corps, and Coast Guard no longer needed draftees.[5] The strength of the active forces plummeted. The army alone sank from a force of 8,268,000 in 1945 to

1,891,000 in 1946, to 991,000 in 1947, and to a low of 554,000 in 1948. A limited draft in 1948–1949 brought the number up to 660,000 in 1949, but in 1950 (before Korea) it sank back to 593,000.[6] Furthermore, it should be remembered that these numbers do not tell the whole story about the weakness of an army afflicted by personnel turbulence, demoralization, and inadequate facilities and resources for serious training.

General Alfred M. Gruenther, head of the Joint Staff of the Joint Chiefs of Staff, briefed Secretary of Defense James Forrestal in February 1948 concerning the state of the armed forces. The army had some 140,000 troops in the Far East, about 100,000 in Europe, and 155,000 at various installations in the United States. The Army general reserve, its forces ready for deployment overseas in the event of a crisis, consisted solely of the 82nd Airborne Division and one other half-strength infantry division, plus miscellaneous supporting units, a grand total of 46,000 men. The Marines could muster eleven battalion landing teams (a bit more than a division).[7] America's land forces were, clearly, in as serious straits as in 1939. The occupation forces were of necessity dispersed and hence could not be trained for serious fighting, and the units at home were busy maintaining installations and coping with new draftees and enlistees.

In order to maintain effective armed forces at a time of deepening cold war (on 15 March 1948 Jan Masaryk committed suicide according to the Communists, was murdered according to most), President Truman asked for and, on 24 June 1948, obtained America's second peacetime conscription law, the Selective Service Act of 1948. The Act provided for twenty-one months' service or (for eighteen-year-olds) one year of voluntary service restricted to the United States. Truman assured Congress and the American people that "selective service would be used only as an interim measure until the solid foundation of universal training can be established."[8] Truman had already accepted his first compromise: a selective service bill in 1948 in return for a deferment of UMT for a year or two.[9]

Few men were actually inducted under the two-year Selective Service Act of 1948—20,000 in the final months of 1948 and fewer than 10,000 in the first half of 1949; 30,000 in all over two years. Yet the Act did a good job of spurring voluntary enlistment. According to the director of Selective Service, within six months after the passage of the Act 200,000 more men had enlisted than in the previous comparable period.[10] True, many if not most of the enlist-

[155]

ments were of the one-year kind and hence not terribly valuable to the active forces. Still, the draft had, as during the Civil War, provided large numbers of men by eliciting eight or ten volunteers for every conscript.

Here was another lesson learned by the Selective Service System which, though useful in a narrow and technical sense, had pernicious long-term consequences. A minimal draft did indeed spur enlistment, but few paused to ponder the long-term consequences of such a policy, of which two would be particularly troublesome in the 1960s. The first was the difficulty of openly drafting a very small proportion of the eligible population (albeit a much larger fraction was being tacitly conscripted). The apparent inequity of this procedure became more and more marked as time went on. Additionally, by volunteering for service a tacit draftee could avoid the more hazardous kinds of duty, since volunteers usually had more choice over their assignments. Thus, during the Vietnam war a further inequity developed as men avoided combat by, ironically, volunteering for military service.

These difficulties were comfortably remote, however. A further political struggle was required to extend the Selective Service Act in 1950, even though no inductions were occurring or envisaged. After a fight over who could order inductions, Congress or the president, the proponents of a zero draft won by a narrow margin, on the very eve of the Korean war in June 1950. Within two months, by August 1950, Selective Service was inducting between 50,000 and 80,000 men a month.[11] For the third time in a bit more than a generation, Selective Service mobilized American manpower for a military buildup that brought expansion of the armed forces to a strength of over three and a half million, even as American industry again geared up for war production.

The Universal Military Training Debate

As early as 1944, President Roosevelt mentioned at a news conference the possibility of a "one year Government training program for youths, not necessarily military, in the postwar period."[12] In January 1945, as World War II drew to a close, he asked Congress to consider a program of Universal Military Training, but did not elaborate on the proposal or attempt to secure its enactment. In July, a report of the House Select Committee on Postwar Military Policy recommended UMT. The report said that the program "should be designed primarily to train men for military service under conditions of modern warfare," that it should be "universal and democratic," consist only of training (not service), and that it should not affect the status of the National Guard.[13]

Even as early as 1944–1945 there was evidence of the ambivalence and uncertainty of the government as a whole and even of some key men within it concerning the purposes of UMT. One group, including the secretary of war, Henry Stimson, the army chief of staff, General George C. Marshall, and the secretary of the navy, James Forrestal, wanted UMT on purely military grounds.[14] Stimson's 15 July 1945 testimony to the House committee referred to above was forthright on this point:

> In the first place, let me speak of universal military training as necessary for the physical protection of our country and its people. . . . No matter how complicated the weapons of war may become, no matter how necessary to the nation's future security are programs for scientific research and industrial mobilization, the disciplined, trained, and patriotic citizenry of a nation remain the bricks of the foundation upon which the other methods and means of security rest.
>
> But in the second place, beyond and above any responsibility attending to her own sovereignty, there now attaches to the United States as a great world power a further duty. . . . To meet our obligation of bearing our full share in preserving world peace, a part of America's present military readiness should be retained.[15]

General Marshall's support for UMT owed a good deal to the influence of one of his few close friends, Brigadier John McAuley Palmer, a staff officer under Pershing who had long advocated the creation of a federalized, Swiss-type National Guard. In 1941 Marshall recalled the seventy-one-year-old general to active duty, and from then until 1946 Palmer worked for the adoption of a system constructed along these lines.

Roosevelt's and later Truman's support for UMT, unlike that of their military advisers, did not rest on purely military grounds. In his memoirs Truman recalled that he had supported the creation of the Civilian Conservation Corps during the 1930s partly because "I thought it might lead to a universal training program, which I advocated throughout my political career."[16] True, his address to Congress on 23 October 1945 did not refer to the nonmilitary advantages of UMT. Rather, he said that the objective would be "to train citizens, so that if and when Congress should declare it necessary for them to become soldiers, they could do so more quickly and more efficiently."[17] Yet in referring to the same same speech in his memoirs, Truman says that "this was not a military training program in the conventional sense. The military phase was incidental to what I had in mind."[18] Truman was not deliberately concealing his views: his 20 December 1946 remarks to the Advisory Commission on Universal Training expressed the same sentiments found in his memoirs: "I want it to be a universal training program, giving our young people a background in the disciplinary approach of getting along with one another, informing them of their physical makeup, and what it means to take care of this Temple which God gave us."[19]

From the very beginning, therefore, a fatal ambivalence afflicted advocates of UMT, particularly the president. Their uncertainty about what should be the purpose of the program prevented the formulation of a coherent and intelligent military training program—one that probably would have required a drastic reorganization and restructuring of the reserve components. A similar ambivalence had afflicted the proposals for conscription into the reserves of the 1920 National Defense Act. Officers then made the case for UMT as

> more or less the universal panacea for all the social ills which beset them. It would strengthen national unity, promote the amalgamation of ethnic groups, and encourage democracy and tolerance. It would be physically beneficial and would virtually eliminate illiteracy in the United States . . .[20]

A more serious training program would have excluded all those physically or mentally unfit for military service, some 30 percent of the young male population, judging by World War II figures. A universal training program, by contrast, would reach all men, and perhaps eventually women as well. Such a program—dominated by egalitarian fervor (see Chapter 6)—could not have been as rigorous as the military training of the war years. During World War II, as during most wars, military training had become increasingly tough and dangerous in order to accustom men to the sensations of the battlefield. Serious military training would have meant a regimen both unpopular and impracticable if anyone besides able-bodied men were inducted.

Despite Palmer's work, Truman's yearly proposals for UMT (the first of which was offered in 1945) had little substance or structure until 1947, when the President's Advisory Commission on Universal Training issued its report, *A Program for National Security*. That document, and the 1951 report of the National Security Training Commission, *Universal Military Training: Foundation of Enduring National Strength*, presented the UMT proposals. The program remained a curious, and to many an unsatisfactory, compromise between a new military manpower system and a social or education scheme.

The commissioners recommended a one-year program, consisting of six months' training followed by a choice of six months' active duty, further training, or enlistment in the reserves.[21] Training would be progressive: participants in the program would be trained up to the brigade or division level, but no arrangement would be made to pass those trained units into the reserves as units. The reason for this was simple: the commissioners were responsible for devising a scheme for UMT, not for restructuring the American military system, and hence they had to make their plans in isolation from those of defense planners generally. Furthermore, one of the avowed purposes of UMT was to bring young men from all over the country together, whereas the essence of militia training is that it is localized. In addition, only the army (which expected to take half of the trainees) had anything like detailed plans for coping with them, let alone utilizing them. Neither the navy nor the air force was eager to burden itself with the task of training and releasing hundreds of thousands of young men a year.

The armed forces would, according to this 1947 proposal, conduct training, but the trainees would *not* be members of the armed forces, and hence would not be subject to martial law.[22] The training would emphasize "moral welfare" and "character guidance"; deferments or exemptions would be pared down to the lowest level possible, and the compulsory training of women would also be considered at a later date.[23] Again, the avowed purpose of UMT was unclear. Was it to provide a pool of trained men for another World War II–type mobilization? Was it to ensure that in the event of nuclear war the United States would contain a large and dispersed pool of trained men to help the nation recover from a strategic bombardment? Was its aim simply to toughen the fiber of American youth?

Throughout the long debate in 1948 over UMT the public opinion polls revealed a consistently high level of support for UMT. Between December 1945 and January 1956 only once did support fall below 65 percent (to 60 percent) and opposition rise above 25 percent (to 33 percent).[24] Universal Military Training had the support of the administration, patriotic and veterans' groups such as the American Legion, and such able and respected statesmen as General George C. Marshall, then serving as secretary of state. Why did it fail?

To begin with, a number of powerful interest groups opposed it, public opinion notwithstanding. Some, such as the Mennonites and the American Farm Bureau, simply opposed conscription root and branch. The representative of the latter group said, "We oppose a program of compulsory military training which leads to regimentation, an authoritarian point of view, and future wars."[25] The mainstream opposition view, however, was that of such organizations as the American Federation of Labor and the Association of American Colleges. These groups accepted the need for sizable increases in the defense buget and even the enactment of the 1948 Selective Service Act, but they opposed UMT as unnecessary and, in fact, illegitimate:

> The American Federation of Labor would favor the application of selective service on a limited and temporary basis solely because of the present emergency with which we are confronted. We do not believe that peacetime conscription is consistent with the American way of life.[26]

One undeniably pro-military group, the National Guard Association (NGA), was only lukewarm to UMT, to the considerable annoyance of the commanders of the Regular Army and the Reserve. Many of the NGA leaders were old-fashioned Midwest Republicans who cherished the ideals of limited government and voluntarism. In addition, no one promised that National Guard members would be exempt from the UMT programs; in fact, NGA members thought it possible that UMT would decrease the number of recruits available to the Guard.[27]

The military arguments for UMT seemed unconvincing. General Marshall's support for UMT gradually shifted to an endorsement of it primarily as a gesture that would impress upon America's allies and enemies her strength and resolve, although he still claimed to support the program on military grounds as well.[28] Even the advocates of UMT had to concede that it would offer only long-term benefits, that it could not provide a tool for America foreign policy in the short term.

More important, perhaps, an alternate and less expensive method of raising America's military prestige and preparing for war was at hand. The newly independent air force was vigorously pressing for the creation of a seventy-group air force (fifteen more than currently existing) as a new bulwark for American security. In 1948 Congress passed an $822 million supplemental appropriation to bring the air force up to sixty-six groups, thereby quashing the prospects for UMT that year. A powerful air force would be cheaper than UMT, an important consideration in view of MIT president Karl Compton's estimate that UMT would add three billion dollars to a budget already rising to twenty billion.[29] Moreover, a seventy-group air force and an expanded active army would, in the view of many (including the secretary of defense), deter major aggression in Europe and provide the means to cope with lesser conflicts on the fringes of or beyond that continent.[30] Universal Military Training might help the United States mobilize for another World War II–type conflict (although many critics pointed out that it was not integrated with any permanent reserve system), but it would not cope with America's immediate strategic difficulties.[31] The choice was between UMT and a seventy-group air force plus the moderately larger active army.[32]

Congress never passed a UMT bill, although the 1951 draft law (signed 13 June 1951) was entitled the Universal Military Training and Service Act. Not only did UMT seem costly and unnecessary in view of the expansion of the air force, but "to many, including most of the Congressmen who then and thereafter were called upon to judge it, it looked like a bad compromise."[33] Universal Military Training would not increase the active forces—the sheer existence of the Selective Service System and its miniscule inductions would do that. It would not provide the well-equipped and trained reserve divisions that Brigadier Palmer called for. The only case for UMT, it seemed, was that it would be a useful social program; and many contended that the corrupting influence of a year's compulsory service (in particular, the exposure of young men to prostitution and alcohol) would outweigh the benefits. Moreover, as Walter Millis put it, "The young will readily accept military training if they think the state really may have need of their services. But once they are told that their government's principal interest is in their 'moral and spiritual welfare' they are likely to lose their enthusiasm."[34]

The Korean war put an end to the concept of UMT, even though the annual draft act was referred to as a Universal Military Training and Service Act until 1967. More important, most young men served in the military during the late 1950s, so that the substance of UMT did take place. The Reserve Forces Act of 1955 strengthened the reserve and increased the number of men who did six months of training and then entered the National Guard or Reserves, a result similar to that which Palmer had hoped for. Until 1957 National Guardsmen did not have to undergo *any* basic training; in the new reserve forces all had at least several months (usually six) of training and active duty.[35]

On the other hand, the machinery for UMT did not exist, nor was any attempt made to resurrect it. During the Korean war and the ensuing American global military buildup, the need was for active forces. The services had neither the resources nor the desire to work on such a large and long-range project as UMT would inevitably have been. President Eisenhower, a long-standing supporter of UMT, was asked about it shortly after taking office. He replied:

> Now, as for the exact position today of UMT, while we are having this kind of a draft call to prosecute a fairly major war over in Korea, I am not prepared to say. . . . There is a commission, as you know, working on that problem. . . . They think it can be done simultaneously; I don't quite see how it can be done.[36]

And there the matter rested. Universal Military Training, a politically attractive if militarily dubious concept, was dead. In its place there stood Selective Service, which filled the ranks of America's active forces for the next seventeen years; its days, however, were also numbered.

DRAFT BY DEFAULT

The practical effect of the Korean era draft and the Reserve Forces Act of 1955 was to introduce UMT, although Eisenhower himself said to Congress in January 1955, when speaking of the reserves, "As in our active forces we will rely as heavily as possible on voluntary service."[37] The New Look strategy of the administration called for substantial increases in the air force, a fairly steady funding of the navy, and decreases in the size of the army, which declined from 1,533,000 in 1953 to 859,000 in 1961 (this was not a negligible force, however: in 1984 the Army was smaller yet, barely 780,000 men).[38]

The lengthy period required to mobilize National Guard units during the Korea Conflict and in 1961 (many units required a full year to become ready for deployment) further convinced defense planners that the reserves were not to be relied upon, thereby undermining a further argument for UMT. Secretary of Defense Robert S. McNamara succeeded during the early 1960s in eliminating four National Guard and four Reserve divisions, plus one thousand smaller units.[39] At the same time, draft calls were increased to build up the active forces—the army numbered 972,000 in 1964, the last pre-Vietnam year. Overall, however, the percentage of eighteen-year-olds in the population entering military service was decreasing.

The United States did not, after the Korean war, reevaluate its military manpower policies. The Selective Service System produced adequate numbers of draftees and, more important, larger numbers of draft-induced volunteers. In some years inductees exceeded volunteers; in 1958, the army took 179,400 draftees and received only 88,300 volunteers. For the most part, however, more men volunteered than were drafted: in 1959, for example, 111,200 were inducted and 130,600 enlisted.[40] The armed forces could expand their numbers easily because of the steady growth in the population of young men caused by the post–World War II baby boom.

In fact, over time a decreasing percentage of young men served in the military. Of twenty-six-year-old men in 1958, 70 percent had undergone military service (including reserve duty). Only eight years later, less than half—46 percent—had served.[41] The Vietnam war barely alleviated the problem (if it can be so termed), even though it doubled the army's total accessions from the 200,000–250,000 level of the prewar period to roughly 500,000 per year from 1966 to 1969. Only 40 percent of the draft-age population served in the military during the Vietnam era (see Chapter 4). The eventual end of the war would allow the problem of selection to surface, and demographics promised that it would be more acute than ever.

The Selective Service System attempted to cope with these developments by extending deferments and adopting a "channeling" policy. In the words of the director of Selective Service:

> The term "channeling" refers to that process through which registrants are influenced to enter and remain in study, in critical occupations, and in other activities in the national health, safety, and interest by deferment or prospect for deferment from military service. Selective Service channels thousands of young men through its deferment procedures into these fields of endeavor where there are short-

ages of adequately trained personnel. Many would not have continued their education at the undergraduate and graduate college level if there had not been a college student deferment program.[42]

This policy was in perfect accord with the original rationale of Selective Service as defined by General Crowder; the problem, however, lay in the fact that the task of the system in the 1960s was in no way similar to that in either World War. During those wars the job was to secure the maximum number of soldiers while preserving the nation's war economy, and the problem was manpower scarcity. Now the task of Selective Service was to send a fraction of the population of young men to fight in Vietnam; the problem, therefore, was a superabundance of manpower.

Selective Service, by its adoption of "channeling," helped subvert its moral authority, for it treated compulsory military service as a useful threat rather than as an appeal to honor and duty. Small wonder, then, that the draft was increasingly unpopular: as if the extreme unpopularity of Vietnam were not enough, Selective Service's methods were objectionable. In 1956, 77 percent of the population supported the draft; in 1970 a bare majority did; in 1972 one survey reported that only 13 percent did.[43]

Undoubtedly, much of the unpopularity of the draft had to do with the chance that draftees would suffer death or mutilation in Vietnam. At the peak of the fighting, a disproportionate number of the forces there (infantrymen in particular) were draftees (see Table 3). Only 30 percent of those killed in action were U.S. Army regulars.[44] Why did draftees do so much of the fighting and dying in Vietnam? Again, the answer can be found in the absence of a true selective service system, the name of the draft bureau notwithstanding. Men were allowed to volunteer for three-year tours of duty; they thereby served one year more than the others in their drafted cohort, but they could often choose their military specialty and, indirectly, the locus of their service. The Navy and Air force benefited greatly from this option. As one Navy volunteer is said to have remarked, "there in't no Viet Cong submarines."

Yet there was more to public opposition to the draft than the fact of the Vietnam war. Sociologists studying the attitudes of young people found that "the young man who gets caught and who serves for two or more years on active duty is likely to consider himself a sucker."[45] The question haunted the government as well—the subtitle of one study of the draft (as remarked above) was "Who Serves When Not All Serve?"

[164]

Table 3.   Percentage of Draftees in Vietnam and in the Army as a Whole, 1967–1972

Year	Draftees as Percentage of Vietnam Strength	Draftees as Percentage Army Overall
1967	49	42
1968	41	39
1969	40	36
1970	39	22
1971	28	28
1972	16	14

Source: U.S. Department of the Army, *Department of the Army Historical Survey 1972* (Washington, D.C.: Government Printing Office, 1974), p. 77.

As a result of the unpopularity of the draft, the Selective Service System had to cope with massive evasion and resistance. During all of World War II (in the course of which well over ten million were inducted) only 72,000 filed claims to be considered conscientious objectors (COs). During 1970–1971, when only 153,000 were inducted, young men filed over 121,000 such claims. In other words, the rate of application for CO status was one hundred times that of World War II.[46] Men devised scores of ways to flunk their draft physicals; as a result, in Massachusetts over 320 men had to be summoned for physicals in order to obtain 100 inductees.[47] Nor were draft evaders on their own: they received support from many, including California judges who had COs cut their families' lawns for two years in order to fulfill the requirements for two years' alternate service, as mandated by law.[48]

Various attempts were made to reform Selective Service. The Military Selective Service Act of 1967, for example, abolished most graduate school deferments and in other ways closed draft loopholes. Upon taking office in 1969, President Richard M. Nixon fired Major General Lewis B. Hershey, who had run the nation's draft since the early days of World War II. More important, starting in 1970 a random selection procedure was established: young men would be called up on the basis of a number lottery. In addition, starting in 1971 only nineteen-year-olds and those whose deferments had expired would be called. Thus a young man's vulnerability to the draft was reduced to one year. All these, however, were merely interim and palliative measures. By 1969 a slow but steady withdrawal from Vietnam was in sight, as was an overall draw-down of American forces. The time seemed ripe to consider an end to the draft.

[8]

The Advent of the All-Volunteer Force

By the late 1960s, changing demography had fundamentally altered the conditions under which the old draft had operated. No longer, as in the 1950s, would virtually every young man serve in the military; rather, even during a war, barely half of them would. The Selective Service System, once a source of national pride and even affection, had become a mistrusted institution, composed, in the popular mind, of fossilized and callous old men. An institution once thought of as representing the best in American politics now had the reputation of representing the worst.

There is some evidence that President Johnson was contemplating an end to the draft, but it was his successor who implemented it. The time seemed ripe: popular discontent with the Vietnam war fed growing discontent with the draft, and the improving demographic picture seemed to promise that conscription would no longer be necessary. President Nixon entered office committed to ending the draft.

On 27 March 1969, President Nixon appointed a commission headed by former secretary of defense Thomas S. Gates to study the prospects for an all-volunteer force. Nixon's 13 May 1969 Special Message to Congress on Reforming the Military Draft (made before the commission submitted its report) revealed that the end of the draft was in sight. This is but one piece of evidence (if evidence be needed) that the creation of the All-Volunteer Force (AVF) stemmed from political considerations rather than from the technical analysis provided by the commission.[1] Be that as it may, in February 1970 the Gates Commission issued its pro-AVF report, which stated: "We unanimously believe that the nation's interests will be better served by an all-volunteer force, supported by an effective stand-by draft, than by a mixed force of volunteers and conscripts; that steps should be taken promptly to move in this. direction."[2]

However, the exigencies of domestic politics alone by no means accounted for the Gates Commission's recommendations; rather, a cluster of considerations led the commissioners to their final report. Perhaps the most important fact was that in 1965 the pool of young men aged seventeen to twenty numbered six and a half million, whereas in 1980 the same age group would contain eight and a half million men.[3] Some simple calculations suggested that if first-term pay were raised to levels commensurate with those in the civilian economy (a move that would cost $2.7 billion), and assuming that higher pay at all levels would induce more reenlistments, the nation could comfortably maintain armed forces of two and a half million men for the foreseeable future.[4] This force level was the "midrange" or most probable projection of the Gates Commission. It would be easy, the commissioners claimed, to maintain a two-million-man force, but possibly difficult to keep up a three-million-man force. Nor would the quality or representativeness of the AVF be a problem: "An all-volunteer force will be manned largely by the same kind of individuals as today's armed forces."[5]

Underlying the analysis and recommendations of the Gates Commission were a set of methodological and ideological assumptions, most of which flowed from the doctrines of liberal (that is, free-market) economists. Such distinguished academics as Milton Friedman and Martin Anderson (later a prominent economic adviser to President Reagan) were either members of the commission or influential advisers to it. The economics-oriented approach has dominated most subsequent manpower studies, including the 1976 *Defense Manpower Commission Report*, Richard Cooper's 1977 RAND study, and the various studies by Brookings Institution experts (Martin Binkin, for example).[6] This dominance of economists in defense policy was not an isolated phenomenon; it was part of a much larger development, the rise of systems analysis, a mode of strategic thought derived from economics that was at its height during the tenure of Robert S. McNamara as secretary of defense during the 1960s.[7]

The commissioners started from the premise that "conscription is a form of taxation, the power to conscript is the power to tax"; the first substantive chapter of the report was entitled "Conscrip-

tion is a Tax."[8] The Gates Commission staff even devised mathe-
matical formulae to calculate the precise dollar cost of the "conscription tax." In this view, there was nothing elevated about
military service, or indeed any kind of national service. The problem of manpower planning was an essentially simple one, which
required only that fixed requirements for certain types of manpower be established and that the most economic means be employed to acquire that manpower.

This peculiar outlook on military service had a contradictory
effect. On the one hand, it seemed liberal in its assertion that free
choice, rather than coercion, should shape an individual's choice to
enter military service. Moreover, the Gates Commissioners were
also responsible for the improved salaries and living conditions
that followed from the creation of an All-Volunteer Force. At the
same time, however, the "conscription is a tax" argument subtly
lowered the status of manpower questions. Manpower became a
commodity, an input into the machinery of national defense, in the
same way that weapons or installations were. The economic approach implied that purely financial motivations could—and ought
to—direct an individual's choice about service; hence the increased
attention to monetary incentives. The consequences of this attitude
would extend beyond the quality of the force recruited for the AVF:
they would include a transformation of the military's self-concep-
tion. Thus, even those (the officer corps) who would probably have
served regardless of whether there was a draft found themselves
influenced by the ethos of the marketplace.

Given the fundamental outlook of the Gates Commissioners, it is
small wonder that the report began with the following assertion:

> A return to an all-volunteer force will strengthen our freedoms,
> remove an inequity now imposed on the expression of the patriotism
> that has never been lacking among our youth, promote the efficiency
> of the armed forces, and enhance their dignity. It is the system for
> maintaining standing forces that minimizes government interference
> with the freedom of the individual to determine his own life in accord
> with his values.[9]

Some, such as Martin Anderson, went even further, speaking of
"the unconscionable agonies of the draft."[10]

Considerations of liberal (or rather, libertarian) doctrine combined with those of egalitarianism: "When not all our citizens can
serve, and when only a small minority are needed, a voluntary

decision to serve is the best answer, morally and practically, to the question of who should serve."[11]

To be sure, the commissioners and their successors were not completely doctrinaire; if a draft were absolutely necessary they would have been willing, in theory, to accept it. Their studies, however, proceeded from the premise that a volunteer force was the most desirable one, and that the only proper manpower question was, in their words, "whether sufficient numbers of capable men could be attracted by voluntary means."[12] The problem was "managing defense manpower," in the words of the Defense Manpower Commission report.[13] Larger issues (discussed in previous chapters) were often slighted by these manpower analysts. The memoirs of General Hershey's successor at Selective Service, Curtis Tarr, for example, contain nothing to indicate that he knew anything of the profound political rationale for local draft boards, as enunciated by Wilson and Crowder. The extensive historical studies of the Gates Commission had one aim only, to prove that peacetime conscription in the United States, of whatever kind, was and always had been illegitimate and unprofitable.

One further peculiarity of the Gates Commission report was its narrow time horizon, limited to ten years (1970–1980). Coincidentally or not, the terminus of this horizon was also the point at which the pool of eligible recruits would begin to shrink. The Gates Commissioners did provide for this problem by advocating a standby or zero draft: registration would continue, but no young men would be called. Here too, however, their rather mechanistic approach betrayed a lack of appreciation for the implications of their analysis. A draft, once ended, could not be easily restarted except in the case of war (as occurred in 1950). From the beginning, the standby draft could not function as a cushion against the failure of the econometric models of the Gates Commission, because political realities precluded it. What occurred instead was a determined and desperate effort on the part of Democratic and Republican administrations to prove that the all-volunteer force was working.

The attitude of the military toward the all-volunteer force was ambivalent. On the one hand, military men were temperamentally inclined to look kindly on volunteers, since voluntarism is one of the highest of the military virtues. On the other hand, many military men (particularly officers in the army, the service most sharply affected by the advent of the all-volunteer force) feared a sharp decline in standards. There was another source of ambivalence as well. Initially, many military men found the end of the draft a welcome removal of an irritant to benign civil-military relations. Calculating, as they did, that the disapprobation of the American public stemmed primarily from the existence of the draft, they were willing to see it disappear. In the longer term, however, they found themselves deprived of a link with society. Ten years after the abolition of the draft, the leaders of the military were no longer so certain that an absence of a draft would guarantee public support.

The decision to turn to the AVF in 1970 may have been tactical and based on short-term considerations, the product of a president's eagerness to have done quickly with an unpopular institution. The choice, however, was consonant with a long (albeit unexamined) tradition of liberal thought. It represented, in addition, the triumph of a particular school of strategic thought rooted in economics.[14]

THE AVF AFTER TEN YEARS

The AVF has not, as of this writing (1984), been tested in war. Enough material has accumulated, however, to make preliminary judgments on over ten years' peacetime experience with a large all-volunteer force. (Although the draft did not formally end until 1973, by 1971 more men were volunteering than being inducted, and during 1972 and 1973 barely 30,000 were being inducted annually.) Criticisms of the All-Volunteer Force fall into four categories, defined by their concern with representativeness, numerical strength, quality, and overall war efficiency.

Of these, the first is easiest to analyze. The All-Volunteer Force has been, and remains, a highly unrepresentative one. In 1984, 25 percent of the force overall is either black or Hispanic, mainly the former, with considerably higher percentages in the army, and particularly in the combat arms. Although the unrepresentativeness of the armed forces is an issue in some quarters, it is not such among the leaders of the minorities overrepresented. From their point of view the armed forces provides their people with both jobs and a means of entering larger American society. Nor is quality an issue, since black soldiers in particular tend today to have higher educational backgrounds than white soldiers. Nonetheless, the armed forces have to confront the moral and political ramifications of the fact that, in the event of a war, as much as 40 percent of the casualties could come from minority groups, particularly blacks. At

[170]

the same time, it is quite clear that the predominantly white middle class sends its sons and daughters to college, not to the armed forces.

Important as the issue of representation is, the problems of numbers, quality, and organizational effectiveness are far more severe, for their consequences are, quite literally, those of life and death. The Gates Commission did not adequately describe the magnitude of the recruiting task it was thrusting upon the armed services. Rather, it suggested that the experience of other countries (notably, Great Britain) indicated that the transition would be a fairly easy one. Although the report made much of Britain's conversion to an all-volunteer armed force during the late 1950s, it failed to examine the implications for Britain of that move. The British 1957 Defence White Paper reshaped overall British military policy; it increased British reliance on a nuclear deterrent and a centralized, airmobile strategic reserve in Great Britain. Above all, the White Paper formulated a policy for an Empire in the process of self-liquidation.[15] The British Army sank from a force of nearly three-quarters of a million in 1956, to half a million in 1960, to fewer than four hundred thousand in 1967.[16] As in the case of Australia, which abolished conscription as it withdrew from Vietnam in 1970, the end of a draft accompanied a drastic curtailment of military commitments, ongoing and envisaged.

The new British forces were more professional than the National Service force, no doubt. They were also far fewer than previously, and British defense planners warned their American colleagues that in a liberal, relatively prosperous society, only a small group of what they termed "the Foreign Legion hard core" could be expected to sign up, no matter what monetary inducements were offered.[17]

The British concept seemed to be vindicated in the course of the 1982 Falklands war, when a force of some 5,000 British professional soldiers routed a force of Argentine draftees nearly twice as numerous. British forces seemed superior in two respects. First, in terms of sheer toughness and military skill, the British were far more adept at waging war in a rough and thoroughly inhospitable environment. Second, British public opinion seemed more willing to tolerate losses from a voluntarily enlisted force than from a drafted one. This is not to suggest that there was callous disregard for the lives of professional soldiers; rather, it meant that the families of those soldiers, and the public at large, accepted the notion that the risks of military service include the risk of death.

[171]

On the other hand, there were reasons to discount the British success. For one thing, the Argentine conscripts were exceptionally poorly led and trained, many of the best Argentine troops having been retained to guard the Chilean border. More important, the British troops could maintain high qualitative standards and long-term enlistments because of their relatively small numbers. One measure of the problem of keeping up a strong AVF is the Military Participation Ratio (MPR) of a country, the number of personnel in its active armed forces divided by total population.[18] In 1984 the MPR of Great Britain, the only major military power besides the United States relying on an AVF, was .571. That of the United States was .910, slightly ahead of France's (.908), which drew more than half of its personnel from conscription, and considerably ahead of the MPR of the Federal Republic of Germany (.803), also conscript.

Despite the high MPR under the All-Volunteer Force, the American armed forces actually suffered a considerable reduction in strength. In 1960 the active forces numbered 2,476,000; the army alone numbered 873,000. Twenty-four years later the numbers are, respectively, 2,136,000 and 780,000.[19] For the Reserves overall the numbers were 4,147,000 in 1960 and 2,169,000 in 1980. These figures include members of the Individual Ready Reserve, who would be needed as fillers in the event of a war. The total figure for the Selected Reserve (those in reserve units doing monthly drills) was 954,000 in 1964, including 269,000 in the Army Reserve and 382,000 in the Army National Guard. In 1983 the Selected Reserve numbered 1,005,000, including 266,000 in the Army Reserve and 417,000 in the Army National Guard.[20] Only the Army National Guard has shown an improvement in quantitative strength under the AVF.

Thus, the AVF in 1984 is barely meeting the low-range projection of the Gates Commission, the two-million manpower level that the commissioners had assumed an AVF would easily achieve. Curiously enough, the problem is not yet a demographic one. 1979 was the peak year for the pool of 18–21-year-old men (with over 8,800,000 of them), and the decade's low will not be reached until 1988, when the 18–21-year-old pool will total slightly over 7,500,000.[21] The Gates Commissioners had projected (correctly) an expanding pool of eligible men through the 1970s, yet at the end of that decade the AVF was in serious trouble, on a number of fronts.

To begin with, the quality of recruits to both the active and the reserve forces deteriorated sharply. The Defense Department has,

Table 4. Armed Forces Qualifying Test Score Classification

AFQT Percentile	Mental Group	General Designation
93–99	I	Superior
65–92	II	Above Average
31–64	III	Average
10–30	IV	Below Average (Marginally Qualified)
0–9	V	Not Qualified

Note: The services are barred by law from recruiting personnel from Group V.
Source: Defense Manpower Commission, *Defense Manpower Commission Staff Studies*, 3 vols. (Washington, D.C.: Government Printing Office, 1976), vol. 3, p. A-6-4.

since World War II, used an Armed Forces Qualifying Test (AFQT) to divide men into five Mental Categories (see Table 4). The precipitous decline in representation of Category I and II personnel following on the institution of the AVF can be seen from Table 5, compiled in 1984. It should be borne in mind that 1964 was the last pre-Vietnam (i.e., peacetime) year. In fact, the situation in the late 1970s was worse than this table (based on 1979 data, with the exception of some 1982 data taken from the 1982 *Military Manpower Task Force Report*) indicates, because an error in test evaluation resulted in understating the number of Category IV recruits by a factor of *six*. Thus, in 1980 48 percent—not 8 percent—of the army's recruits were in the lowest acceptable Mental Category.[22]

The discovery of this statistical error produced, not surprisingly, a considerable furor. Secretary of the Army Clifford Alexander

Table 5. AFQT Classifications of Department of Defense and Army Personnel, 1964–1982

Mental Category	Percentage							
	Department of Defense				Army			
	1964	1972	1979	1982	1964	1972	1979*	1982
I and II	38	35	29	37	34	34	20	32
III	47	48	66	50	45	48	70	49
IV	15	17	5	13	21	18	9	19

*Percentages for 1979 total less than 100 because of rounding.
Source: William Schneider, "Personnel Recruitment and Retention: Problems and Prospects for the United States," *Annals of the American Academy of Political and Social Science* 457 (September 1981): 169; and Military Manpower Task Force, *A Report to the President on the Status and Prospects of the All Volunteer Force* (Washington, D.C.: Government Printing Office, 1982), pp. II-7, II-8.

protested that the AFQT was nearly forty years old, lasted barely three-quarters of an hour, and represented only three parts out of twelve in the Armed Services Vocational Aptitude Battery (ASVAB) tests. He declared that "the experts say it is not an intelligence test."[23] These arguments, however, proved incorrect. The army's own consultants (and more important, perhaps, the army's NCO corps) believed that the AFQT scores did indeed predict performance and aptitude for soldiering. They maintained that, on the basis of their own and other countries' experience, AFQT scores were better indicators of performance than the other usual measure, a high school degree.[24] Charles Moskos, the foremost student of American enlisted men and women, declared: "The evidence is unambiguous that . . . higher educated and higher aptitude soldiers do better in low skill jobs as well as high skill jobs. This confirms what every NCO has always known."[25] Earlier government studies had found evidence that supported this contention, although no administration was willing to endorse it. They found this the case, despite biased and sloppy survey methodology which tended to obscure the facts. The Defense Manpower Commission, for example, sent out survey teams composed alternately of a man and a woman and a black and a white to discuss the integration of women into the armed forces, race relations, and the overall aptitude level of recruits. The interviewers recorded their puzzlement that interviewees sometimes anticipated their questions with stock answers, or seemed to be providing a "party line" generally favorable to the AVF.[26]

The AFQT was a general aptitude test, not a vocational one. As had long been known, the duller soldier could be trained in his tasks, so long as extra time and attention were given him and, if necessary, he could be recycled through training.[27] What bothered the services was the time, money, and effort substandard recruits required for training and the difficulty such recruits had in learning new skills or improvising. A more serious objection had to do with combat readiness. The great strength of the intelligent, partially college-educated draftee was his ability to plug the gaps when key personnel, officers, or NCOs were incapacitated. In less urgent circumstances the college-educated draftee was an invaluable company clerk or orderly.

The embarrasing AFQT score revelations led the Defense Department temporarily to stop publishing them in the annual reports. Officials instead concentrated on percentages of recruits with high school degrees, although even here the statistics were not encouraging. In 1981 less than 70 percent of the armed services' recruits had high school diplomas; in the army, a few more than half did.[28] The services preferred high school graduates not so much for their education as for the indication a high school degree gave of maturity and sociability.[29] Yet over time (in particular, since World War II), high school graduation had become more and more common, and less and less an indication of those desirable characteristics. Congress reacted to these developments in 1981 by mandating certain maximum levels for Category IV personnel (20 percent by 1983) and minimum levels for high school graduates (65 percent).

Both measures of quality, Mental Category and high school graduate, are artificial but suggestive. Better indicators of the quality of the AVF are the attrition rate of nearly one-third (that is, one-third of first-term enlistees did not complete a three-year term), recurrent recruiting scandals involving coaching and falsification of test scores, and the pervasive negative opinion of NCOs as revealed in private questioning by nongovernmental researchers.[30] By 1980 the AVF was simply recruiting a worse-quality soldier than it ever did under the draft, a trend that showed in such things as high failure rates among tank gunners (in a test of over one thousand M-60 tank crews, 28 percent in the United States and 21 percent in Europe did not know how to aim the tank gun using the battle sight).[31]

In the early 1980s, however, an economy in recession and an armed force given substantial pay increases by the Reagan administration (11.7 percent in 1981, 14.3 percent in 1982) made possible the recovery of some ground lost in the late 1970s. The army was able to hold its intake of Category IV personnel to 12 percent, and in the Department of Defense as a whole the figure was held to 8 percent—a better performance in this regard than at any time since 1964. Increased recruiting of women (who, on average, tended to have higher scores and educational levels than their male counterparts) also improved the figures. Nonetheless, Secretary of Defense Weinberger admitted in his annual report to Congress for fiscal year 1985 that "the more stringent limitations on AFQT Category IV (below average) accessions restrict our flexibility and could present a problem in future years, particularly for the Army."[32]

These successes were reinforced by a concurrent effort of the military (particularly the army) to reprofessionalize itself, to restore traditional military values and virtues. This effort, associated primarily with the army chief of staff, General Edward C. Meyer, included the reinvigoration of the regimental system, cohort training (whereby two-hundred-man companies stay together from basic training to discharge several years later), and lengthened command tours. Nonetheless, the services did not have the manpower required by their force structure. Battleships were sent to sea only partially manned; army divisions were forced to rely increasingly on Reserve and National Guard units. The Reagan administration's program for military expansion ran afoul of the realities of manpower constraints; thus, plans for adding a seventeenth division to the army had to be radically altered and deferred in 1983. When these plans finally emerged in 1984, they called for the transformation of two divisions (the 7th and the 25th) into light divisions about 60 percent the size of regular infantry divisions and the creation of yet another light division. The economic recovery of the mid-1980s, Congressional reluctance to continue substantial pay increases, the shrinking manpower pool, and the Reagan administration's own plans for an expansion of the force render the future of the AVF dubious. The Reagan administration's plans include a programmed expansion of the navy to six hundred ships, the addition of an army division, and continued increases in the size of the air force. Overall, the administration expects to add approximately 40,000 active duty and 100,000 Reserve slots between 1983 and 1985.[33]

The shortfalls in manpower led Defense planners to two other measures beyond acceptance of low-quality recruits: the large-scale recruitment of women, and the "Total Force" concept. Women, who comprised less than 2 percent of the army during World War II and for years afterward, made up some 7.5 percent of it in 1981. Under the Reagan administration the Department of Defense increased the total percentage of women in the active force to an unprecedented level—9.3 percent of enlisted personnel, 8.9 percent of officers. Women were assigned to all units except infantry, armor, combat engineer, and some air defense and field artillery units.[34] This meant that women would, in fact, be in combat in the event of war, given their participation in signal and transportation units that, of necessity, work close to the front.

Most senior officers were ambivalent toward this experiment. Women are usually more intelligent and docile than male recruits, but their introduction into field units poses a host of problems, among them the need for separate sanitary facilities, morale problems caused by sexual envy or desire, an annual pregnancy rate of

15 percent, resistance of many of the women to their transfer to "nontraditional" jobs, and the prospect of female participation in combat.[35] This use of women in the armed forces was unprecedented for any peacetime army, including Israel's, which keeps its female recruits in an equivalent of the Women's Army Corps (abolished in the United States in 1975) and carefully insulates women from combat, no matter what their jobs.

The increasing use of women in the general-purpose military eroded the combat exclusion policy of the various services. If women were to have truly equal opportunity, including opportunity to rise to the highest levels of command, they could not be excluded from jobs that are associated with promotion. Moreover, a policy of combat exclusion was increasingly strained by the realities of modern combat, which include the extension of the area of danger to locations well behind the front lines. This difficulty was a latent one: although public opinion polls revealed a consistent opposition to the use of women in combat, none of the minor military tests of the early 1980s—the deployment of Marines in Lebanon, the rescue *cum* invasion of Grenada in 1983—brought the problem to the fore.

One must conclude, however, that overall the influx of women into "nontraditional" areas of military service has detracted from military effectiveness. Commanders already burdened with the usual difficulties of training find themselves coping with the problem of sexual harassment and favoritism, a greater need for privacy, and sexual misconduct. At the purely physical level, women are simply incapable of meeting the upper body strength requirements still demanded in many areas of military service. When an attempt was made to introduce sex-blind physical strength tests for various jobs, pressure by feminist groups forced the armed services to reduce their requirements, and even to allow admittedly unqualified personnel into physically demanding jobs.[36]

The large-scale introduction of women has had other effects as well. Combat exclusion policies mean that a significant portion of the administrative force cannot be called upon to serve as infantry replacements in the event of emergencies such as were common during the higher-intensity episodes of World War II and the Korean war. At a more subtle level, mixed units have lost the benefits of what is known as "male bonding," the perhaps juvenile but nontheless essential camaraderie of the kind found in the average high school locker room. Sexual envy and pity interfere with the harmonious workings of units that have to operate for prolonged periods away from home, under conditions of periodic stress.[37]

The armed forces also attempted to cope with their drop in numbers by embracing the Total Force concept, which mandated the interweaving of active and reserve units. In the words of the army chief of staff in 1981, "We rely on the reserve components today as never before."[38] The Defense Manpower Commission Report in 1976 made it clear that the move to the Total Force was linked to the establishment of the AVF. Government officials rather disingenuously argued that the Total Force decision (1970) was made primarily in order to give the Reserve components a sense of purpose; in fact, the Total Force concept was essential if the AVF was to meet most of its main missions.[39]

The need to use reserve units suppressed the army's long-standing mistrust of them and of the state-controlled National Guard. This was particularly true when, in 1975, Secretary of Defense James Schlesinger ordered an increase in the army's organizational strength from thirteen divisions to sixteen and Senator Sam Nunn obtained the passage of legislation that converted 11,000 support troops in the army in Europe to combat forces. The Nunn Amendment resulted in the creation of two additional brigades, each organizationally attached to complete divisions in the United States.[40]

By 1984 only half of the army's sixteen divisions have all of the maneuver (infantry, armor, and artillery) units they would need for war. Four divisions consist of only two active duty brigades (drawing the needed third brigade from the National Guard), and four others would each need from one to three battalions of reservists to reach wartime strength (a division would normally consist of some eleven battalions).[41] Fully nineteen reserve maneuver battalions would be required to "round out" the active force. In 1981, two-thirds of the army's combat engineers, three-fifths of its medical units, almost half of its field artillery, armor, and infantry units, and over a third of its aviation assets were in the National Guard or Reserves.[42] By 1984, dependence on the Reserves is even greater—some 68 percent of the tactical support the total force would require comes from the Reserves. Thus, no major military operation could be undertaken without a Reserve mobilization, and all of its attendant delays and political problems.

This increased reliance on Reservists comes in spite of the fact that the Selected Reserve (those units that actually train regularly in local armories) has advanced little since 1964. In the mid-60s, when dependence on the Reserves was less than during the 1970s and 1980s, the Army National Guard had 386,000 men, or 12,000 more than in 1980 and only slightly less than in 1983 (417,000).[43] An energetic and costly recruiting campaign increased the number of Selected Reserve members during the early 1980s, although the creation of new units (including a new National Guard division plus additional Air National Guard squadrons) soaked up the increased manpower.

The composition of the Reserves changed dramatically between the 1960s and the 1980s. In 1970 the National Guard and Reserve consisted of 55 percent college-trained men, but by 1975 the figure had dropped to scarcely 6 percent.[44] True, more of the Reservists in 1975—two out of three, in fact—were veterans, compared to one out of three in 1970.[45] This led, however, to more frequent mismatches between military skill and rank.

Under the war plans of the 1980s, many of the military's Reserve units were "scheduled to deploy within ten days of mobilization."[46] In short, Reserve units were expected to maintain the same level of readiness and fitness as their active counterparts. The problems with this assumption were many. For one thing, it was and remains uncertain how swift and complete a Reserve mobilization could be, for the United States (unlike other countries dependent on reserve mobilizations, such as Israel) does not practice sudden reserve call-ups. As during past Reserve mobilizations (in 1961, for example), one could expect many Reservists to petition for hardship exemptions from call-ups, or simply to delay their appearance at mobilization centers.

Moreover, it it unreasonable to think that reserve units, particularly those composed of non–prior service soldiers, are likely to be nearly as proficient as their active duty counterparts. In the words of one of the army's foremost trainers:

> Reserve Component Training suffers from the Army's failure to make a realistic assessment of what can be expected from the Reserve Components in an emergency, and from the Reserve Components' promise of more than they can deliver. . . . After all the call-up problems have been accommodated and the unit is assembled in a field environment even company-size units would require at least thirty days of concentrated training to be prepared for combat. . . . Statements that Reserve Component units should be as ready to fight as Active Army units are self-serving and self-defeating . . .[47]

[179]

The author goes on to argue that reserve training should concentrate on proficiency at the individual, squad, platoon, and company levels, and that attempts to demand more of reserve units only serve to endanger the lives of those who serve in them.

Comparisons with the Israel Defense Forces, which rely heavily on reserve units, are misleading. First, the IDF draws its recruits almost exclusively from a force that has completed three or more years of training on active duty, unlike the men who have augmented the depleted U.S. Reserve forces in the 1980s. Many Israeli reservists (again, unlike their counterparts in the United States in the 1980s) are the veterans of several wars against the same opponents they currently face. Secondly, IDF reserve units have always had—and know they have—a real likelihood of engaging in military action. This invaluable sense of urgency does not and cannot obtain in the United States. The relative paucity of American Reserve training with live ammunition is but one example of this. Finally, even the IDF relies increasingly on a substantial active duty force to bear the brunt of its military operations. Its active forces now number fully 172,000 men and women, or a third of its Total Force. This is a considerable departure from the much more heavily reserve-dependent IDF forces of the 1950s and 1960s.[48]

If the Selected Reserve is short (for even at their increased 1980s levels the Army Reserve and National Guard are below wartime strength),[49] the situation in the Individual Ready Reserve (IRR) is even worse. These men, unaffiliated with local units but retaining a reserve obligation, would be necessary as individual fillers and replacements in the event of war. By various estimates the IRR pool (about 70 percent of which could be expected to be available in the event of war) was somewhere between a quarter and a third of a million men short in 1980. In 1984 the situation is little improved, as Department of Defense officials concede that four months into a mobilization the army would find itself short 168,000 men in combat enlisted skills alone.[50] In addition, reliance on the IRR means reliance, in wartime, on an individual replacement system similar to that which disrupted unit cohesion in World War II, Korea, and Vietnam.

Because of reserve shortfall, any mobilization would be likely to repeat, in some measure, the experience of World War II, in which partial units were filled up with recent draftees and superannuated reservists. The result in World War II was that whole units had to be retrained at the pace of the least-experienced soldier, that is, the draftee (Chapter 3). Measures such as transferring men wholesale from the Standby Reserve to the Individual Ready Reserve concealed rather than ameliorated the problem.[51]

By most standards, then, the AVF was not ready for a major war in the late 1970s, and only marginally so by the early 1980s. Reliance on reserve units and, worse, on undermanned reserve units means that as in World War II, 1950, and 1961, units will require extensive retraining before deployment, because new troops will have to be inserted into units to fill the ranks.[52] To deploy any major force overseas would require a reserve mobilization, with all the attendant political difficulties of such a move.

The large-scale incorporation of women has created numerous morale and disciplinary problems, in addition to raising the spectre of women dying in combat, or being captured and raped. It has limited the flexibility of commanders, who have to envisage the possibility of turning their service troops into infantrymen at short notice (as during World War II and during the retreat of the 1st Marine Division from Chosin Reservoir in 1950–1951).

The increased number of dull-witted soldiers puts technical problems in the way of maintaining complicated equipment. What is worse, however, it presents the prospect of disaster through failure to provide line units with resourceful and intelligent soldiers. Even though brighter recruits appeared in the early 1980s, the fact remains that the All-Volunteer Force is not attracting into the enlisted ranks the college-educated—or even the college-bound—soldier.[53]

As military sociologists, particularly Charles Moskos, have repeatedly pointed out, the high first-term pay levels of the All-Volunteer Force are transforming the nature of military service. High pay enables soldiers to live off base, and barracks assume the aspect of semi-private dormitories. The prestige of the noncommissioned officer, the backbone of armies since Roman times, has fallen as his pay relative to that of the trainee has decreased. As pay has grown, and as recruiting campaigns have emphasized the armed services' advantages for vocational training, the soldier's calling has become a job, much like any other. This is a perilous condition, for in wartime the soldier has a far grimmer set of duties, a far more difficult environment in which to live and work, than the automotive mechanic or crane operator.[54]

These realities are as comfortably remote from the United States in 1984 as they have ever been. It is instructive in this regard to consider the 11 November 1942 speech of General Leslie McNair, the mild and scholarly commander of the Army Ground Forces during World War II on whose shoulders rested the responsibility of training the armies that would liberate Europe. On that day, the eve of the invasion of North Africa, the first major ground action of the United States in Europe, McNair attempted to convey to the American people the real nature of the task they had given him, and the harsh measures it would require: "Our soldiers must have the fighting spirit. . . . We must lust for battle; our object in life must be to kill; we must scheme and plan day and night to kill. . . . The struggle is for survival—kill or be killed."[55] By contrast, the American defense establishment convinced itself in the early 1980s that superior American technology and the improvements in the size and quality of America's armed forces would prevent war from occurring: "Now we can be confident that should war break out, our men will have equipment that is at least equal to, and in many cases superior to, that of the Soviets. For that very reason, *it is increasingly unlikely we will have to test any of it in combat*" (emphasis mine).[56] The confidence expressed in the AVF by a succession of secretaries of defense reflects the same distance from the realities of war and of the organizational requirements it would impose.

By the early 1980s it was clear that the AVF was deficient, although only a war could show just how badly off it was. Its difficulties, moreover, can only increase as the pool of men from whom it can pick shrinks in size. Members of the high command, in particular the chief of staff of the army, openly called for a draft, and draft registration has been reintroduced.[57] For a time the recession of the early 1980s and substantial increases in pay have reduced pressure to return to conscription, but it can reasonably be expected that eventually demography, strategic necessity, and economic recovery will conspire to force a return to a draft.[58] What *kind* of draft, however, remains as open a question as it was almost forty years ago.

[9]

Conclusion

The purpose of this book has not been to propose a specific plan for dealing with America's military manpower problems. Rather, its purpose has been to expose the nature of the problem that has confronted the United States since World War II. Before grappling with the immediate problem, therefore, we must step back and consider its dimensions.

I have said that in devising systems of military service, all countries must resolve two clusters of claims, those of foreign *cum* military policy on the one hand, those of justice or ideology on the other. A nation must, moreover, adapt as well as possible in peacetime to the exigencies of war, bearing in mind that war alters all of the conditions, particularly the political conditions, under which a system of military service works. An examination of the history of American military manpower policy reveals the truth of the contention that the United States *cannot avoid* certain irresolvable manpower difficulties. The elements of the dilemma are these:

(1) The United States must maintain a large standing force for all-out conventional war on the European continent. An expansible force (such as the *Reichswehr*) will not do, because such a system requires years to reach full war readiness. A Swiss-type militia system would not work, because American troops must be deployed overseas (the army today keeps over a third of its men in foreign countries, most of them in Europe).[1] In addition, even high-quality militia-type units would require some time (from a few weeks to a few months) to reach the quality of standing forces.

The United States must also prepare to fight small wars. For this purpose, marine forces alone will not suffice: The Marines possess only three divisions and cannot, for both military and political reasons, be committed *in toto* to one small war. The other light units of the army—particularly the 82nd Airborne Division and the 101st Airmobile Division—are unlikely to be sent overseas because, as during the Korean war, they will form a strategic reserve. Special Forces and Ranger units are small and only suitable for specialized operations. In addition, the army has long opposed the use of special units to fight counterinsurgency warfare, as its opposition to the growth of Special Forces during the early stages of the Vietnam war indicated. Thus, the army needed for small wars must be entirely professional, volunteer, and hardy.

(2) The American regime is at once liberal and egalitarian. Thus, a substantial and vocal portion of the public will be unhappy no matter what policy is adopted. The cleavages in American opinion about the draft run across party lines, not along them. Thus, it will be difficult for a president to obtain the undivided support of his party for any draft.

This two-cornered dilemma has obstructed any comprehensive approach to the military manpower problem. The last such approach was President Truman's UMT scheme, and that was successfully opposed by Congress. He and his successors accepted instead a continuation of the draft under the old name of Selected Service.

The post-1948 draft was nothing like Selective Service as created by General Crowder. It did not extend to all able-bodied men, only to those aged eighteen to twenty-six; it did not entail, as it had during World War I and World War II, the abolition of voluntarism. In fact, the director of Selective Service's report for the years 1948–1950 recorded with pride the success of a small-scale draft in increasing enlistments. Thus, postwar selective service was a typically "liberal" draft—that is, a minimal draft for the purpose of inducing men to enlist. The influence of the original conception of selective service persisted, however, as the channeling policy of the early 1960s reveals.

The history of America's postwar draft is one of inertia and improvisation—the modification of a system brilliantly tailored to one set of military needs and political circumstances but unsuited for others. Its collapse was inevitable, given the circumstances. The AVF, a daring experiment, was a poorly conceived solution to the multiple dilemmas of American military manpower policy: hope for its success rested on the short-range fluctuations of demographic trends, the general state of the economy, and on a simplistic set of free-market assumptions. Its failure has been marked not by protests and riots, but by a perceptible decay in the efficiency of the American armed forces and a decrease in their size.

Is there a solution to these multiple dilemmas? A lottery draft promises only to cure some sort-term difficulties. In the long run, liberal and egalitarian criticism of a limited draft (say, of one in four eligible young men) would make any administration eager to gain political favor by returning to an AVF as soon as possible. The public would continue to see the draft as an arbitrary and onerous burden, for unlike death and taxes, a lottery draft would be eminently escapable.

National service proposals present other problems, practical and theoretical. The difficulty and expense of finding and administering make-work jobs for two million young men or four million young men and women would be immense. More important, the concept of national service is profoundly antagonistic to American ideology. The theory of national service is that everyone owes a year's unpaid or poorly paid labor to the state, in other words, *corvée*. Whether such a proposal would be constitutional or not (for compulsory labor might well be considered "involuntary servitude"), it would likely meet with indignation from parents and children.

Universal military service presents practical problems also. It would add well over one million men a year to the armed forces, and thus be enormously costly in pay, support, and equipment. It would prove organizationally hard to manage, for it would require a large increase in the NCO and officer cadre. If military service were shorter than two years, personnel turbulence could well disrupt unit cohesion. The problems involved in sending draftees to fight small wars would remain.

Universal Military Training as proposed in 1948 always lacked a clear rationale. It is likely that the armed forces would oppose devoting human and material resources to a program that would not augment their ready forces. Still, UMT comes closer to a solution of the manpower dilemma than the other possibilities mentioned.

The requirements of a successful military manpower policy are these:

[185]

(1) The system must be consistent with both liberalism and egalitarianism. In other words, service should be brief and limited, but all or almost all young men should serve. The program must have a clear military rationale.

(2) The system must produce effective forces for both total and small wars: this means that the standing army must consist of volunteers.

(3) The system must not be excessively costly, nor may it place excessive organizational and manpower burdens on the armed forces.

One solution would be a resurrection of the plan advanced by George Washington and Alexander Hamilton in "Sentiments on a Peace Establishment," which advocated compulsory universal militia service. Modified versions of this system were proposed repeatedly in the 1940s.[2]

The merits of such a system are that it would impose equal and tolerable service on young men; it would create a large and effective reserve army; it would retain a volunteer standing force, one that would consist of high-quality personnel because of the likelihood—in fact, the certainty—that a reserve draft would spur enlistments in the standing forces; it could endure for decades, unlike an AVF or low-level draft; it would create a cadre of reserve NCOs and commissioned officers for wartime mobilization; and it would be in accord with American traditions and institutions.

Such a system would entail a number of serious practical problems, however. The National Guard would have to be permanently federalized, in order to ensure that the Reserves not only would be efficient, but would have the respect of regular officers. The states could be allowed to raise their own militias (which they would need in wartime anyway, after the mobilization of the National Guard) from the conscripts. Such a system would be costly, although savings could be effected by a return to low first-term pay for recruits, low reserve duty pay, and perhaps a return to the army to thirteen balanced divisions. It is even possible that not all able-bodied young men could be taken. An effort would therefore have to be made to make sure that the most privileged—the scions of the middle and upper classes—would serve. As noted in the case of Switzerland (Chapter 6), the political effects of universal service can be obtained even if only 60 percent of the eligible pool of young men serves, provided that the wealthiest and most politically active parts of the population serve and expect to serve.

A large and effective reserve army would not be easy to create.

Weapons, tactical doctrine, and discipline would have to be adapted to the capacities of part-time soldiers; large amounts of equipment would have to be purchased and training facilities built for them. Current sophisticated weapon systems such as the F-15 and F-16 fighter bombers and the M-1 tank might cost too much to be distributed to the mass reserve force. If so, it might be wise to act on the suggestion of some National Guard officers that cheaper mass-produced weapons be put into the hands of the new federal National Guard. Thus, the United States would deploy a relatively small, high-quality professional army to fight small wars and serve as a front line of defense in large ones. The mass army, consisting of conscript Guardsmen, would be deployed overseas only in the event of war declared by Congress.

Such a system might seem excessive because it would create more forces than are needed at any given time. It would, however, establish a durable system of service consistent with American values; a force suited, moreover, to the contingency of all-out war. The two alternatives to such a policy are to maintain a fragile AVF or to reduce its size sharply and turn it into a professional force. The British have shown that it is possible to sustain a professional army, but only if it is small. In the American context, assuming a military participation ratio of .6 or slightly better (the British average), this would mean a force of 1,400,000, or some 600,000 fewer than today. Most of the manpower cuts would have to come from the army, and would probably necessitate withdrawal from Europe of all but a token force. One result, of course, would be a fundamental alteration of American foreign policy.

CONSCRIPTION AND STATESMANSHIP

An overhaul of the military manpower system along the lines of a universal militia draft would require enormous effort and political skill. It would require courage and political adroitness to pry the National Guard loose from state control, although the power of the National Guard Association to block such an action is today probably far weaker than during the days of General Walsh in the 1930s and 1940s. It would require rare eloquence and persistence to make the armed forces, historically disinclined to believe in the efficiency of reserve forces, treat them seriously, as more than adjuncts or fillers for the standing forces. Above all, it would require energy and mastery of American rhetoric (using the word in its nonpejorative sense) to convince the American people of the need for such a system, of its suitability for our military needs and congruence with our political traditions.

A useful model in this regard is that of Richard Burdon Haldane (see Chapter 4). His transformation of the Militia and Volunteers into the Territorial Army—though less successful than it might have been—is a model of how militia organizations that have acquired deep, local political roots can be transformed by patient political skill. On the other hand, the experience of Britain before World War I offers as much discouragement as hope. Despite the best efforts of acute minds, the British were unable to devise, much less implement, a military system to solve the dilemmas that that country faced, dilemmas resembling those of the United States today.

There is no one form of military service that will satisfy both military needs and the more political claims of justice—and indeed, as we have seen, those military needs have a certain political component. The claims of liberty and equality are insistent and must be met, as the sorry history of military substitution and the Vietnam-era Selective Service System show. Of all systems, the militia type of military service would seem to be most in accord with the Anglo-American type of regime, although it has practical and perhaps theoretical deficiencies. In any case, Ralph Barton Perry's sixty-year-old warning that "the American military system must be popular," that it must be carefully considered and deliberately adopted, remains as true as ever.[3] The free man does not wish to become a soldier; the democratic man abhors unequal burdens; the military man would like to ignore their claims, but cannot. It is the task of the statesman to reconcile the three, and to do so in a way likely to last.

Perhaps the worst system of military service is that which changes constantly, which invites paralyzing debates and accusations of inadequacy or injustice, which tacitly encourages manipulators of rules to evade service and thereby to undermine the moral basis of military obligations. As no one would wish to transform the judicial system every decade, so no one should desire to do the same to the system of military service. As the author of *Federalist* No. 62 said of the dangers of mutability in government:

> But the most deplorable effect of all is that diminution of attachment and reverence which steals into the hearts of the people, towards a political system which betrays so many marks of infirmity,

and disappoints so many of their faltering hopes. No government, any more than an individual, will long be respected without being truly respectable; nor be truly respectable, without possessing a certain portion of order and stability.[4]

The difficult task, therefore, is to devise a system that is not merely fair and effective, but durable as well.

The true dilemmas (as opposed to the short-term difficulties) of America's military manpower system are several and profound, the claims of policy analysts and government officials notwithstanding. These dilemmas are rooted in the nature of the American regime and America's place in the world. The debate on military manpower in the United States has not turned on these issues. It has, rather, been characterized by the development of arcane and improbable models, unthinking reliance on the ethics and efficiency of the marketplace, resort to simplistic assertions about American political traditions, manipulation of statistical information, and, above all, a myopic preoccupation with short-term problems and trends. It has been my purpose in this book to demonstrate the continuing truth of Marshal St.-Cyr's dictum that the laws governing military recruitment are political institutions. To ignore this truth is to invite turmoil at home and defeat abroad.

Notes

1. When I speak of the World Powers I refer to those states capable of projecting major forces into Europe and other major regions of the world simultaneously—of sustaining, in short, a global war. Today, only the United States and the Soviet Union qualify as World Powers. Great Britain was one through World War II, France was one in the eighteenth century, and Germany very nearly became one at the end of the nineteenth century and the beginning of the twentieth century. By Great (or "medium") Powers I refer primarily to contemporary European states, although others (China, for example) fit this category as well. Great Powers are those states that exercise a considerable regional influence and that can offer even the World Powers a serious struggle in their (the Great Powers') own vicinity. By Minor (or "small") Powers I refer to countries able perhaps to put up serious resistance to invasion, but generally incapable of projecting power into their region: for example, Finland, Tunisia, and Thailand. The above classification follows that used by Martin Wight in his classic study *Power Politics* (1946; rev. ed. New York: Holmes & Meier, 1978).

2. For the most part this book treats armies, the main land forces of a country. For historical and technical reasons, most navies, air forces, and gendarmeries in most states (including the United States) have made little or only limited use of conscripts. Such services either have skill requirements that preclude the use of draftees, or sufficient glamour and rewards (for example, the imparting of vocational skills) to attract adequate numbers of volunteers to fill their ranks.

3. See, for example, "We Must Reinstate the Draft," *New York Times*, 25 February 1982, p. A31.

4. See an article by Joseph Califano, "Doubts about an All Volunteer Army," *New Republic* 168:9 (3 March 1973): 9–11.

5. Louis Jules Trochu, *L'Armée Francaise en 1867* (Paris: Amyot, 1867), pp. 39–40 (quotation: p. 39).

6. Polybius, *The Rise of the Roman Empire* (Book VI of *Histories*), trans. Ian Scott-Kilvert (Harmondsworth: Penguin, 1979), pp. 302–338; Aristotle, *Politics*, trans. Benjamin Jowett (New York: Modern Library, 1943), pp. 271–272 (Book VI, chap. 7).

7. *Report of the President's Commission on an All-Volunteer Armed Force* (Washington, D.C.: Government Printing Office, 1970), pp. 23–24.

8. Richard V. L. Cooper, *Military Manpower and the All-Volunteer Armed Force* (Santa Monica: RAND, 1977), pp. 5–7.

[191]

9. Samuel P. Huntington, *Political Order in Changing Societies* (New Haven: Yale University Press, 1968), p. 12.

10. Catherine McArdle Kelleher, "Mass Armies in the 1970s: The Debate in Western Europe," *Armed Forces and Society* 5:1 (Fall 1978): 3–30.

11. See the discussion in Morris Janowitz, "Military Service and Citizenship in Western Societies," *Armed Forces and Society* 2:2 (Winter 1976): 185–204.

12. Alexis de Tocqueville, *Democracy in America* (New York: Anchor, 1969), pp. 270–276.

13. See Otto Hintze, "Military Organization and State Organization," in Felix Gilbert, ed., *The Historical Essays of Otto Hintze* (New York: Oxford University Press, 1975), pp. 178–215. This is the theme of Hans Delbrueck's magistral *Geschichte der Kriegskunst im Rahmen der politischen Geschichte* (Berlin: Georg Stilke, 1920).

14. M. R. D. Foot, *Men in Uniform* (New York: Praeger, 1961), p. 30.

15. See Jean Colin, *The Transformations of War*, trans. L. H. R. Pope-Hennessy (1912; rpt. Westport: Greenwood, 1977), pp. 199–200; J. F. C. Fuller, *Armament and History* (New York: Charles Scribner's Sons, 1945), pp. 18–19; Cyril Falls, *A Hundred Years of War* (New York: Collier, 1953), p. 22.

1. Constraints: Necessity and Choice

1. Germany deployed substantially more troops in the opening battles of August 1914, but only because the German General Staff was far more willing than the French to use reserve formations.

2. Numbers drawn from International Institute for Strategic Studies, *The Military Balance, 1982–1983* (London, 1983).

3. See Douglas Edward Leach, *Arms for Empire* (New York: Macmillan, 1973), pp. 8–40.

4. See Viktor Suvorov (pseud.), *Inside the Soviet Army* (New York: Macmillan, 1982), pp. 234–238 for an account of Soviet senior draftee/NCO training.

5. On the place of NCOs in the German Army see Herbert Rosinski, *The German Army*, 2d ed. (New York: Praeger, 1966), pp. 99–103. For an interesting comparison of the relative strength of the NCO corps in various nineteenth-century European armies see Nicholas Golovine, *The Russian Army in the World War* (New Haven: Yale University Press, 1931), p. 29.

6. Martin Wight, *Power Politics*, ed. Hedley Bull and Carsten Holbraad (New York: Holmes & Meier, 1978), p. 56.

7. Definition derived in part from Cyril Falls, *A Hundred Years of War* (New York: Collier, 1953), pp. 130–133; C. E. Callwell, *Small Wars* (London: HMSO, 1906), pp. 21–24.

8. See Raymond Aron, *The Imperial Republic*, trans. Frank Jellinek (Englewood Cliffs: Prentice-Hall, 1974), esp. pp. 1–159, 252–260. On America as an imperial power see George Liska, *Imperial America* (Baltimore: Johns Hopkins University Press, 1967), pp. 3–35; Robert W. Tucker, *Nation or Empire?* (Baltimore: Johns Hopkins University Press, 1968). On contemporary problems of limited war see Robert E. Osgood, *Limited War* (Chicago: University of Chicago Press, 1957); and, by the same author, *Limited War Revisited* (Boulder: Westview Press, 1979).

9. Thucydides, *The Peloponnesian War*, trans. Rex Warner (Harmondsworth: Penguin, 1972), p. 161.

10. Richard Clutterbuck, *The Long, Long War: Counterinsurgency in Malaya and Vietnam* (New York: Praeger, 1966), pp. 9–10.

11. See Jean Gottman, "Bugeaud, Gallieni, Lyautey: The Development of French Colonial Warfare," in Edward Meade Earle, ed., *The Makers of Modern Strategy* (Princeton: Princeton University Press, 1943), pp. 234–259.

12. See the yearly reports on the fighting in Afghanistan put out by the International Institute for Strategic Studies, London, in its annual *Strategic Survey*.

13. This question is part of a much larger debate on whether foreign policy has its own logic, determined by the nature of international politics, or is driven by internal politics. It takes a particularly sharp form in the dispute among German scholars over the outbreak of World War I, with Gerhard Ritter among others arguing for the *Primat der Aussenpolitik*—the inexorable logic of foreign policy—and Eckart Kehr and Fritz Fischer arguing for the *Primat der Innenpolitik*—the preeminence of domestic factors.

14. See Ellen Jones and Fred W. Grupp, "Political Socialization in the Soviet Military," *Armed Forces and Society* 8:3 (Spring 1982): 355–384.

15. See John Shy, *A People Numerous and Armed: Reflections on the Military Struggle for American Independence* (New York: Oxford University Press, 1976), pp. 163–179, 216–217.

16. Alexis de Tocqueville, *Democracy in America*, trans. George Lawrence (New York: Anchor, 1969), 2:645–654.

17. This obfuscatory use of the term "democratic" is particularly evident in the pre–World War I and post–World War II debates, even in discussion among political scientists. See William L. Ransom, ed., "Military Training: Compulsory or Volunteer," *Proceedings of the Academy of Political Science* 6:4 (July 1916); and Paul Russell Anderson, ed., "Universal Military Training and National Security," *The Annals of American Political and Social Science* 241 (September 1945). Both volumes are invaluable for the study of the political theory of conscription in liberal-democratic states.

18. See the massive studies conducted by Samuel Stouffer and his associates, *The American Soldier* (Princeton: Princeton University Press, 1949), vols. 1 and 2.

19. See Samuel P. Huntington, *The Soldier and the State: The Theory and Politics of Civil-Military Relations* (Cambridge: Harvard University Press, 1957), pp. 59–97.

20. Professional isolation is recommended by Huntington in the interest of "objective civilian control." *The Soldier and the State*, p. 94.

21. Tocqueville, *Democracy in America*, 1:308.

22. See Stouffer et al., *The American Soldier*, 2:59–241; F. M. Richardson, *Fighting Spirit: A Study of Psychological Factors in War* (London: Leo Cooper, 1978), p. 144.

23. Jean Larteguy, *The Centurions*, trans. Xan Fielding (New York: E. P. Dutton, 1962), pp. 307–326.

24. On British problems in World War I see Winston S. Churchill, *The World Crisis*, vol. 5, *The Aftermath* (New York: Charles Scribner's Sons, 1929), pp. 40–59. On American difficulties during World War II see Omar N. Bradley and Clay Blair, *A General's Life* (New York: Simon & Schuster, 1983), pp. 447–448. The Stouffer studies also vividly depict the rapid fall in morale once the war ended, as men grew impatient to return home.

25. C. P. Stacey, *Arms, Men, and Governments: The War Policies of Canada, 1939–1945* (Ottawa: Department of National Defence, 1970), pp. 397–484.

26. The degree of social prestige in Swiss society attached to high military rank can be seen in such stories as Friedrich Duerrenmatt's *Der Richter und sein Henker* (Hamburg: Rowohlt, 1955).

27. See Karl Haltiner and Ruth Meyer, "Aspects of the Relationship between Military and Society in Switzerland," *Armed Forces and Society* 6:1 (Fall 1979): 49–81.

28. See the testimony of Grenville Clark, a prominent New York lawyer and one of the leaders of the pre–World War I Plattsburg movement, in U.S. Congress, Senate, Committee on Military Affairs, *Compulsory Military Training and Service. Hearings before the Senate Committee on Military Affairs*, 76th Cong., 3d sess., 1940, pp. 10–12.

2. *Military Service and the Mass Army: 1776–1914*

1. Summary statements of this view can be found in many textbooks; for rather more sophisticated views, see R. R. Palmer, "Frederick the Great, Guibert, Bülow: From Dynastic to National War," in Edward Meade Earle, ed., *The Makers of Modern Strategy* (1943; rpt. Princeton: Princeton University Press, 1971), p. 51; and Otto Hintze, "Military Organization and State Organization," in Felix Gilbert, ed., *The Historical Essays of Otto Hintze* (New York: Oxford University Press, 1975), pp. 205–206. See Eric Robson, "The Armed Forces and the Art of War," *The New Cambridge Modern History*, vol. 7, ed. J. O. Lindsay (Cambridge: Cambridge University Press, 1957), pp. 163–190, esp. pp. 171–174.

2. Alfred Vagts, *A History of Militarism* (New York: Meridan, 1959), p. 129.

3. Palmer, "Frederick the Great," p. 72.

4. See Anthony L. Wermuth, "A Critique of Savage and Gabriel," *Armed Forces and Society* 3:3 (May 1977): 482–483.

5. Two bitter expositions of this view are Richard A. Gabriel and Paul L. Savage, *Crisis in Command: Mismanagement in the Army* (New York: Hill & Wang, 1978) and Cecil B. Currey, *Self-Destruction: The Disintegration and Decay of the United States Army during the Vietnam Era* (New York: W. W. Norton, 1981).

6. Cyril Falls, *A Hundred Years of War* (New York: Collier, 1953), p. 22.

7. Ibid.

8. On the subject matter of this chapter see Andre Corvisier, *Armies and Societies in Europe, 1494–1789*, trans. Abigail T. Siddal (Bloomington: Indiana University Press, 1979); and Richard A Preston and Sydney F. Wise, *Men in Arms*, 2d rev. ed. (New York: Praeger, 1970), pp. 179–199. See also J. W. Fortescue, *A History of the British Army*, vol. 3 (London: Macmillan, 1911), p. 535; Spenser Wilkinson, *The French Army before Napoleon* (Oxford: Oxford University Press, 1915), p. 85.

9. A. M. Nikolaieff, "Universal Military Service in Russia and Western Europe," *Russian Review* 8:2 (April 1949): 117–118; Vasili Klyuchevsky, *Peter the Great*, trans. Lilian Archibald (New York: Vintage, 1958), p. 84.

10. Herbert Rosinski, *The German Army*, ed. Gordon Craig, 2d ed. (New York: Praeger, 1966), p. 33; Ernst Huber, *Heer und Staat* (Hamburg: Hanseatische Verlaganstalt, 1938), p. 92.

11. Wilkinson, *The French Army*, p. 85.

12. Ibid., p. 72.

13. Huber, *Heer und Staat*, pp. 91–92.

14. Christopher Duffy, *The Army of Maria Theresa* (London: Davis & Charles, 1977), pp. 47–62.

15. Samuel F. Scott, *The Response of the Royal Army to the French Revolution* (Oxford: Oxford University Press, 1978), pp. 18–19. See also Gerhard Ritter, *Frederick the Great*, trans. and ed. Peter Paret (Berkeley: University of California Press, 1974).

16. Rosinski, *The German Army*, pp. 36–37.

17. Wilkinson, *The French Army*, p. 86.

18. Emile G. Leonard, *L'Armée et ses problemes au XVIIIe siècle* (Paris: Librairie Plon, 1958), p. 287.

19. Huber, *Heer und Staat*, pp. 94–98.

20. Max Jaehns, *Geschichte der Kriegswissenschaften vornehmlich in Deutschland*, vol. 3 (Munich: Oldenburg, 1891), p. 220.

21. Hans Delbrueck, *Geschichte der Kriegkunst im Rahmen der politischen Geschichte*, vol. 4 (Berlin: Georg Stilke, 1920), p. 452.

22. Leonard, *L'Armée et ses problemes*, pp. 102, 204; J. F. C. Fuller, *British Light Infantry in the Eighteenth Century* (London: Hutchinson, 1925), p. 77.

23. Maruice Saxe, *Reveries on the Art of War*, ed. and trans. Thomas R. Phillips (1732; Harrisburg: Military Service Publishing, 1944), p. 32.

24. Corvisier, *Armies and Societies*, p. 113 (table).

25. See the detailed treatment in Martin van Creveld, *Supplying War* (Cambridge: Cambridge University Press, 1977), pp. 24–39.

26. Saxe, *Reveries*, p. 86.

27. Leonard, *L'Armée et ses problemes*, p. 135.

28. See Jean Colin, *L'Infanterie au XVIIIe siècle: la tactique* (Paris: Berger-Levrault, 1907).

29. On this topic see Jean Colin, *L'Education militaire de Napoleon* (Paris: Chapelot, 1901), pp. 4–82.

30. Ibid., p. 72.

31. See Tom Wintringham, *The Story of Weapons and Tactics* (Boston: Houghton Mifflin, 1943).

32. Frederick the Great, *Oeuvres*, 28:5, 29:57–65; Fuller, *British Light Infantry*, p. 62; Jaehns, *Geschichte der Kriegswissenschaften*, pp. 2234–2236.

33. Rosinski, *The German Army*, p. 38.

34. Alexis de Tocqueville, *Democracy in America*, trans. George Lawrence (New York: Anchor, 1969), 2:658–659.

35. Hoffman Nickerson, *The Armed Horde, 1793–1939* (New York: G. P. Putnam's Sons, 1940), p. 67.

36. J. L. Talmon, *The Origins of Totalitarian Democracy* (New York: Praeger, 1960), pp. 95–96, 232–247.

37. "Die Invasion war gescheitert. Sie ist abgewehrt worden nicht mit den Mitteln der Revolution, nicht mit einem bewaffneten Volkaufgebot, sondern wesentlich mit den Resten des alten koeniglichen Kriegstaats, namentlich mit den sachlichen Mitteln der Festungen und der Artillerie." Delbrueck, *Geschichte*, 4:456. Leonard, *L'Armée et ses problemes*, pp. 350–351 points out that the officer corps of the Revolutionary armies resembled that of the royal navy in length of service, education, and social background. See also Colin, *L'Education militaire de Napoleon*, pp. 37–39.

38. Delbrueck, *Geschichte*, 4:462. See his general discussion, pp. 461–473. Also, see Charles Oman, *Studies in the Napoleonic Wars* (London: Methuen, 1929), p. 89.

39. Oman, *Studies in the Napoleonic Wars*, pp. 86–88; Ramsay W. Phipps, *The Armies of the First French Republic*, 5 vols. (Oxford: Oxford University Press, 1926–1929), 1:218–244; Delbrueck, *Geschichte*, 4:459.

40. See R. R. Palmer, *Twelve Who Ruled* (Princeton: Princeton University Press, 1970), pp. 57, 180, 335–340; Nickerson, *Armed Horde*, p. 109.

41. Delbrueck, *Geschichte*, 4:481–484; Vagts, *Militarism*, pp. 126–127; Nickerson, *Armed Horde*, pp. 108–109.

42. Gerhard Ritter, *The Sword and the Scepter*, trans. Heinz Worden, 4 vols. (Coral Gables: University of Miami Press, 1969), 1:48. See also Walter Goerlitz, *History of the German General Staff, 1657–1945*, trans. Brian Battershaw (New York: Praeger, 1953), p. 34; Huber, *Heer und Staat*, pp. 120, 124; Delbrueck, *Geschichte*, 4:46.

43. William O. Shanahan, *Prussian Military Reforms, 1786–1813* (New York: Columbia University Press, 1945), pp. 117–122; Ritter, *Sword and Scepter*, 1:72–74.

44. Goerlitz, *German General Staff*, p. 18; Shanahan, *Prussian Military Reforms*, pp. 107, 133–135, 179–182.

45. Ritter, *Sword and Scepter*, 1:76, 275. See also Curt Jany, *Geschichte der Preussischen Armee*, vol. 4 (1928–1933; rpt. Osnabrueck: Biblio Verlag, 1967), pp. 1–114; Shanahan, *Prussian Military Reforms*, p. 16.

46. On the British military system in the eighteenth century see Fortescue, *History of the British Army*, 4:83–84, 217–218, 639–640, 884; 5:198–222; 6:180–183. See also Michael Glover, *Wellington's Army in the Peninsula* (New York: Hippocrane Books, 1977), p. 30.

47. Glover, *Wellington's Army*, pp. 24, 115.

48. Ibid., p. 69.

49. Michael Howard, *Studies in War and Peace* (New York: Viking Press, 1971), pp. 51–56.

50. David G. Chandler, *The Campaigns of Napoleon* (New York: Macmillan, 1966), p. 348. An excellent summary of Wellington's tactics can be found in Oman, *Studies in the Napoleonic Wars*, p. 99. John Keegan's chapter on Waterloo in *The Face of Battle* (New York: Viking, 1976) analyzes in depth the psychological mechanisms at work.

51. For accounts of Moore's background and achievements, see Fortescue, *History of the British Army*, vol. 3; Fuller, *British Light Infantry*; Beatrice Brownrigg, *The Life and Letters of Sir John Moore* (New York: D. Appleton, 1923); J. F. Maurice, ed., *The Diary of Sir John Moore* (London: Edward Arnold, 1904); J. F. C. Fuller, *Sir John Moore's System of Training* (London: Hutchinson, 1925); Carola Oman, *Sir John Moore* (London: Hodder and Stoughton, 1953). For a splendid fictionalized account of the results of Moore's training, see C. S. Forester, *Rifleman Dodd* (Boston: Little, Brown, 1933).

52. Brownrigg, *Life and Letters*, p. 142; Fuller, *Sir John Moore's System of Training*, pp. 118–161.

53. Maurice, ed., *Diary of Sir John Moore*, 2:82; see also Fuller, *Sir John Moore's System of Training*, pp. 85–94.

54. From Roger Parkinson, *Moore of Corunna* (London: Hart-Davis MacGibbon, 1976), pp. 126–127.

55. See the summary of the Soult Law of 1832 in Douglas Porch, *Army and Revolution: France, 1815–1848* (London: Routledge & Kegan Paul, 1974), pp. 61–78.

56. H. d'Ideville, *Le Maréchal Bugeaud d'après sa correspondance intime et des documents inédits*, 3 vols. (Paris: Firmin Didot, 1882), 2:241.

57. Ibid., p. 216. See also p. 217.

58. Ardant du Picq, *Etudes sur le combat*, 8th ed. (Paris: Librairie Chapelot, 1914), pp. 113, 152, 358. For background and evaluations of his work see J. F. C. Fuller, *War and Western Civilization, 1832–1932* (London: Dicksworth, 1932), pp. 79–91, 103–107, 154–157, 185; Stefan T. Possony and Etienne Mantoux, "Du Picq and Foch: The French School," in Earle, ed., *Makers of Modern Strategy*, pp. 206–233.

59. Du Picq, *Etudes*, pp. 132–135.

60. Ibid., pp. 258–265.

61. See Michael Howard, *The Franco-Prussian War* (New York: Metheun, 1961), pp. 18–39; Thoumas, *Les Transformations de l'Armée francaise*, 2 vols. (Paris: Berger Levrault, 1887), 1:134. The Austrians adopted conscription in 1868, the French in 1872, the Japanese in 1873, the Russians in 1874, and the Italians in 1875.

62. Colmar von der Goltz, *The Nation in Arms*, trans. Philip A. Ashworth (London: W. H. Allen, 1887), pp. 17, 18.

3. Systems of Military Service and Total War

1. Jacques van Doorn, *The Soldier and Social Change* (London: Sage, 1975), p. 21; see also pp. 19, 54–56. Even Michael Howard, in *War and European History* (Oxford: Oxford University Press, 1976), pp. 94–135, distinguishes between "The Wars of the Nations" and "The Wars of the Technologists"—although he points out that both wars were fought by masses of conscripts.

2. J. F. C. Fuller, *The Dragon's Teeth* (London: Constable, 1932), p. 212. See also his *The Reformation of War* (London: Hutchinson, 1923); and *Armored Warfare: Lectures on F. S. R. III* (Harrisburg: Military Service Publishing, 1943), a widely reprinted text that influenced Guderian and other German panzer generals.

3. Fuller, *Armored Warfare*, p. 61.

4. J. F. C. Fuller, *Machine Warfare* (London: Hutchinson, 1942), p. 8.

5. Charles Moran, *The Anatomy of Courage* (Boston: Houghton Mifflin, 1967), pp. 164–166.

6. Charles de Gaulle, *Vers l'armée de métier* (Paris: Berger-Levrault, 1934), p. 152.

7. Ibid., p. 39; also pp. 40–42, 50–53; Charles de Gaulle, *The Edge of the Sword*, trans. Gerard Hopkins (1932; London: Faber & Faber, 1960), pp. 48, 65.

8. De Gaulle, *Armée de métier*, p. 44.

9. Hans von Seeckt, *Gedanken eines Soldaten* (Leipzig: K. F. Koehler, 1935), pp. 55–60, 79. The two crucial essays in this volume are "Moderne Heere" (1928) and "Grundsaetze moderner Landesverteidigung" (1930). See also his *Die Reichswehr* (Leipzig: R. Kittler, 1933).

10. Seeckt, *Gedanken*, p. 75.

11. J. R. M. Butler, *Grand Strategy*, vol. 2, *September 1939–June 1941* (London: HMSO, 1957), pp. 38–40; Gavin Long, *The Six Years War* (Canberra: Australia War Memorial, 1973), p. 26. The Israeli Army also uses civilian skills and specialized training to make the most of its reservists: see Edward Luttwak and Dan Horowitz, *The Israeli Army* (New York: Harper & Row, 1975), p. 190. Also see Harold Wool, *The Military Specialist* (Baltimore: Johns Hopkins University Press, 1968), pp. 14–25; Marvin A. Kreidberg and Henry G. Merton, *History of Military Mobilization in the U.S. Army* (Washington, D.C.: Department of the Army, 1955), pp. 379, 622–625.

12. John McAuley Palmer, *America in Arms* (New Haven: Yale University Press, 1941), p. 203.

13. Eli Ginzberg et al., *The Lost Divisions* (New York: Columbia University Press, 1959), p. 54; also pp. 16–29, 55–57.

14. James Digby, "New Weapons Technology and Its Impact on Intervention," in Ellen P. Stern, ed., *The Limits of Military Intervention* (London: Sage, 1977), p. 126.

15. In addition to Doorn, see Martin Binkin and Irene Kyriakopoulos, *Youth or Experience: Manning the Modern Military* (Washington, D.C.: Brookings, 1979), pp.

15–24; Wool, *Military Specialist*, pp. 16–17. In fact, when Binkin's and Wool's figures are combined, it would seem that there was no decline in the percentage of combat arms soldiers between the two World Wars.

16. Kent Roberts Greenfield, *U.S. Army in World War II: The Organization of Ground Combat Troops* (Washington, D.C.: Department of the Army, 1947), pp. 190–193; S. L. A. Marshall, *Men against Fire* (New York: William Morrow, 1947), pp. 15–18; Samuel A. Stouffer et al., *The American Soldier*, vol. 1, *Adjustment during Army Life* (Princeton: Princeton University Press, 1949), pp. 293–295.

17. See Frederick Martin Stern, *The Citizen Army* (New York: St. Martin's, 1957), pp. 17–18, 32–52. This book is a valuable, if overly passionate, argument for the militia system.

18. Samuel P. Huntington, *The Soldier and the State: The Theory and Politics of Civil-Military Relations* (Cambridge: Harvard University Press, 1957), p. 37: "The shift in the officer corps from amateurism to professionalism was virtually always associated with the shift from career soldiers to citizen soldiers." For the social consequences of this transformation, which included the isolation of the professional officer corps, see ibid., pp. 19–97.

19. See the excellent discussion in Erwin Haeckel, "Military Manpower and Political Purpose," Adelphi Paper no. 72 (London: International Institute for Strategic Studies, 1970), esp. p. 12.

20. See Viktor Suvorov (pseud.), *Inside the Soviet Army* (New York: Macmillan, 1982), pp. 215–217, 224–231, for a more vivid account than one usually finds in the standard texts. On the experience of the 65th Division see Robert R. Palmer et al., *The U.S. Army in World War II: The Procurement and Training of Ground Combat Troops* (Washington, D.C.: Department of the Army, 1948), pp. 482–488.

21. Suvorov, *Inside the Soviet Army*, pp. 221–223, 234–238. On the German Army see Martin van Creveld, "Fighting Power: German Military Performance, 1914–1945" (Washington, D.C.: C & L Associates, 1980), pp. 137–143.

22. See, for example, John McAuley Palmer, *Statesmanship or War* (New York: Doubleday, 1972).

23. Quoted in Hans Rudolf Kurz, *Operationsplanung Schweiz* (Thun: Ott, 1974), p. 22.

24. Adam Roberts, *Nation in Arms* (New York: Praeger, 1976), p. 51; Urs Schwarz, *The Eye of the Hurricane* (Boulder: Westview, 1980), pp. 3, 18–24. Alfred Ernst, *Die Konzeption der schweizerischen Landesverteidigung 1815 bis 1966* (Frauenfeld: Huber, 1971), pp. 138–139, 142.

25. Roberts, *Nation in Arms*, p. 107. This and the following discussion are derived from Kurz's thorough study, *Operationsplanung Schweiz*, pp. 6, 17–19, 28–29. See also General Halder's request for invasion plans reproduced in Edgar Bonjour, *Geschichte der schweizerischen Neutralitaet*, vol. 3 (Basel: Helbing & Lichtenhahn, 1974), pp. 43–44.

26. Kurz, *Operationsplanung Schweiz*, p. 66.

27. This and other figures from the current Swiss army come from the International Institute for Strategic Studies, *Military Balance, 1980–1981*, p. 38. There is valuable background in Robert C. Hasenbohler, "The Swiss Militia," in Louis Zurcher and Gwyn Harries Jenkins, eds., *Supplementary Military Forces* (London: Sage, 1978), pp. 239–258.

28. P. Beurer et al., *Sicherheitspolitik und Armee* (Frauenfeld: Huber, 1976), p. 165.

29. See the description in Karl Brunner, *Die Landesverteidigung der Schweiz* (Frauenfeld: Huber, 1966), pp. 282–337.

30. Roberts, *Nation in Arms*, pp. 52–53.

31. See the discussion in Ernst, *Konzeption*, pp. 351–375.

32. Ibid., p. 407.

33. Beuer et al., *Sicherheitspolitik*, p. 112.

34. Haeckel, "Military Manpower," p. 23.

35. See Roberts, *Nation in Arms*, pp. 97–273.

36. Walter Hubatsch, *Weseruebung* (Berlin: Musterschmidt, 1960), p. 129. See also Telford Taylor, *The March of Conquest* (New York: Simon & Schuster, 1958), pp. 82–154. T. K. Derry, *The Campaign in Norway* (London: HMSO, 1952), p. 100.

37. See Anthony F. Upton, *Finland, 1939–1940* (London: Davis Poynter, 1974), esp. pp. 51–56; Carl Gustaf Mannerheim, *Memoirs*, trans. Eric Lewenhaupt (New York: E. P. Dutton, 1954), pp. 265–273, 324–373.

38. German reports from IV Corps, Bock's 6th Army, quoted in L. F. Ellis, *The War in France and Flanders, 1939–1940* (London: HMSO, 1953), p. 326; also see pp. 19–21, 249–293. See also Norman H. Gibbs, *Grand Strategy*, vol. 1, *Rearmament Policy* (London: HMSO, 1976), pp. 443–477, 503–521, 525–527.

39. Edward A. Shils and Morris Janowitz, "Cohesion and Disintegration in the Wehrmacht in World War II," *Public Opinion Quarterly* 12 (Summer 1948): 285, 287.

40. John Dickinson, *The Building of an Army* (New York: Century, 1922), p. 335.

41. John Terraine, *To Win a War: 1918, the Year of Victory* (London: Sidgwick & Jackson, 1978), p. 85; also see pp. 85–87, 104, 129, 186–187. See also A. J. Smithers, *Sir John Monash* (London: Leo Cooper, 1973); and Malcom Falkins, "General Sir John Monash," in Michael Carver, ed., *The War Lords* (Boston: Little, Brown, 1976), pp. 134–143.

42. See Terraine, *To Win a War*, p. 86; Luttwak and Horowitz, *Israeli Army*, pp. 203–204. The Australians were regarded by friend and foe as some of the best soldiers on either side in both World Wars. See also John McAuley Palmer, *America in Arms* (New Haven: Yale University Press, 1941), p. 49.

43. See John H. Faris, "The Impact of Basic Combat Training," in Nancy L. Goldman and David R. Segal, eds., *The Social Psychology of Military Service* (London: Sage, 1976), pp. 13–26.

44. Worst of all, incompetent Guard officers were much more difficult to purge than their Regular counterparts. See Forrest C. Pogue, *George C. Marshall: Ordeal and Hope, 1939–1942* (New York: Viking, 1965), pp. 98–101.

45. Defense Manpower Commission, *Defense Manpower Commission Staff Studies and Supporting Papers*, vol. 2 (Washington, D.C.: Government Printing Office, 1976), pp. E13–E15, E47. All National Guard units, however, are supposed to be ready for service if given thirteen weeks of refresher training.

46. Franz von Gaertner, *Die Reichswehr in der Weimarer Republik* (Darmstadt: Fundus, 1969), pp. 87–89.

47. These options are described exceedingly well in Walter Bernhardt, *Die deutsche Aufruestung, 1934–1939* (Frankfurt am Main: Bernard & Graefe, 1969), pp. 60–69.

48. Ibid., pp. 125–129. Robert M. Kennedy, "The German Campaign in Poland (1939)," Department of the Army Pamphlet No. 20-255 (Washington, D.C.: Government Printing Office, 1956), p. 25; also pp. 18–24.

49. See B. H. Liddell Hart, *The German Generals Talk* (1948; New York: Morrow, 1979), p. 24 and (generally) pp. 23–27; also Shils and Janowitz, "Cohesion and Disintegration," pp. 297–299, and Fuller, *Machine Warfare*, pp. 55–56.

50. These and other figures in this paragraph are taken from Kreidberg and Merton, *Military Mobilization*. Mark Skinner Watson, *U.S. Army in World War II: Chief of Staff: Prewar Plans and Preparation* (Washington, D.C.: Department of the

Army, 1950), pp. 148–49, 204. A convenient summary can be found in Kent R. Greenfield, *The Historian and the Army* (New York: Kennikat, 1954), pp. 61–71. Pogue, *Marshall: Ordeal and Hope*, p. 159. See also Dickinson, *Building of an Army*, p. 125; Watson, *Chief of Staff*, pp. 16–26; Forrest C. Pogue, *George C. Marshall: Education of a General, 1880–1939* (New York: Viking Press, 1963), pp. 204–214; Palmer et al., *Procurement*, pp. 433–434.

51. Stouffer et al., *The American Soldier*, 1:269.

52. Palmer et al., *Procurement*, p. 467. On officer recruitment see Watson, *Chief of Staff*, pp. 209, 226, 263; Palmer et al., *Procurement*, pp. 92, 106; Omar Bradley, *A Soldier's Story* (New York: Henry Holt, 1955), p. 33.

53. Greenfield et al., *Organization*, p. 39. Compare General Bradley's description of the 1st Division and the 28th Division (National Guard): *A Soldier's Story*, pp. 14–15, 154.

54. Watson, *Chief of Staff*, p. 212; also pp. 94–96.

55. Pogue, *Marshall: Ordeal and Hope*, pp. 91–104, esp. p. 96; William J. Slim, *Defeat into Victory* (London: Cassell, 1956), p. 23.

56. Numbers are taken from C. P. Stacey, *Six Years of War* (Ottawa: Ministry of National Defence, 1955), p. 34; G. McClymont, *Official History of New Zealand in the Second World War, 1939–1945*, vol. 1, *To Greece* (Wellington: Department of Internal Affairs, 1959), p. 2; Gavin Long, *Australia in the War of 1939–1945*, vol. 1, *To Benghazi* (Canberra: Australian War Memorial, 1952), p. 14. Statistics in the following paragraphs are taken from these official histories. See also C. P. Stacey, *Arms, Men, and Governments: The War Policies of Canada, 1939–1945* (Ottawa: Department of National Defence, 1970), p. 48.

57. McClymont, *To Greece*, p. 3; Long, *Six Years*, p. 477; Stacey, *Six Years*, p. 51.

58. Stacey, *Six Years*, p. 48.

59. Enoch H. Crowder, *The Spirit of Selective Service* (New York: Century, 1920), pp. 60, 156. See also H. M. D. Parker, *Manpower: A Study of War-Time Policy and Administration* (London: HMSO, 1957), p. 141; Byron Fairchild and Jonathan Grossman, *U.S. Army in World War II: The Army and Industrial Manpower* (Washington, D.C.: Department of the Army, 1959), pp. 16, 219; Stacey, *Arms, Men, and Governments*, p. 403; Kreidberg and Merton, *Military Mobilization*, p. 262; Dickinson, *Building of an Army*, p. 129.

60. Quoted in Kreidberg and Merton, *Military Mobilization*, p. 253.

61. Henry L. Stimson and McGeorge Bundy, *On Active Service in Peace and War* (New York: Harper & Row, 1947), p. 484. See also Seeckt, *Die Reichswehr*, p. 38; Fuller, *The Reformation of War*, p. 248; Fairchild and Grossman, *Army and Industrial Manpower*, pp. 198–199, 219–244.

62. Alan Bullock, *Hitler: A Study in Tyranny*, rev. ed. (New York: Harper & Row, 1962), pp. 332–333. See Joachim Fest, *Hitler*, trans. Clara Winston (New York: Random House, 1975), pp. 491–493; Bernhardt, *Die deutsche Aufruestung*, pp. 34–39, 69–74; Kennedy, "The German Campaign in Poland," pp. 18–23.

63. Stacey, *Arms, Men, and Governments*, p. 33. On Britain see the extended discussion in Peter Dennis, *Decision by Default: Peacetime Conscription and British Defense, 1919–1939* (Durham: Duke University Press, 1972), pp. 206–225. On the United States see Stimson and Bundy, *On Active Service in Peace and War*, pp. 345–348; Watson, *Chief of Staff*, pp. 186–198; Pogue, *Marshall: Ordeal and Hope*, p. 57.

64. McClymont, *To Greece*, p. 45. See the Australian account in Long, *To Benghazi*, p. 88.

65. See Palmer, *Statesmanship or War?* and *Washington, Lincoln, Wilson: Three War*

Statesmen (New York: Doubleday, 1930), pp. 3–135, 263–281, 375–401. Short summaries can be found in Emory Upton, *The Military Policy of the United States* (Washington, D.C.: Government Printing Office, 1904), pp. vii–xv; Palmer, *America in Arms*, pp. 10–62, 108–118.

66. See Luttwak and Horowitz, *The Israeli Army*, pp. 76–79, 156, 180; Gunther E. Rothenburg, *The Anatomy of the Israeli Army* (London: B. T. Batsford, 1979), pp. 82–84. In 1967 a division commander led one of three division-sized task forces in the Sinai; in 1973 one of the top generals on the Golan Heights was also a reservist.

4. *Systems of Military Service and Small Wars*

1. The memorandum is reprinted in John K. Dunlop, *The Development of the British Army, 1899–1914* (London: Methuen, 1938), p. 307. This book and Paul Kluke, *Heeresaufbau und Heerespolitik Englands von Burenkrieg bis zum Weltkrieg* (Munich: Oldenbourg, 1932) are the standard works on the period.

2. A succinct summary of late Victorian military reform can be found in Correlli Barnett, *Britain and Her Army, 1509–1970* (Harmondsworth: Penguin, 1970), pp. 295–312.

3. Dunlop, *Development*, p. 27. A summary of these developments can be found in Jay Luvaas, *The Education of an Army: British Military Thought, 1815–1940* (Chicago: University of Chicago Press, 1964), pp. 98–101.

4. Brian Bond, ed., *Victorian Military Campaigns* (London: Hutchinson, 1967), p. 18; for a general discussion, see pp. 17–23. For the opposite view see Barnett, *Britain and Her Army*, p. 324.

5. C. E. Callwell, *Small Wars* (London: HMSO, 1906), p. 21.

6. Ibid., p. 320; also pp. 29–33.

7. Ibid., p. 33.

8. Ibid., pp. 57, 71, 79, 80, 97, 151.

9. Ian Hamilton, *Listening for the Drums* (London: Faber & Faber, 1944), pp. 210–211. Callwell, *Small Wars*, p. 388; see also ibid., pp. 389–398.

10. Callwell, *Small Wars*, pp. 212, 219, 225, 287–288. For a vivid fictional account of the Afghanistan debacle see George MacDonald Fraser's fanciful *Flashman* (London: Barrie & Jenkins, 1969).

11. Callwell, *Small Wars*, pp. 109, 122–123.

12. Ian Hamilton, *Compulsory Service* (London: John Murray, 1910), p. 57.

13. John Keegan, "Regimental Ideology," in Geoffrey Best and Andrew Wheatcroft, eds., *War, Economy, and the Military Mind* (London: Croom Helm, 1976), p. 11. See also G. F. R. Henderson, *The Science of War* (London: Neill Malcom, 1905), pp. 379, 385, 392–393 on the importance of the voluntary principle and the regimental tradition. John Bayne's *Morale: A Study of Men and Courage* (London: Cassell, 1967) is an excellent study of the regimental system at work in the years just before World War I.

14. J. F. C. Fuller, *The Conduct of War, 1789–1961* (New Brunswick: Rutgers University Press, 1961), p. 140. See also Barnett, *Britain and Her Army*, pp. 341–347; Michael Howard, *Studies in War and Peace* (New York: Viking, 1971), pp. 86–88; Ampthill, "The Position of the Militia as the Constitutional Force of Great Britain," *Journal of the Royal United Services Institute* 69:473 (February 1924): 9.

15. For the conventional view of the army of the Spanish-American War period see Walter Millis, *The Martial Spirit* (New York: Viking Press, 1965). A very per-

suasive revisionist account is Graham A. Cosmas, *An Army for the Empire* (Columbia: University of Missouri Press, 1971) esp. pp. 11, 47–51. See also John M. Gates, *Schoolbooks and Krags* (Westport: Greenwood, 1973), pp. 54–78. Gates's book is the only thorough account of the Philippine War.

16. William Addleman Ganoe, *The History of the United States Army* (New York: D. Appleton, 1932), p. 397; Elihu Root, *The Military and Colonial Policy of the United States*, ed. Robert Bacon (Cambridge: Harvard University Press, 1916), pp. 8–9, 58.

17. Department of War, *Annual Report of the War Department, 1900* (Washington, D.C.: Government Printing Office, 1901), vol. 1, pt. 3, p. 21. Of those serving during the period of heaviest fighting (June 1898–June 1901), some 62,000 were regulars and some 50,000 United States Volunteers. Casualty figures are taken from Richard E. Welch, *Response to Imperialism* (Chapel Hill: University of North Carolina Press, 1979), pp. xiii, 42; population figures from Root, *Military and Colonial Policy*, p. 146, and U.S. Census data (1970); troop deployments and additional casualty data from R. E. Dupuy and William H. Baumer, *The Little Wars of the United States* (New York: Hawthorn Books, 1968), pp. 92–92, and the *Annual Report* of the War Department for the years 1898–1903. The figures cited are conservative, i.e., if anything they minimize the relative size of the war.

18. Welch, *Response to Imperialism*, p. 57; Gates, *Schoolbooks and Krags*, p. 7. On the parallel administration instituted by the guerrillas see Department of War, *Annual Report, 1900*, vol. 1, pt. 5, esp. p. 61. It is interesting to compare Filipino tactics with modern anticolonial warfare such as that in Indochina and Algeria. See Peter Paret, *French Revolutionary Warfare from Indochina to Algeria* (London: Pall Mall, 1964), pp. 9–20. See a copy of a captured guerrilla pamphlet in Department of War, *Annual Report, 1900*, vol. 1, pt. 5, pp. 72–76.

19. Frederick Funston, *Memories of Two Wars* (New York: Charles Scribner's Sons, 1914), p. 314. Funston was the leader of the audacious operation that resulted in Aguinaldo's capture.

20. Ganoe, *History*, pp. 410, 416; Gates, *Schoolbooks and Krags*, p. 111; Welch, *Response to Imperialism*, p. 30.

21. Gates, *Schoolbooks and Krags*, p. 143. For general discussion, see ibid., pp. 130–48.

22. Ibid., p. 212; also pp. 205–211, 260. See Dupuy, *Little Wars*, p. 85. In the Batangas region, for example, 10,000 Americans captured 1,000 insurgents and induced 3,700 more to surrender.

23. Welch, *Response to Imperialism*, pp. 55–63, 87, 118–132. Also see Samuel Eliot Morison, Frederick Merk, and Frank Freidel, *Dissent in Three American Wars* (Cambridge: Harvard University Press, 1970), pp. 65–96; Glenn Elliott Shealey, "American Domestic Reaction to the Philippine Insurrection, 1899–1900" (senior honors thesis, Williams College, 1969). See Gates, *Schoolbooks and Krags*, pp. 82–84, 171–175, on torture. The American military command did, contrary to popular belief, court-martial soldiers on such charges, although undoubtedly many escaped justice.

24. See Allan R. Millett, *Semper Fidelis: The History of the United States Marine Corps* (New York: Macmillan, 1980), pp. 147–266; Russell F. Weigley, *History of the United States Army* (New York: Macmillan, 1967), pp. 295–354.

25. Dunlop, *Development*, p. 18.

26. See the summary in Denis Hayes, *Conscription Conflict* (London: Sheppard, 1949), p. 31. The best summaries are in Kluke, *Heeresaufbau*, pp. 25–28, 45–53; and Barnett, *Britain and Her Army*, pp. 355–370. On the views of the British General

Staff, see Kluke, *Heeresaufbau*, pp. 187–189. The chief of the general staff from 1904 to 1906, Neville Lyttelton, opposed Arnold-Foster's scheme for creating a short-service army for home defense and large expeditions and another for colonial defense: see Neville Lyttelton, *Eighty Years* (London: Hodder & Stoughton, 1928), pp. 272–272. See also J. E. Tyler, *The British Army and the Continent, 1904–1914* (London: Edward Arnold, 1938), p. 19.

27. Richard Burdon Haldane, *Autobiography* (New York: Doubleday, 1929), pp. 196, 198. The best account of Haldane's tenure as secretary of state for war is Edward M. Spiers, *Haldane: An Army Reformer* (Edinburgh: University of Edinburgh Press, 1980).

28. Haldane, *Autobiography*, p. 205. Most scholars agree with Haldane's assertion that he did intend the Territorials' role to go well beyond Home Defense. See Howard, *Studies*, p. 96; Kluke, *Heeresaufbau*, p. 104.

29. Richard Burdon Haldane, *Before the War* (London: Cassell, 1920), p. 174. See also Barnett, *Britain and Her Army*, p. 366; William Robertson, *Soldiers and Statesmen, 1914–1918* (New York: Charles Scribner's Sons, 1926), 1:35; Paul M. Kennedy, *The Rise and Fall of British Naval Mastery* (London: Allen Lane, 1976), p. 193; Spiers, *Haldane*, pp. 172–173.

30. Haldane, *Before the War*, p. 171.

31. See C. E. Callwell, *Field Marshal Sir Henry Wilson: His Life and Diaries* (New York: Charles Scribner's Sons, 1927), 1:99, 118–120, 134; Howard, *Studies*, p. 97.

32. For an account of the National Service League see Hayes, *Conscription Conflict*, pp. 36–135. See also C. G. Coulton, *The Case for Compulsory Military Service* (London: Macmillan, 1917), p. 267; Lord Roberts's preface to a study of the Swiss military system, C. Delme Radcliffe, *A Territorial Army in Being* (London: John Murray, 1908), pp. viii–x; Kluke, *Heeresaufbau*, pp. 126–132; Hayes, *Conscription Conflict*, p. 44; Frederick Sleigh Roberts, ed., *Facts and Fallacies* (London: John Murray, 1911), pp. 31–34. The second and third chapters of Roberts's book were written by Leo Amery and J. A. Crumb (a professor of modern history at Queen's College, University of London). Spiers, *Haldane*, p. 178. A fairly typical proposal can be found in Spenser Wilkinson, *Britain at Bay* London: Constable, 1909), pp. 153–165. Another such proposal is sketched in Roberts, *Facts and Fallacies*, pp. 158–160.

33. See Hamilton, *Compulsory Service*, pp. 101–113. Haldane's introduction (pp. 9–42) plays down the use of the Territorials in a Continental war (see esp. pp. 35–36). Compare Coulton, *Compulsory Military Service*, p. 215.

34. Charles à Court Repington, *Imperial Strategy* (London: John Murray, 1906), p. 17. See, for example, Frederick Sleigh Roberts, *Lord Roberts' Message to the Nation* (London: John Murray, 1912), p. 28.

35. Wilkinson, *Britain at Bay*, p. 12; Roberts, *Facts and Fallacies*, pp. 64, 67, 151–152; Haldane in Hamilton, *Compulsory Service*, pp. 11, 80.

36. Repington, *Imperial Defense*, p. 35. See also Wilkinson, *Britain at Bay*, p. 144.

37. Haldane, *Autobiography*, pp. 200, 208–209, 297–298. For German evaluations see Kluke, *Heeresaufbau*, p. 113; "A German General Staff Appreciation of the British Army in 1912," *Journal of the Royal United Services Institute* 65:459 (August 1920): 605–607. The Germans at Mons thought the BEF heavily equipped with machine guns. In fact, the BEF had the same number as did the Germans (two per battalion); it was the excellence of their riflery, not weapons superiority, that made up for the scantiness of the BEF's numbers. Spiers's evaluation can be found in *Haldane*, pp. 81–82. See also Kluke, *Heeresaufbau*, pp. 120–121; John French, *1914* (Boston: Houghton Mifflin, 1919), pp. 304–306; Horace Smith-Dorrien, *Memories of Forty-Eight Years'*

Service (London: John Murray, 1925), pp. 368–369, 374–375; Winston S. Churchill, *The World Crisis, 1911–1914* (New York: Charles Scribner's Sons, 1924), pp. 12, 159, 253; William Robertson, *From Private to Field Marshal* (Boston: Houghton Mifflin, 1921), pp. 190, 229; Robertson, *Soldiers and Statesmen*, 1:64.

38. James F. Schnabel, *Policy and Direction: The First Year* (Washington, D.C.: U.S. Army, Office of the Chief of Military History, 1972), p. 43; J. Lawton Collins, *War in Peacetime* (Boston: Houghton Mifflin, 1969), p. 67; Matthew B. Ridgway, *The Korean War* (New York: Doubleday, 1967), pp. 34–35.

39. Director of Selective Service, *Selective Service under the 1948 Act Extended, July 9, 1950–June 19, 1951* (Washington, D.C.: Government Printing Office, 1953), p. 32. On manpower issues see Harry S. Truman, *Years of Trial and Hope* (New York: Doubleday, 1956), pp. 338–348, 386, 463. Numbers come from the official history: Roy E. Appleman, *South to Naktong, North to Yalu* (Washington, D.C.: Army, Office of the Chief of Military History, 1961), pp. 197, 264, 381, 606; Walter G. Hermes, *Truce Tent and Fighting Front* (Washington, D.C.: U.S. Army, Office of the Chief of Military History, 1966), p. 58; Collins, *War in Peacetime*, pp. 79–80; Director of Selective Service, *Selective Service under the 1948 Act Extended* (Washington, D.C.: Government Printing Office, 1953), pp. 3–14; in addition see Director of Selective Service, *Selective Service under the 1948 Act* (Washington, D.C.: Government Printing Office, 1951), pp. 1–140 (for the period 24 June 1948 to 9 July 1950); Director of Selective Service, *Annual Report for Fiscal Year 1953* (Washington, D.C.: Government Printing Office, 1954), p. 89, esp. table.

40. Pat Meid and James Yingling, *Operations in West Korea* (Washington, D.C.: Historical Division, Headquarters, U.S. Marine Corps, 1972), pp. 499–502. On the use of recruits see Schnabel, *Policy and Direction*, p. 122; Meid and Yingling, *Operations*, pp. 499–502; Collins, *War in Peacetime*, p. 98.

41. S. L. A. Marshall, *Pork Chop Hill* (New York: William Morrow, 1956), p. 291. See also his comments on pp. 14–20, 59; and Hermes, *Truce Tent*, pp. 186, 334, 349–351. On the importance of small-unit cohesion see S. L. A. Marshall, *Men against Fire* (New York: William Morrow, 1947). On Korea specifically, see James H. Toner, "American Society and the American Way of War: Korea and Beyond," *Parameters* 11:1 (March 1981): 79–91.

42. George C. Gallup, *The Gallup Poll, 1949–1958* (New York: Random House, 1972), pp. 960, 1019; Edward Suchman et al., "Attitudes towards the Korean War," *Public Opinion Quarterly* 17 (Summer 1953): 173–179, 182. For other polling data see Gallup, *Gallup Poll, 1949–1958*, pp. 942, 932, 972, 1034, 1120. A 29 July 1950 poll—*before* Inchon—found that 41 percent expected the war to end in six months or less, and 67 percent expected it to end in a year or less. Ibid., p. 928.

43. See Abraham F. Lowenthal, *The Dominican Intervention* (Cambridge: Harvard University Press, 1972); Jerome N. Slater, "The Dominican Republic, 1961–1966," in Barry M. Blechman and Stephen S. Kaplan, eds., *Force without War* (Washington, D.C.: Brookings Institution, 1978), pp. 289–342.

44. These numbers and dates are taken from Allan R. Millet, ed., *A Short History of the Vietnam War* (Bloomington: Indiana University Press, 1978); Guenter Lewy, *America in Vietnam* (New York: Oxford University Press, 1978); William C. Westmoreland, *A Soldier Reports* (New York: Doubleday, 1976); *The Pentagon Papers: The Defense Department History of the United States Decision-Making in Vietnam*, Senator Gravel edition (Boston: Beacon Press, 1971), vols. 1–4.

45. Michael Charlton and Anthony Moncrieff, *Many Reasons Why* (New York: Hill & Wang, 1978), p. 115. On Johnson's desire to avoid reserve mobilization in order to

keep the conflict under control, see Herbert Y. Schandler, *The Unmaking of a President* (Princeton: Princeton University Press, 1977), pp. 30, 39, 102–103, 229, 293. See also *Pentagon Papers*, 4:483.

46. Westmoreland, *A Soldier Reports*, p. 392.

47. Lewy, *America in Vietnam*, p. 118. For the effects of American manpower policies see Westmoreland, *A Soldier Reports*, p. 392; Director of Selective Service, *Semiannual Report for the period July 1 to December 31, 1971* (Washington, D.C.: Government Printing Office, 1971), p. 52. See also Lawrence M. Baskir and William A. Strauss, *Chance and Circumstance* (New York: Alfred A. Knopf, 1978), pp. 52–56, 149–151; Lewy, *America in Vietnam*, pp. 159–160. See *Armed Forces and Society* 3:3 (May 1977) for a spirited debate about the meaning of the Vietnam experiences of the United States Army.

48. Robert Thompson, *No Exit from Vietnam* (New York: David McKay, 1970), pp. 127, 134–135, 122. See also his *Defeating Communist Insurgency* (New York: Praeger, 1966), pp. 20, 58–62, 105, 127; Lewy, *America in Vietnam*, p. 118; Richard M. Pfeffer, ed., *No More Vietnams?* (New York: Harper & Row, 1968), pp. 163–164. For a fascinating critique of America's strategy in Vietnam see Harry G. Summers, *On Strategy* (Novato, Calif.: Presidio, 1982).

49. See Maynard Parker, "Vietnam: The War That Won't End," *Foreign Affairs* 53:2 (January 1975): 353–361 for an excellent summary of Abram's tactics and strategy. See also Westmoreland, *A Soldier Reports*, pp. 290–291; Lewy, *America in Vietnam*, pp. 98–99; *Pentagon Papers*, 4:528; Baskir and Strauss, *Chance and Circumstance*, p. 122.

50. Baskir and Strauss, *Chance and Circumstance*, pp. 4–5, 9.

51. Anthony Lake, ed., *The Vietnam Legacy* (New York: New York University Press, 1976), p. 123. See also Peter Osnos's similar observations in ibid., pp. 69, 112.

52. Charlton and Moncrieff, *Many Reasons Why*, pp. 162–165. See also Steven Kelman, *Push Comes to Shove* (Boston: Houghton Mifflin, 1970), pp. 117–120.

53. Lake, *Legacy*, pp. 129–130, 136. See also Hazlel Erskine, "The Polls: Is War a Mistake?" *Public Opinion Quarterly* 34 (Spring 1970): 134–150; John E. Mueller, *War, Presidents and Public Opinion* (New York: John Wiley, 1973), pp. 148–152. This is the analysis presented in Allen H. Barton, "The Columbia Crisis: Campus, Vietnam and the Ghetto," *Public Opinion Quarterly* 32 (Fall 1968): 333–351. For proof that the opposition to the war correlated with conscription see John E. Mueller, "Trends in Popular Support for the Wars in Korea and Vietnam," *American Political Science Review* 65:2 (June 1971): 366. See also Lewy, *America in Vietnam*, p. 73; Leslie H. Gelb and Richard K. Betts, *The Irony of Vietnam: The System Worked* (Washington, D.C.: Brookings Institution, 1979), p. 219.

54. George H. Gallup, *Public Opinion, 1972–1977*, p. 990; Roger B. Handberg, "'The Vietnam Analogy': Student Attitudes on War," *Public Opinion Quarterly* 36 (Winter 1972–1973): 613.

55. Henry Stanhope, *The Soldiers: An Anatomy of the British Army* (London: Hamish Hamilton, 1979), pp. 17–19.

56. Ibid., Richard Clutterbuck, *The Long, Long War: Counterinsurgency in Malaya and Vietnam* (New York: Praeger, 1966), p. 146; Edgar O'Ballance, *Malaya: The Communist Insurgent War, 1941–1960* (Hamden: Archon Books, 1966), p. 133. The security forces numbered 300,000: of these only 40,000 were regulars, with only 25,000 British (the other regulars being Gurkhas and other non-British imperial troops).

57. Ridgway, *Korean War*, pp. 88–92; see also his memoirs, *Soldier* (New York: Harper & Brothers, 1956), pp. 204–206.

58. Clutterbuck, *The Long, Long War,* p. 51.

59. See Jac Weller, *Fire and Movement: Bargain Basement Warfare in the Far East* (New York: Thomas Y. Crowell, 1967), esp. pp. 13–95.

60. A point made informally to the author by several former high-ranking British officials.

61. See V. G. Kiernan, *From Conquest to Collapse: European Empires from 1815 to 1960* (New York: Pantheon, 1982).

62. George Armstrong Kelly, *Lost Soldiers: The French Army and Empire in Crisis, 1947–1962* (Cambridge: MIT Press, 1965); Paul-Marie de la Gorce, *The French Army: A Military-Political History,* trans. Kenneth Douglas (New York: Braziller, 1962), p. 376. See also Bernard B. Fall, *Street without Joy* (Harrisburg: Stackpole, 1961).

63. Kelly, *Lost Soldiers,* pp. 33, 52–53.

64. John Talbott, *The War without a Name: France in Algeria, 1954–1962* (New York: Knopf, 1980), p. 205.

65. See Douglas Porch, *The Portuguese Armed Forces and the Revolution* (London: Croom Helm, 1977), pp. 61–72.

66. Alexis de Tocqueville, *Democracy in America,* trans. George Lawrence (New York: Anchor, 1969), p. 657.

67. Lewy, *America in Vietnam,* p. 116; see also Lewis W. Walt, *Strange War, Strange Strategy* (New York: Funk & Wagnall's, 1970), pp. 105–112.

68. See John Stewart Ambler, *Soldiers against the State: The French Army in Politics* (New York: Doubleday, 1968), p. 382; Kelly, *Lost Soldiers.*

69. Adolphe Thiers, *Discours parlementaires,* 16 vol. (Paris: Calmann Levy, 1879–1889), 8:187.

5. *Military Service and Republican Ideology: Civic Obligations and the Citizen-Soldier*

1. Jean Jacques Rousseau, *On the Social Contract,* trans. Judith R. Masters (1762; New York: St. Martin's, 1978), p. 116.

2. Adam Smith, *The Wealth of Nations* (1776; New York: Modern Library, 1937), pp. 63–65.

3. Adam Smith, *Lectures on Jurisprudence* (1766; Oxford: Oxford University Press, 1978), p. 540.

4. Ibid., p. 230.

5. Ibid., p. 543.

6. Smith, *Wealth of Nations,* p. 666.

7. Ibid., p. 658.

8. Smith, *Lectures,* p. 230.

9. Smith, *Wealth of Nations,* p. 667.

10. Edward Gibbon, *Decline and Fall of the Roman Empire,* ed. J. B. Bury (London: Methuen, 1909), pp. 10–11.

11. Samuel P. Huntington, *The Soldier and the State: The Theory and Politics of Civil-Military Relations* (Cambridge: Harvard University Press, 1957), p. 144.

12. Woodrow Wilson, *The Messages and Papers of Woodrow Wilson,* ed. Albert Shaw (New York: Review of Reviews, 1924), 2:826–827 (speech of 8 September 1919 in Sioux Falls, South Dakota).

13. William James, "The Moral Equivalent of War," in *Memories and Studies* (New York: Longmans, Green, 1911), p. 288.

14. This led in the United States to the lowering of the voting age to eighteen, on the basis of the slogan, "If you're old enough to fight you're old enough to vote." See also J. M. Main, ed., *Conscription: The Australian Debate, 1901–1970* (Melbourne: Cassell Australia, 1970), p. 143.

15. Ralph Barton Perry, *The Plattsburg Movement* (New York: E. P. Dutton, 1921), p. 260. He goes on to discuss the civic virtues inculcated by military training.

16. William Blackstone, *Commentaries on the Laws of England* (New York: E. Ducy-kinck, 1827), Book 1, chap. 13.

17. Jack Franklin Leach, *Conscription in the United States: Historical Background* (Rutland, Vt.: Charles E. Tuttle, 1952), p. 26. See also John Remington Graham, *A Constitutional History of the Military Draft* (Minneapolis: Ross & Haines, 1971), pp. 78–80.

18. Blackstone, *Commentaries*, Book 1, chap. 13.

19. Wilson, *Messages and Papers*, 1:78 (speech of 8 December 1914).

20. Heinrich von Treitschke, *Politics*, trans. Blanche Dugdale and Torben de Bille (New York: Macmillan, 1916), 2:402.

21. Ibid., pp. 186–187 (speech in Congress, 31 January 1916).

22. Ibid., p. 130 (speech of 4 November 1915).

23. Quoted in Russell Weigley, *Towards an American Army: Military Thought from Washington to Marshall* (New York: Columbia University Press, 1962), pp. 26–27.

24. Paul Russell Anderson, ed., "Universal Military Training and National Security," *The Annals of the American Academy of Political and Social Science* 241 (September 1945): 16.

25. See Selective Service System, *The Selective Service Act: Its Legislative History, Amendments, Appropriations, Cognates, and Prior Instruments of Security* (Washington, D.C.: Government Printing Office, 1954), 2:1. See also Leach, *Conscription*, p. vii. For a modern attack on Selective Service on the same grounds see Graham, *Constitutional History*.

26. See the opinions reprinted in John Whiteclay Chambers, ed., *Draftees or Volunteers* (New York: Garland, 1975), pp. 281, 285.

27. Ibid., p. 72; J. L. Granatstein and J. M. Hitsman, *Broken Promises: A History of Conscription in Canada* (Toronto: Oxford University Press, 1977), p. 15.

28. The story of the tension between the professionals (particularly Emory Upton) and the advocates of a citizen force (for example, General John McAuley Palmer) is traced in three books: T. Harry Williams, *The History of American Wars from 1745 to 1918* (New York: Knopf, 1981), and Russell Weigley's *History of the United States Army* (New York: Macmillan, 1976) and *Towards an American Army*.

29. Alexander Hamilton, John Jay, and James Madison, *The Federalist* (1787–1788; New York: Modern Library, 1937), p. 176. See numbers 8, 22, and 29. See also John Stuart Mill, *Collected Works*, J. M. Robson, ed. (Toronto: University of Toronto Press, 1972), 17:1796, 1802.

30. See for example, Alexander Hamilton, *Works*, ed. Henry Cabot Lodge (New York: G. P. Putnam's Sons, 1904), 7:556. This is Hamilton's 1799 plan. His plan of 1783 (a memorandum for Washington's famous "Sentiments on a Peace Establishment") is at 6:479–482.

31. Eugen Weber, *Peasants into Frenchmen: The Modernization of Rural France, 1870–1914* (London: Chatto & Windus, 1979), pp. 298–302.

32. See, for example, Theodore Roosevelt, *Fear God and Take Your Own Part* (New York: George H. Doran, 1916).

33. Theodore Zeldin, *France, 1848–1945* (Oxford: Oxford University Press, 1977), 2:905.

34. Treitschke, *Politics*, 2:440.

35. *In Pursuit of Equity: Who Serves When Not All Serve?* Report of the National Advisory Commission on Selective Service (Washington, D.C.: Government Printing Office, 1967), p. 59; Robert S. McNamara, *The Essence of Security* (New York: Harper & Row, 1968), pp. 127–128, 131–138.

36. Quoted in John O'Sullivan and Alan M. Meckler, ed., *The Draft and Its Enemies* (Urbana: University of Illinois Press, 1974), p. 31.

37. Leslie C. Jauncey, *The Story of Conscription in Australia* (London: George Allen & Unwin, 1935), p. 75.

38. For World War I see William L. Ransom, ed., "Military Training: Compulsory or Volunteer," *Proceedings of the Academy of Political Science* 6:4 (July 1916): 47; Wilson, *Messages and Papers*, 1:160. On postwar proposals see *A Program for National Security*, Report of the President's Advisory Commission on Universal Training (Washington, D.C.: Government Printing Office, 1947), pp. 71–76. See also President Truman's speech of 23 October 1945, reprinted in Chambers, *Draftees or Volunteers*, p. 377.

39. O'Sullivan and Meckler, *Draft*, pp. 216, 219.

40. Edward A. Fitzpatrick, *Universal Military Training* (New York: McGraw Hill, 1945), p. 211.

41. See the arguments advanced by Alexander Meiklejohn, President of Amherst College, in Ransom, "Military Training," p. 175.

42. See Reinhard Hoehn, *Die Armee als Erziehungsschule der Nation: Das Ende einer Idee* (Bad Harzburg: Verlag fuer Wissenschaft, Wirtschaft, und Technik, 1963), pp. 441–470, 493–502. For a detailed critique of the army's ability to educate see Anderson, "Universal Military Training," pp. 113–122.

43. Colonel Samuel H. Hays, "A Military View of Selective Service," in Sol Tax, ed., *The Draft: A Handbook of Facts and Alternatives* (Chicago: University of Chicago Press, 1967), p. 17. On Project 100,000 see Anne Hoiberg, "Military Staying Power," in Sam C. Sarkesian, ed., *Combat Effectiveness* (Beverly Hills: Sage, 1980), p. 218.

44. Fitzpatrick, *Universal Military Training*, p. viii.

45. James, *Memories and Studies*, p. 288.

46. Ibid., p. 291.

47. See a copy of a Selective Service memorandum reprinted in Chambers, *Draftees or Volunteers*, pp. 494–495.

6. *Military Service and Republican Ideology: Liberalism and Egalitarianism*

1. Thomas Hobbes, *Leviathan* (1651), chap. 17.
2. John Locke, *Second Treatise of Government* (1690), paragraph 124.
3. Hobbes, *Leviathan*, chap. 21.
4. Ibid.
5. Locke, *Second Treatise*, paragraph 139.
6. Hobbes, *Leviathan*, chap. 21.

7. Michael Walzer, *Obligations: Essays on Disobedience, War and Citizenship* (New York: Simon & Schuster, 1970), p. 89.

8. Ibid., p. 118.

9. See Leslie C. Jauncey, *The Story of Conscription in Australia* (London: George Allen & Unwin, 1935), pp. 215–238. According to Jauncey over two-fifths of the Australian soldiers serving overseas voted against conscription.

10. See the accounts in Richard D. Challenger, *The French Theory of the Nation in Arms, 1866–1939* (New York: Russell & Russell, 1965); and David B. Ralston, *The Army of the Republic: The Place of the Military in the Political Evolution of France, 1871–1914* (Cambridge: MIT Press, 1967).

11. Ralph Barton Perry, *The Free Man and the Soldier: Essays on the Reconciliation of Liberty and Discipline* (New York: Charles Scribner's Sons, 1916), p. 9.

12. Thucydides, *The Peloponnesian War*, trans. Rex Warner (Harmondsworth: Penguin, 1972), p. 146.

13. G. F. R. Henderson, *The Science of War* (London: Neill Malcom, 1905), p. 379. See also ibid., pp. 365–434. Henderson gives considered yet warm praise for American volunteers in *Stonewall Jackson and the American Civil War* (1898; New York: Longmans Green, 1949), p. 13, 25, 36, 421, 468, 603–605, 623. Sherman thought the volunteers of the first part of the Civil War the best. William T. Sherman, *Memoirs* (1875; Bloomington: Indiana University Press, 1957), 1:382.

14. Woodrow Wilson, *The Messages and Papers of Woodrow Wilson*, ed. Albert Shaw (New York: Review of Reviews, 1924), 1:398 (speech of 18 May 1917).

15. Speech of 17 August 1940. In John Whiteclay Chambers, ed., *Draftees or Volunteers* (New York: Garland, 1975), p. 322.

16. Manifesto quoted in Jauncey, *Story*, p. 172.

17. Abraham Lincoln, *The Collected Works of Abraham Lincoln* (New Brunswick: Rutgers University Press, 1953), 6:447.

18. Ibid., p. 445.

19. Ibid., p. 448.

20. Pierre van Paassen, *Days of Our Years* (New York: Dial, 1939), pp. 64–65.

21. See, for example, William L. Ransom, ed., "Military Training: Compulsory or Volunteer," *Proceedings of the Academy of Political Science* 6:4 (July 1916): 148.

22. Edward A. Fitzpatrick, *Universal Military Training* (New York: McGraw Hill, 1945), p. 279.

23. Quoted in Chambers, *Draftees or Volunteers*, p. 227.

24. Quoted in Walter Millis, ed., *American Military Thought* (Indianapolis: Bobbs-Merrill, 1966), p. 12.

25. *A Program For National Security*, Report of The President's Advisory Commission on Universal Training (Washington, D.C.: Government Printing Office, 1947), p. 72.

26. Daniel Webster, *Letters of Daniel Webster*, ed. C. H. van Tyne (New York: McClure, Phillips, 1902), p. 65. This famous speech, a classic liberal denunciation of military service, was written in December 1814, but apparently never delivered.

27. See Harvey A. De Weerd, *President Wilson Fights His War: World War I and the American Intervention* (New York: Macmillan, 1968), p. 213.

28. Quoted in Fitzpatrick, *Universal Military Training*, p. 222.

29. Chambers, *Draftees or Volunteers*, p. 398.

30. Fitzpatrick, *Universal Military Training*, p. 210.

31. Chambers, *Draftees or Volunteers*, p. 398.

32. Lincoln, *Works*, 6:448.

33. Selective Service System, *Backgrounds of Selective Service*, Special Monograph No. 1, "A Historical Review of the Principle of Citizen Compulsion in the Raising of Armies" (Washington, D.C.: Government Printing Office, 1947), 1:181.

34. Theodore Zeldin, *France, 1848–1945* (Oxford: Oxford University Press, 1977), 2:878.

35. Bernard Schnapper, *Le Remplacement Militaire en France* (Paris: SEVPEN, 1968), pp. 57, 64.

36. See Ralston, *Army of the Republic*, pp. 36–39.

37. See especially his speech of 21 October 1848: Adolphe Thiers, *Discours Parlementaires*, 16 vols. (Paris: Calmann Levy, 1879–1889), 8:190–193.

38. Ibid., p. 240.

39. Ibid., p. 173.

40. Ibid., p. 166.

41. Zeldin, *France*, 2:886.

42. Schnapper, *Remplacement*, pp. 64, 201–205.

43. Jack Franklin Leach, *Conscription in the United States: Historical Background* (Rutland, Vt.: Charles E. Tuttle, 1952), p. 177.

44. Alexis de Tocqueville, *Democracy in America*, trans. Henry Reeve (New York: Vintage, 1945), 2:286.

45. Leach, *Conscription*, p. 455.

46. Treitschke said of France's abolition of the one-year volunteer provision that it represented the triumph of equality over culture. Heinrich von Treitschke, *Politics*, trans. Blanche Dugdale and Torben de Bille (New York: Macmillan, 1916), 2:441.

47. Ralph Barton Perry, *The Plattsburg Movement* (New York: E. P. Dutton, 1921), p. 48.

48. In Ransom, "Military Training," p. 155.

49. See, for example, James Fallows, *National Defense* (New York: Random House, 1981), p. 136.

50. Russell F. Weigley, *History of the United States Army* (New York: Macmillan, 1967), p. 168.

51. Perry, *Free Man*, p. 228. See also Seth Cropsey, "Women in Combat?" *Public Interest* 61 (Fall 1980): 58–59; James Webb, "Women Can't Fight," *The Washingtonian* (November 1979).

52. See Walzer, *Obligations*, pp. 121–125.

53. Thomas Jefferson, *The Writings of Thomas Jefferson* (Washington, D.C.: Thomas Jefferson Memorial Association, 1907), 13:261 (letter to Colonel James Monroe, 18 June 1813).

54. Russell Weigley, *Towards an American Army: Military Thought from Washington to Marshall* (New York: Columbia University Press, 1962), p. 234.

55. See John J. McCloy's description of UMT in Paul Russell Anderson, ed., "Universal Military Training and National Security," *The Annals of the American Academy of Political and Social Science* 241 (September 1945): 28. Canada also toyed with UMT. See J. L. Granatstein and J. M. Hitsman, *Broken Promises: A History of Conscription in Canada* (Toronto: Oxford University Press, 1977), pp. 247–248.

56. Jauncey, *Story*, p. 100. See also C. Delme-Radcliffe, *A Territorial Army in Being* (London: John Murray, 1908).

57. *In Pursuit of Equity: Who Serves When Not All Serve?* Report of the National

Advisory Commission on Selective Service (Washington, D.C.: Government Printing Office, 1967), pp. 23, 158.

58. Chambers, *Draftees or Volunteers*, p. 369.

59. *In Pursuit of Equity*, p. 38.

60. Ibid., pp. 28, 39.

61. Curtis W. Tarr, *By the Numbers: Reform of the Selective Service System, 1970–1972* (Washington, D.C.: National Defense University Press, 1981), pp. 45–47.

62. A. A. Calwell, quoted in J. M. Main, ed., *Conscription: The Australian Debate, 1901–1970* (Melbourne: Cassell Australia, 1970), p. 138.

63. Speech of 14 August 1940, quoted in Chambers, *Draftees or Volunteers*, p. 323.

64. "A Citizen Assembly Discusses a Draft," *New York Times*, 21 September 1981, p. 23.

7. American Manpower Policy, 1940–1970

1. Maurice Matloff, "The 90-Division Gamble," in Kent Roberts Greenfield, ed., *U.S. Army in World War II: Command Decisions* (Washington, D.C.: Department of the Army, 1960), pp. 365–382; Kent Roberts Greenfield, *The Historian and the Army* (New York: Kennikat, 1954), pp. 60–85.

2. Samuel Stouffer et al., *The American Soldier*, vol. 2, *Combat and Its Aftermath* (Princeton: Princeton University Press, 1949), p. 273. See also R. R. Palmer et al., *U.S. Army in World War II: Procurement of Ground Combat Troops* (Washington, D.C.: Department of the Army, 1948), pp. 228–231.

3. Kent Roberts Greenfield, *U.S. Army in World War II: The Organization of Ground Combat Troops* (Washington, D.C.: Department of the Army, 1947), p. 193.

4. Stouffer, *American Soldier*, 2:90.

5. Director of Selective Service, *Selective Service and Victory: Fourth Report of the Director of Selective Service, 1944–1945, with a Supplement for 1946–1947* (Washington, D.C.: Government Printing Office, 1948), pp. 159, 321–322.

6. Russell F. Weigley, *History of the United States Army* (New York: Macmillan, 1967), p. 569.

7. Walter Millis, ed., *The Forrestal Diaries* (New York: Viking, 1951), pp. 374–375.

8. Speech of 17 March 1948. Harry S. Truman, *Public Papers of the Presidents of the United States, 1948* (Washington, D.C.: Government Printing Office, 1964), p. 188.

9. Walter S. Millis, *Arms and the State: A Study in American Military History* (New York: G. P. Putnam's Sons, 1956), pp. 215, 219.

10. Director of Selective Service, *Selective Service under the 1948 Act: June 24,194 8–July 9, 1950* (Washington, D.C.: Government Printing Office, 1951), pp. 31, 132, 248.

11. Director of Selective Service, *Selective Service under the 1948 Act Extended: July 9, 1950–June 19, 1951* (Washington, D.C.: Government Printing Office, 1957), pp. 5, 244.

12. Theodore Paullin, ed., *Sourcebook on Peacetime Conscription* (Philadelphia: American Friends Service Committee, 1944), p. 10.

13. Director of Selective Service, *Selective Service and Victory*, p. 56.

14. Millis, ed., *The Forrestal Diaries*, p. 15.

15. Henry L. Stimson and McGeorge Bundy, *On Active Service in Peace and War* (New York: Harper & Bros., 1947), pp. 597–598.

16. Harry S. Truman, *Memoirs*, vol. 1, *Year of Decisions* (New York: Doubleday, 1955), p. 153.

17. Harry S. Truman, *Public Papers of the Presidents of the United States, 1945* (Washington, D.C.: Government Printing Office, 1961), p. 410.

18. Truman, *Memoirs*, 1:511.

19. Harry S. Truman, *Public Papers of the President of the United States, 1946* (Washington, D.C.: Government Printing Office, 1962), p. 509.

20. Samuel P. Huntington, *The Soldier and the State* (New York: Vintage, 1964), p. 509.

21. President's Advisory Commission on Universal Training, *A Program for National Security* (Washington, D.C.: Government Printing Office, 1947), p. 55.

22. Ibid., p. 53.

23. Ibid., pp. 41–42; National Security Training Commission, *Universal Military Training: Foundation of Enduring National Strength* (Washington, D.C.: Government Printing Office, 1951), p. 71.

24. Samuel P. Huntington, *The Common Defense* (New York: Columbia University Press, 1961), p. 240.

25. U.S. Congress, Senate, Committee on Armed Services, *Universal Military Training. Hearings before the Senate Committee on Armed Services*, 80th Cong., 2d sess., 1948, p. 138. Henceforth cited as *UMT Hearings*.

26. Ibid., p. 842.

27. See Martha Derthick, *The National Guard in Politics* (Cambridge: Harvard University Press, 1965), pp. 97–101.

28. *UMT Hearings*, pp. 7–10; Warner R. Schilling et al., *Strategy, Politics, and Defense Budgets* (New York: Columbia University Press, 1962), p. 149; Millis, ed., *Forrestal Diaries*, pp. 377, 384, 432.

29. By other estimates, UMT would cost four billion dollars. See *UMT Hearings*, p. 69; Millis, *Forrestal Diaries*, pp. 388, 426–427.

30. Ibid., p. 432.

31. A point hammered home by Oswald Garrison Villard in Paul Russell Anderson, ed., "Universal Military Training and National Security," *The Annals of the American Academy of Political and Social Science* 241 (September 1945): 35. Villard also insisted that conscription was antithetical to American ideals—that many immigrants had come to the United States to avoid conscription.

32. Huntington, *Common Defense*, p. 371.

33. Millis, *Arms and the State*, p. 307.

34. Ibid., p. 309.

35. Derthick, *National Guard*, p. 143. For general discussion, see U.S. Congress, House, Committee on Armed Services, *History of United States Military Policy on Reserve Forces, 1775–1957* (Washington, D.C.: Government Printing Office, 1957).

36. News conference of 25 February 1953. Dwight D. Eisenhower, *Public Papers of the Presidents of the United States, 1953* (Washington, D.C.: Government Printing Office, 1960), p. 68.

37. 13 January 1955 Special Message to Congress on National Security Requirements. Dwight D. Eisenhower, *Public Papers of the Presidents of the United States, 1955* (Washington, D.C.: Government Printing Office, 1959), p. 75. See also ibid., letter to the secretary of defense on national security requirements, 5 January 1955, pp. 3, 5.

38. Eisenhower summarizes The New Look in his memoirs, *Mandate for Change* (New York: Doubleday, 1963), pp. 451–453.

39. Weigley, *History of the United States Army*, p. 532.

40. Department of Defense statistics provided to author by the assistant secretary of defense for manpower, reserve affairs, and logistics.

41. The President's Commission on an All-Volunteer Armed Force, *Studies Prepared for the President's Commission on an All-Volunteer Armed Force*, 2 vols. (Washington, D.C.: Government Printing Office, 1970), vol. 2, p. III-1-2.

42. Director of Selective Service, *Annual Report, 1966* (Washington, D.C.: Government Printing Office, 1967), p. 16.

43. Kenneth J. Coffey, *Strategic Implications of the All-Volunteer Force: The Conventional Defense of Central Europe* (Chapel Hill: University of North Carolina Press, 1979), p. 17.

44. William C. Westmoreland, *A Soldier Reports* (New York: Doubleday, 1976), p. 392. In 1969, 88 percent of the riflemen in Vietnam were draftees: Coffey, *Strategic Implications*, p. 48.

45. Eli Ginzberg, quoted in Coffey, *Strategic Implications*, p. 7.

46. Ibid., p. 8. In New York (ibid., p. 11), at one point 77 out of 100 examinees were disqualified. The highest national average was 55 out of 100.

47. Curtis W. Tarr, *By the Numbers: The Reform of the Selective Service System, 1970–1972* (Washington, D.C.: National Defense University Press, 1981), p. 12.

48. Ibid., p. 59.

8. *The Advent of the All-Volunteer Force*

1. Richard M. Nixon, *Public Papers of the Presidents of the United States, 1969* (Washington, D.C.: Government Printing Office, 1971), pp. 258, 365.

2. The President's Commission on an All-Volunteer Armed Force, *Report of the President's Commission on an All-Volunteer Armed Force* (Washington, D.C.: Government Printing Office, 1970), p. iii. Henceforth cited as *Gates Commission Report*.

3. Ibid., p. 146.

4. Ibid., pp. 6–7.

5. Ibid., pp. 12, 36.

6. This has been noted by other observers as well. See John B. Keeley, ed., *The All-Volunteer Force and American Society* (Charlottesville: University of Virginia Press, 1978), p. xii.

7. Cooper begins his RAND study by eulogizing two of the founders of systems analysis, Charles Hitch and Roland McKean: Richard V. L. Cooper, *Military Manpower and the All-Volunteer Armed Force* (Santa Monica: RAND, 1977), pp. 5–7. The Defense Manpower Commission uses the lingo of systems analysis and insists on the importance of cost-effectiveness criteria: Defense Manpower Commission, *Defense Manpower: The Keystone of National Security* (Washington, D.C.: Government Printing Office, 1976), pp. 279–280 (henceforth cited as *DMC Report*). On systems analysis see Alain C. Enthoven and K. Wayne Smith, *How Much Is Enough? Shaping the Defense Program, 1961–1969* (New York: Harper & Row, 1971). I have presented a critique of systems analysis as a mode of strategic thought in "Guessing Game: A Reappraisal of Systems Analysis," in Samuel P. Huntington, ed., *The Strategic Imperative* (Cambridge: Ballinger, 1982).

8. *Gates Commission Report*, pp. 23–24, 122.

9. Ibid., p. 6.

10. *DMC Report*, p. 46.

11. *Gates Commission Report*, p. 14.

12. Curtis W. Tarr, *By the Numbers: The Reform of the Selective Service System, 1970–1972* (Washington, D.C.: National Defense University Press, 1981), p. 4.

13. *DMC Report*, p. 71.

14. See Charles C. Moskos, "Making the All-Volunteer Force Work: A National Service Approach," *Foreign Affairs* 60:1 (Fall 1981): 22.

15. See Correlli Barnett, *Britain and Her Army, 1509–1970* (Harmondsworth: Penguin, 1970), pp. 486–487.

16. The President's Commission on an All-Volunteer Armed Force, *Studies Prepared for the President's Commission on an All-Volunteer Armed Force*, 2 vols. (Washington, D.C.: Government Printing Office, 1970), vol. 2, p. III-3-14 henceforth cited as *Gates Commission Studies*.

17. Tarr, *By the Numbers*, p. 127. See also Jonathan Alford, "Deterrence and Disuse: Some Thoughts on the Problem of Maintaining Volunteer Forces," *Armed Forces and Society* 6:2 (Winter 1980): 247–256.

18. MPRs derived from International Institute for Strategic Studies, *The Military Balance, 1981–1982* (London: International Institute for Strategic Studies, 1981). In this and in much of what follows, I am drawing from (and updating) my article, "Why We Need a Draft," *Commentary* 73:4 (April 1982).

19. Department of Defense, *Selected Manpower Statistics, Fiscal Year 1980* (Washington, D.C.: Directorate for Information, Operations, and Reports, 1981), pp. 81–82.

20. Ibid., pp. 238–239.

21. Department of Defense statistics supplied to author by office of the assistant secretary of defense for manpower, reserve affairs, and logistics, prepared 22 September 1981.

22. U.S. Congress, House, Committee on Appropriations, *Department of Defense Appropriations for 1981. Hearings before a Subcommittee of the House Committee on Appropriations*, 96th Cong., 2d sess., 1981, p. 316.

23. U.S. Congress, House, Committee on Armed Services, *Status of Army Manpower. Hearings before the House Committee on Armed Services*, 96th Cong., 2d sess., 1981, pp. 7–8.

24. Maxwell R. Thomson, "Recruiting the Force Is a Two-Way Street," *Army* 31:10 (October 1981): 211–213.

25. Keeley, ed., *All-Volunteer Force*, p. 72.

26. *DMC Staff Studies*, vol. 3, p. E-41. The report nonetheless concluded that "the quality of the active forces, expressed in terms of educational level and mental category, has improved in comparison with the pre-AVF draft years" (p. 10).

27. See William L. Hauser, *America's Army in Crisis: A Study in Civil-Military Relations* (Baltimore: Johns Hopkins University Press, 1973), p. 141.

28. Department of Defense, *Annual Report to the Congress, Fiscal Year 1982* (Washington, D.C.: Government Printing Office, 1981), p. 271.

29. See Robert G. Yerks, "Manning the Force in the 1980s: Time of Success and Challenge," *Army* (October 1981). In 1976 only 23 percent of eighteen-year-olds did *not* receive high school degrees (Defense Manpower Commission, *Staff Studies*, 3 vols. [Washington, D.C.: Government Printing Office, 1976], vol. 3, p. D-3; henceforth cited as *DMC Staff Studies*).

30. See Department of Defense, *Annual Report, 1982*, p. 273; Kenneth J. Coffey, *Strategic Implications of the All-Volunteer Force: The Conventional Defense of Central Europe* (Chapel Hill: University of North Carolina Press, 1979); U.S. Congress, Sen-

ate, Committee on Armed Services, *Recruiting in the United States Army. Hearing before a Subcommittee of the Senate Committee on Armed Services, 96th Cong., 1st sess.,* 1980, esp. pp. 3, 45–54.

31. U.S. Congress, House, Committee on Armed Services, *Status of Army Manpower, 96th Cong., 2d sess., 1981,* p. 33.

32. Department of Defense, *Annual Report to the Congress, Fiscal Year 1985* (Washington, D.C.: Government Printing Office, 1984), p. 76.

33. Ibid., pp. 74, 84.

34. Department of Defense, *Annual Report, Fiscal Year 1985,* p. 90; U.S. Congress, House, Committee on Armed Services, *Women in the Military. Hearings before a Subcommittee of the House Committee on Armed Services,* 96th Cong., 1st and 2d sess., 1981, p. 113.

35. Ibid., pp. 79–80, 110; Coffey, *Strategic Implications,* pp. 52–55. On the external pressures brought to bear on the services see *DMC Report,* pp. 250–251. On women in combat see Seth Cropsey, "Women in Combat?" *The Public Interest* 61 (Fall 1980): 58–89; George Gilder, "The Case against Women in Combat," *Parameters* 9:3 (September 1979): 81–86; James Webb, "Women Can't Fight," *The Washingtonian* (November 1979); Eliot A. Cohen, "Likely Effects of the E.R.A. on the Armed Forces of the United States," in U.S. Congress, Senate, Committee on Judiciary, *Hearings before a Subcommittee of the Senate Committee on the Judiciary,* 98th Cong, 1st sess., 1 November 1984.

36. See "Women in the Military," *Washington Post,* 22 October 1984, p. A14.

37. See the perceptive remarks by an *advocate* of women in the military, Mady Wechsler Segal, "The Argument for Female Combatants," in Nancy Loring Goldman, ed., *Female Soldiers—Combatants or Noncombatants?* (Westport: Greenwood, 1982), p. 278. See also Glenn Gray, *The Warriors: Reflections on Men in Battle* (1959; New York: Harper, 1970), pp. 59–97 (chap. entitled "Love: War's Ally and Foe"); Edward Shils and Morris Janowitz, "Cohesion and Disintegration in the Wehrmacht," reprinted in Edward Shils, *Center and Periphery* (Chicago: University of Chicago Press, 1975), pp. 351–352, 355–356, 359–360, 365; Eliza G. C. Collins, "Managers and Lovers," *Harvard Business Review* 61:5 (September–October 1983): 142–153. A story on the rites of Harvard's male athletic teams gives an insight into the matter of male bonding: Jennie Kassanoff, "The Rite to Bare All," *The Harvard Independent,* 10 November 1983, p. 7. A fascinating study by the Royal Netherlands Navy which was avowedly intended to prove that sexually integrated crews could work produced unanticipated (i.e., negative) results. Project Group on Women in the Royal Netherlands Navy, "Sailing with Women," Department of Social Research of the Royal Netherlands Navy, July 1982.

38. Edward C. Meyer, "The Challenge of Change," *Army* (October 1981): 15.

39. See *DMC Report,* p. 40; also, Center for Military History, *Department of the Army Historical Survey, Fiscal Year 1971* (Washington, D.C.: Center for Military History, 1973), p. 69.

40. Coffey, *Strategic Implications,* p. 118; *DMC Staff Studies,* vol. 2, pp. A-17–A-25g; *DMC Report,* p. 40.

41. Emmet H. Walker, Jr., "Manpower Climbs, Equipment Lags in the Army National Guard," *Army* (October 1981): 112–113.

42. John Turley, "Mobilization Manpower: A Credible Force or an Empty Promise?" *Military Review* 61:8 (August 1981): 4.

43. Department of Defense, *Selected Manpower Statistics,* pp. 238–239.

44. *DMC Staff Studies,* vol. 3, p. D-3.

45. Ibid., pp. E-4–E-5.

46. Department of Defense, *Annual Report, 1985*, p. 114.

47. Lieutenant General Arthur S. Collins, *Common Sense Training* (San Rafael, Calif.: Presidio, 1978), pp. 189–195. The author was issued this book as a cadet in ROTC. For a sample of just some of the mobilization problems the armed forces would face, see "Rosters for Army May Be Incorrect," *New York Times*, 13 March 1985, p. A18, summarizing a General Accounting Office report that approximately one-fifth of the names and addresses on mobilization lists for reserve units in five parts of the country were incorrect.

48. A good brief description of the current Israel Defense Forces can be found in Richard Gabriel, *Operation Peace for Galilee* (New York: Hill & Wang, 1984).

49. U.S. Congress, Senate, Committee on Armed Services, *Reinstitution of Procedures for Registration under the Military Selective Service Act. Hearings before a Subcommittee of the Senate Committee on Armed Services*, 96th Cong., 1st sess., 1979, pp. 7, 78.

50. Ibid., p. 78; Congressional Budget Office, *The Selective Service System: Mobilization Capacities and Options for Improvement* (Washington, D.C.: Government Printing Office, 1978); William R. Berkman, "The Reserves and Mobilization Readiness," *Army* (October 1981): 129–130; Coffey, *Strategic Implications*, pp. 78–83; Kenneth J. Coffey, *Manpower for Military Mobilization* (Washington, D.C.: American Enterprise Institute, 1978); Martin Binkin, *U.S. Reserve Forces* (Washington, D.C.: Brookings Institution, 1974). Among the imponderables are, what percentage of IRR members would heed a recall and how fast? How much would they retain of the skills? How much retraining or training would they need?

51. For some of the measures used to inflate the IRR, see Department of Defense, *Annual Report to the Congress, Fiscal Year 1984* (Washington, D.C.: Government Printing Office, 1983), pp. 104–105. On mobilization generally, see Robert J. Pirie, "The All-Volunteer Force Today: Mobilization Manpower," in Andrew J. Goodpaster et al., *Towards a Consensus on Military Service* (New York: Pergamon, 1982), pp. 113–130.

52. Coffey, *Strategic Implications*, pp. 136–137; Department of Defense, *Manpower Requirements Report, Fiscal Year 1984* (Washington, D.C.: Government Printing Office, 1983), p. 27.

53. I am indebted to Martin Binkin of the Brookings Institution for the observation that soldiers have not, by and large, been using their post–Vietnam era benefits to attend college. According to his information, of some 715,000 veterans separated from the service between 1977 and 1983, all of whom were eligible for college tuition aid under the Veterans Education Assistance Program, only 33,000 had enrolled in college. This would indicate that scarcely 5 percent of veterans were going on to college after service.

54. See Charles Moskos, "The Enlisted Man in the All-Volunteer Army" (unpublished paper, Northwestern University, Evanston, Illinois, January 1984). See also his chapter in Goodpaster et al., *Towards a Consensus*, pp. 131–151.

55. Quoted in E. J. Kahn, *McNair* (Washington, D.C.: Infantry Journal, 1945), p. 8.

56. Department of Defense, *Annual Report, 1985*, p. 6.

57. American Enterprise Institute, "A Conversation with General E. C. Meyer: The Army of the Future" (Washington, D.C.: American Enterprise Institute, 1981), pp. 11–12, 16.

58. For the most recent assessments see Military Manpower Task Force, *A Report to the President on the Status and Prospects of the All-Volunteer Force* (Washington, D.C.:

Government Printing Office, 1982); Andrew J. Goodpaster et al., *Toward a Consensus on Military Service: Report of the Atlantic Council's Working Group on Military Service* (Washington, D.C.: Atlantic Council, 1982); Brent Scowcroft, ed., *Military Service in the United States* (Englewood Cliffs: Prentice-Hall, 1982).

9. Conclusion

1. Department of Defense, *Selected Manpower Statistics, Fiscal Year 1980* (Washington, D.C.: Directorate for Information, Operations, and Reports, 1981), p. 60.

2. For Washington's "Sentiments on a Peace Establishment" see John McAuley Palmer, *Washington, Lincoln, Wilson: Three War Statesmen* (New York: Doubleday, 1930). Hamilton evidently helped Washington draft this proposal, as is evident from his *Works* (12-volume Federal edition, ed. Henry Cabot Lodge [New York: G. P. Putnam's Sons, 1904], 6:479, 482; 7:22–47). Theodore Roosevelt put forward proposals for a similar program during the opening stages of World War I in his rambunctious book, *Fear God and Take Your Own Part* (New York: George H. Doran, 1916).

3. Ralph Barton Perry, *The Plattsburg Movement* (New York: E. P. Dutton, 1921), p. 265.

4. Alexander Hamilton, John Jay, and James Madison, *The Federalist* (1787–1788; New York: Modern Library, 1937), p. 407.

Selected Bibliography

Some of the following works are listed because they were particularly valuable for the writing of this book, others because I think they are at once outstanding and easily overlooked. This bibliography omits most standard works in civil-military relations, military sociology, and the like. For further references (including standard works on various aspects of military manpower questions), consult the notes to this volume; also see Martin Anderson, *Conscription: A Select and Annotated Bibliography* (Stanford: Hoover Institution Press, 1976).

Anderson, Paul Russell, ed. "Universal Military Training and National Security." *Annals of American Political and Social Science* 241 (September 1945). A summary of elite thought about the problem of conscription during one of the critical periods of American manpower policy.

Bayne, John. *Morale: A Study of Men and Courage*. London: Cassell, 1967. An excellent study of the British military manpower system in its prime, on the eve of World War I.

Callwell, C. E. *Small Wars*. London: HMSO, 1906. The British General Staff primer on the subject, which explains much about the British adherence to an all-volunteer army.

Crowder, Enoch H. *The Spirit of Selective Service*. New York: Century, 1920. An authoritative account by the father of Selective Service of the administrative and political rationale for it.

Defense Manpower Commission. *Defense Manpower: The Keystone of National Security* and *Defense Manpower Commission Staff Studies and Supporting Papers* (3 volumes). Washington, D.C.: Government Printing Office, 1976. Valuable chiefly as an example of how bias—in this case, an attempt to prove that the AVF was flourishing, when in fact it was very badly off—can distort an official study.

Delbrueck, Hans. *Geschichte der Kriegskunst im Rahmen der politischen Geschichte*. Volume 4. Berlin: Georg Stilke, 1920. Still one of the most thoughtful discussions of the relationship between political ideas, the nature of war, and military service. This volume should shortly appear in English translation.

Department of Defense. *Selected Manpower Statistics*. Washington, D.C.: Directorate for Information, Operations, and Reports. An annual compilation (by fiscal year) of military manpower statistics, both contemporary and historical.

Director of Selective Service. *Selective Service* . . . The annual (in some cases semi-annual) reports of the Director of Selective Service to Congress from the beginning of World War I through the end of the draft in the early 1970s provide not only factual information, but insight into the psychology of the administrators of Selective Service.

Erickson, John. "Soviet Military Manpower Policies." *Armed Forces and Society* 1:1 (November 1974). A clear summary of Soviet practices and attitudes.

Ernst, Alfred. *Die Konzeption der schweizerischen Landesverteidigung 1815 bis 1966.* Frauenfeld: Huber, 1971. A solid introduction to the Swiss system of military service, by one of the men who helped shape it.

Feld, Maury. "Military Professionalism and the Mass Army." *Armed Forces and Society* 1:2 (Winter 1975).

Foot, M. R. D. *Men in Uniform.* New York: Praeger, 1961. One of the first comparative studies of military service, now somewhat outdated, but valuable nonetheless.

Gerhardt, James M. *The Draft and Public Policy: Issues in Military Manpower Procurement, 1945–1970.* Columbus: Ohio State University Press, 1971. A standard work.

von der Goltz, Colmar. *The Nation in Arms.* Philip A. Ashworth, trans. London: W. H. Allen, 1887. The case for the modern cadre/conscript system, made by a German soldier and scholar/publicist.

Goodpaster, Andrew J., et al. *Toward a Consensus on Military Service: Report of the Atlantic Council's Working Group on Military Service.* Washington, D.C.: The Atlantic Council, 1982. A generally pessimistic assessment of the All-Volunteer Force, which should be compared with the Military Manpower Task Force report (below).

Haeckel, Erwin, "Military Manpower and Political Purpose." Adelphi Paper No. 72. London: International Institute for Strategic Studies, 1970. An excellent discussion of the dilemmas created for modern states by different types of military service.

Hamilton, Ian. *Compulsory Service.* London: John Murray, 1910. A brilliant polemic for the voluntary system by the ill-fated commander of the Dardanelles expedition in World War I.

Hintze, Otto. "Military Organization and State Organization." In Felix Gilbert, ed., *The Historical Essays of Otto Hintze.* New York: Oxford University Press, 1975. A seminal essay that includes discussion of the relationship between systems of military service and political culture.

James, William. "The Moral Equivalent of War." In *Memories and Studies.* New York: Longmans, Green, 1911. The classic formulation of the case for nonmilitary national service, which is cited far more often than it is read.

Keegan, John. "Regimental Ideology." In Geoffrey Best and Andrew Wheatcroft, eds., *War, Economy, and the Military Mind.* London: Croom Helm, 1976. A succinct and powerful statement of the case for the British regimental system.

Kelleher, Catherine M. "Mass Armies in the 1970s: The Debate in Western Europe." *Armed Forces and Society* 5:1 (Fall 1978): 3–30. A description of the dilemmas of the modern European cadre/conscript army.

Kiernan, V. G. *From Conquest to Collapse: European Empires from 1815 to 1960.* New York: Pantheon, 1982. An idiosyncratic but highly informative survey of the systems of military service used by the European powers to subjugate extra-European peoples.

Kreidberg, Marvin A., and Henry G. Merton. *History of Military Mobilization in the*

Selected Bibliography

U.S. Army. Washington, D.C.: Department of the Army, 1955. A basic reference work.

Military Manpower Task Force. *A Report to the President on the Status and Prospects of the All-Volunteer Force.* Washington, D.C.: Government Printing Office, 1982. A predictably optimistic assessment of the All-Volunteer Force.

Moskos, Charles C. "Making the All-Volunteer Force Work: A National Service Approach." *Foreign Affairs* 60:1 (Fall 1981). A telling indictment of the econometric approach to the study of military manpower.

Nickerson, Hoffman. *The Armed Horde, 1793–1939.* New York: G. P. Putnam's Sons, 1940. A curious mixture of polemics and scholarship, this book places excessive blame on the conscript system and underestimates its durability.

O'Sullivan, John, and Alan M. Meckler, eds. *The Draft and Its Enemies.* Urbana: University of Illinois Press, 1974. Perhaps the best of the various readers on the subject.

Palmer, John McAuley. *America in Arms.* New Haven: Yale University Press, 1941. One of a number of studies by America's most important advocate of militia conscription.

Palmer, Robert R., et al. *The U.S. Army in World War II: The Procurement and Training of Ground Combat Troops.* Washington, D.C.: Department of the Army, 1948. Much of this material is still valid, and a valuable counterweight to the wholly unrealistic official estimates of how fast the United States can mobilize.

Perry, Ralph Barton. *The Free Man and the Soldier: Essays on the Reconciliation of Liberty and Discipline.* New York: Charles Scribner's Sons, 1916. The most thoughtful collection of essays I have seen on the philosophical dilemmas posed by military service in a liberal state, written by an academic who briefly turned soldier.

du Picq, Ardant. *Etudes sur le Combat.* 8th edition. Paris: Librairie Chapelot, 1914. There are many editions (and translations) of this pioneering work in military sociology, which is informed by practical experience, survey research, and historical knowledge.

The President's Commission on an All-Volunteer Armed Force. *Report of the President's Commission on an All-Volunteer Armed Force.* Washington, D.C.: Government Printing Office, 1970. The basic document of the Gates Commission, and vital to an understanding of the assumptions lying behind the adoption of the All-Volunteer Force.

Ransom, William L., ed. "Military Training: Compulsory or Volunteer." *Proceedings of the Academy of Political Science* 6:4 (July 1916). See comments on the Anderson collection (above).

Roberts, Frederick Sleigh. *Facts and Fallacies.* London: John Murray, 1911. A powerful argument for conscription on the eve of World War I, by Britain's foremost general of the time. It is an attack on Hamilton's *Compulsory Service* (above).

von Seeckt, Hans. *Gedanken eines Soldaten.* Leipzig: K. F. Koehler, 1935. The most thoughtful case for the modern volunteer professional army, by the man who rebuilt the German Army after World War I.

Shanahan, William O. *Prussian Military Reforms, 1786–1813.* New York: Columbia University Press, 1945. The standard work on the subject, this book punctures the myth that the cadre/conscript system formed the basis of Prussian military renewal following the disasters of Jena and Auerstaedt.

Trochu, Louis Jules. *L'Armée francaise en 1867.* Paris: 1867. A remarkably balanced assessment of the merits and defects of an all-volunteer force, written by a French general on the eve of the Franco-Prussian War.

[221]

U.S. Congress. Senate. Committee on Military Affairs. *Compulsory Military Training and Service. Hearings before the Senate Committee on Military Affairs.* 76th Cong. 3rd sess. 1940. These hearings reveal virtually all varieties of American attitudes toward military service.

Walzer, Michael. *Obligations: Essays on Disobedience, War, and Citizenship.* New York: Simon & Schuster, 1970. A collection of thoughtful essays on the place of military service in liberal society, shaped by the author's absorption in the problems posed by the Vietnam war.

Weigley, Russel F. *Towards an American Army: Military Thought from Washington to Marshall.* New York: Columbia University Press, 1962. An extremely useful summary of the American military's attitudes—pro and con—toward conscription.

Wool, Harold. *The Military Specialist.* Baltimore: Johns Hopkins University Press, 1968. An extremely influential econometric study of military manpower.

Index

Library of Congress Cataloging in Publication Data

Cohen, Eliot A.
  Citizens and soldiers.

  (Cornell studies in security affairs)
  Bibliography: p.
  Includes index.
  1. Military service, Voluntary—United States.   2. Military service,
Compulsory—United States.   I. Title.   II. Series.
UB323.C56   1985   355.2'236   84-14266
ISBN 0-8014-1581-0 (alk. paper)